THE WORLDS OF JOSEPH SMITH

THE WORLDS OF JOSEPH SMITH

A BICENTENNIAL CONFERENCE AT THE LIBRARY OF CONGRESS

EDITED BY JOHN W. WELCH

BRIGHAM YOUNG UNIVERSITY PRESS
PROVO, UTAH

Also from Brigham Young University Press:

Personal Writings of Joseph Smith, edited by Dean C. Jessee

Opening the Heavens: Accounts of Divine Manifestations, 1820–1844, edited by John W. Welch

Prepared for publication by BYU Studies

Cover and jacket design by Bjorn W. Pendleton

Opinions expressed in this publication are the opinions of the authors and their views should not necessarily be attributed to The Church of Jesus Christ of Latter-day Saints, Brigham Young University, or BYU Studies.

Library of Congress Cataloging-in-Publication Data

The worlds of Joseph Smith : a bicentennial conference at the Library of Congress / edited by John W. Welch.
    p. cm. — (BYU studies)
    Includes index.
    ISBN 0-8425-2636-6 (hard cover : alk. paper)
    1. Smith, Joseph, 1805–1844—Congresses. I. Welch, John W. (John Woodland)
    II. Series: BYU Studies monographs.

BX8695.S6W68 2006
289.3092—dc22   2005037059

Printed in the United States of America

10 9 8 7 6 5 4 3 2 1

Contents

Introduction

On May 5–6, 2005, a conference entitled "The Worlds of Joseph Smith" was held in the Coolidge Auditorium at the Library of Congress in honor of the bicentennial of Joseph Smith's birth on December 23, 1805. This international symposium, cosponsored by the Library of Congress and Brigham Young University, brought scholars together from several countries and many universities to discuss and commemorate the life and work of Joseph Smith (1805–1844). This volume contains the papers that have emerged from this conference.

The idea for this conference began with a conversation between Robert Millet and Gerald McDermott, who had just been involved in the academic celebration at the Library of Congress in honor of Jonathan Edward's three-hundredth birthday. Agreeing that a conference on Joseph Smith sounded promising, Millet contacted people at Brigham Young University and in the Public Affairs office of The Church of Jesus Christ of Latter-day Saints to begin discussing the possibility. An initial contact was also made with Senator Robert Bennett's office.

At about the same time, James Hutson, Director of the Manuscripts Division of the Library of Congress, had directed an exhibition sponsored by the Library entitled "Religion and the Founding of the American Republic." During its travels around the country, this exhibition was on display for three months at Brigham Young University at the time of the Salt Lake City Winter Olympics in 2002. In bringing this exhibition to Provo, Utah, Hutson had worked with John Welch, editor of *BYU Studies,* who hosted this event at the Harold B. Lee Library.

These strands came together when Hutson and Millet conferred with each other and the two of them readily agreed that a conference on Joseph Smith cosponsored by the Library of Congress and Brigham Young University would be of great interest to scholars as well as to the general public. With that encouragement, an organizing committee consisting of Hutson, Millet, and Welch, together with Richard Bushman and Richard Turley, was formed, and plans were laid.

The conference was organized into five plenary sessions, which are reflected here in the five parts of this book. Except for session three, each session began with a principle paper and was followed by papers from three respondents. The five worlds in relation to which the experiences and contributions of Joseph Smith were examined included (1) the surrounding world of his day, (2) the formative world of the past, (3) the personal world of touching human souls, (4) the transcendent world of theology, and (5) the progressing world of the future.

The opening greeting by James Billington, Librarian of the Library of Congress, set the stage warmly and succinctly for this memorable conference and this resulting volume. He said:

> It is really a great pleasure on behalf of my colleagues here at the Library of Congress to welcome you to this symposium cosponsored by Brigham Young University celebrating the bicentennial of the birth of Joseph Smith.
>
> In 1819, John Adams, who as president had signed the legislation creating the Library of Congress, informed a correspondent, Adamon Kronium, "The science of theology is indeed the first philosophy—the only philosophy that comprehends all philosophies, all science. It is the science of the universe and its ruler, and what other object of knowledge can there be?" So, I think Adams would be pleased that present-day Americans continue to be interested in theology and religion as an important part of American history and an important part of life. He would not be surprised at the passions, of course, that these subjects generate.

Since the Library of Congress is really the world's largest repository of stored knowledge and the mint record of American creativity (thanks to copyright deposit and the deposit of so many of our creative figures), it is an ideal forum for an intellectually rigorous exploration of religion and its impact on society. In recent years we have hosted conferences and mounted exhibits on the following subjects: "Was Rome Reborn?" (an exhibition of the treasures of the Vatican library); "In the Beginning Was the Word" (discussing the Russian Orthodox Church's archives here in North America and its interaction with Native Alaskan cultures); "Let There be Light" (on William Tyndale and the making of the English Bible); and "Religion and the Founding of the American Republic." In 2003 the Library cosponsored with Yale University a symposium marking the tricentennial of the birth of Jonathan Edwards, and most recently the Library cosponsored "From Haven to Home— 350 Years of Jewish Life in America."

It is, therefore, extremely appropriate and welcome that we continue to examine significant religious movements and the lives of important religious personalities, particularly when they impact so directly and reflect in so many ways important things of our own broader history as Americans. So today we bring together leading scholars to investigate the career of Joseph Smith, founder of The Church of Jesus Christ of Latter-day Saints, to determine his influence on America and the world. I have no doubt that the papers delivered at this conference will deepen our knowledge of Joseph Smith.

The richness of the Library of Congress's collections is never better illustrated or better used than in illuminating subjects on which it might be assumed that our collections will be weak. We recently had an exhibit of Winston Churchill and discovered that we had seventeen letters of Winston Churchill, which we had not known in the course of properly preparing for the exhibit. These letters described his experiences in the trenches of World War I, about which relatively little had been known.

We also have strong holdings on the Mormons and on the LDS Church. Proof of this are the documents in the cases in the foyer just outside this auditorium. Among those documents are treasures including Joseph Smith's 1829 copyright application for the Book of Mormon and an accompanying printer's proof sheet of the title page of the Book of Mormon, which experts tell us is the actual first printed document in Mormon history.

So we are happy to host this symposium. I am certain that it will be an intellectual feast for everyone. I extend appreciation from all at the Library of Congress to all involved in this conference, particularly to Brigham Young University with whom we have had such an excellent sponsorship of this gathering. Thank you and good conference.

Many people deserve special recognition for making this conference so successful, including leaders of the hosting institutions, participating scholars, curators, technicians, volunteers, and employees. Thousands were able to view the proceedings, either in person or over the Internet. This volume makes it possible for readers to explore further the assertions, references, conclusions, and implications of these engaging presentations.

Several interesting points of discussion, consensus, and divergence arose in this conference. While all agreed that the sincerity and significance of Joseph Smith was not to be doubted, people wondered, Can he best be understood in an American context or transnationally? Should he be approached through the tools of Enlightenment rationality or Romantic sensibilities? How should, or how can, his effulgent approach to religion be characterized? How and why have his seminal ideas become so influential in the lives of his many adherents? What do his prophetic insights and promises offer to people today the world over?

At the end of the conference, one of the participating scholars remarked, "Something very important has happened at this conference. We will arrive at some point in the future when we will look back and say, 'This development began at the Library of Congress.'" We hope that this volume will be a clear and useful point of departure for everyone involved in that ongoing quest to assess and know the many worlds relevant to Joseph Smith.

Richard L. Bushman
James H. Hutson
Robert L. Millet
Richard E. Turley Jr.
John W. Welch

Part 1

Joseph Smith in His Own Time

As scholars look back on Joseph Smith two hundred years after his birth, several historical questions capture their immediate attention. How was Joseph Smith shaped or constrained by his moment in history? How much was Joseph Smith a product of his own time? To what extent can he be explained in terms of the prevailing attitudes of his day? Is it more illuminating to think of him as a critic or as a product of American culture? Should he be seen as an American prophet or in a larger world setting? In many areas of historical inquiry, America as an analytical category has been replaced by transnational analyses that situates everything from the Puritans to abolition in a larger world context; should Joseph Smith be located in a broader framework than the national? After all is said and done, what "world" was the world of Joseph Smith?

Joseph Smith's Many Histories

Richard L. Bushman

In 1992 my wife, Claudia, published a book titled *America Discovers Columbus: How an Italian Explorer Became an American Hero.*[1] The book argued that until the American Revolution, Columbus was almost completely neglected in histories of the British colonies. Not until three centuries after the fact did North Americans honor him as the discoverer of America. Even in 1792, it required a stretch of the imagination to give him the credit, since he never touched foot on the North American continent and for centuries the British had distanced themselves from the hated Spanish exploiters of the New World. But after attaining independence, the newly formed United States needed a new link to their European past besides their one-time oppressors, the British. And so Columbus was elected as grandfather of the new nation, sharing the honors with George Washington, the father, with whose name Columbus was imperishably linked through the title of the nation's capital, Washington, District of Columbia.

Claudia's Columbus story reminds us that our histories are detachable. Every nation, every institution, every person can be extricated from one history and attached to another, often with perfect plausibility. Each of us has many histories. The histories I refer to are not the events of our lives, but the various cultural contexts that produce us and explain who we are—our many different pasts.

Imagine that upon meeting a person you first learn he is of Italian descent and grew up on a New Jersey farm. Think further if he told you he went to the University of Chicago, then to medical school, and that he had converted to Mormonism. Each of those little identity fragments connects our friend to a history and a cultural context; viewing him through each history, we find a new side to his character. Similarly for each of us, our complexity and the interwoven nature of history gives us freedom to select from a number of histories in explaining who we are.

I wish to explore, in broad general terms, the histories to which historians have attached Joseph Smith. As you can imagine, the context in which he is placed profoundly affects how people see the Prophet, since the history selected for a subject colors everything about it. Is he a money-digger like hundreds of other superstitious Yankees in his day, a religious fanatic like Muhammad was thought to be in Joseph's time, a prophet like Moses, a religious revolutionary like Jesus? To a large extent, Joseph Smith assumes the character of the history selected for him. The broader the historical context, the greater the appreciation of the man. If Joseph Smith is described as the product of strictly local circumstances—the culture of the Burned-over District, for example—he will be considered a lesser figure than if put in the context of Muhammad or Moses. Historians who have been impressed with Joseph Smith's potency, whether for good or ill, have located him in a longer, more universal history. Those who see him as merely a colorful character go no farther than his immediate environment for context. No historians eliminate the local from their explanations, but, on the whole, those who value his genius or his influence, whether critics or believers, give him a broader history as well. I want to talk first about the way historians have sought the Prophet's larger meaning by assigning him a history, and then examine the histories to which Joseph Smith attached himself.

Histories Assigned to Joseph Smith

Writers have always put Joseph Smith in his American or Yankee context. He himself once boasted of his Vermont heritage and said that he was a son of the American Revolution.[2] His 1838 history begins with an account of his birth in Sharon and tells of the conditions in New York prompting him to pray for divine guidance about the churches. His visions seem to grow naturally out of the New England and New York religious landscapes. In that spirit, Mormons are happy to call Joseph Smith an "American Prophet." (They proudly tell the story of Leo Tolstoy inquiring about Mormonism, what he called the "American religion."[3])

Mormons, of course, attach Joseph Smith to American history differently than non-Mormon historians do. Mormons call Joseph Smith American in an attempt to win the affection of the American people. They want Joseph to be received with the generosity exemplified in Robert Remini's charming biography of the Prophet.[4] Non-Mormon historians are more likely to use the term to mean that Joseph Smith and his revelations were products of an American environment. Fawn Brodie approvingly quoted Alexander Campbell, the first of Joseph's major critics, saying: "This prophet Smith, through his stone spectacles, wrote on the plates of Nephi, in his Book of Mormon, every error and almost every truth discussed in New York for the last ten years."[5] Brodie and Campbell thought Joseph Smith was no more than a product of his American environment; he absorbed his culture, digested it, and transferred his views into the Book of Mormon, whereas Mormons consider Joseph a prophet with an American accent.

Both Mormons and non-Mormons agree then that Joseph has an American history, whether as a setting to the revelations, as Mormon historians say, or as the source for the Book of Mormon and the revelations, as the critics maintain. But in the nineteenth century, historians of all stripes also agreed that Joseph was more than American. Something about his life and accomplishments transcended his time and place. Critics and supporters alike knew he was more than a small-town, rural visionary, whether for good or ill. His effectiveness in building a church and attracting followers made him more than a local crackpot. The Boston Unitarian Josiah Quincy said Joseph Smith might eventually be seen as "the most powerful influence" of the nineteenth century "upon the destinies of his [American] countrymen."[6] Joseph had to have a broader history to explain his extraordinary powers, and both critics and friends supplied him with one.

To reveal what he truly was, Mormons linked Joseph to the history of biblical prophets. He was another Moses or Paul. They assigned him the historical role of restoring the pure gospel after a long period of apostasy.[7] Joseph started the work of preparing the world for the Second Coming of Christ. Though he had a local and national history, to be sure, Mormons saw Joseph's true history extending back to the New Testament and the loss of Christ's original gospel. To be comprehended, Joseph had to be viewed from two historical perspectives—one national and the other a transnational history of apostasy and restoration.[8] And it was the transnational perspective that made him significant.

Critical nineteenth-century historians assigned him a different transnational history. They saw in Joseph a late manifestation of a long line of false prophets and gave him a distinguished place in the horrible history of fanaticism. "False prophet" and "fanatic" were preformed categories based on prejudices that Joseph's critics automatically snapped into place. Campbell devoted a full page to a list of examples: the Egyptian magicians who withstood Moses; ten false Messiahs of the twelfth century; Munzer, Stubner, and Stork in the Reformation; Ann Lee (Anna Leese), founder of the Shakers; and a Miss Campbell who claimed to have come back from the dead. Alexander Campbell saw Joseph as a member of an ancient and populous company of religious frauds as well as a product of Yankee culture.[9]

One decade after Campbell, J. B. Turner, a professor at Illinois College near Nauvoo, published a volume called *Mormonism in All Ages*. Turner argued that Joseph Smith was an incarnation of a type who appeared, as the title said, in all ages. Turner proposed that throughout human history people had been deluded by religious charlatans. Such fanatics were supported by their gullible followers and ruled by fire and sword like their ultimate embodiment, Muhammad. Fanatics went beyond intolerance to coercion.[10] Violence, according to this deeply engrained stereotype, was the fanatic's natural method.

Recent scholarship has shown how deeply rooted the stereotype has been in western civilization—as deeply rooted as racism—going back at least to Luther, who denounced the peasant uprisings of the sixteenth century and supported crushing them as a manifestation of fanaticism.[11] Tragically, the antifanatics, inflamed by their hatred of fanaticism, have resorted to violence to quell their enemies as often as the fanatics have taken up arms in the cause of their faith. Religious fanaticism has been one of those vicious stereotypes that justify forcible repression. As the Mormons were to learn, once demonized as fanatics, they could be stripped of their rights and expelled from society without scruple.

Throughout the nineteenth century, this combination of an American context and a broader history was the standard pattern of critical histories. While Mormon historians talked of apostasy and restoration, nearly every non-Mormon account featured the requisite list of false prophets and fanatics followed by scornful accounts of Joseph Smith's obvious borrowings from Yankee culture. His history was both American and universal. He was a local phenomenon but was also linked to "all ages," as Turner put it, and it was this link that made Smith important.[12] He was dangerous, terrible—and grand. Mormons were attacked not only because of what they were but also because of what they represented—a fearful tradition going back in time.

Then at the turn of the century in 1903, I. Woodbridge Riley published *The Founder of Mormonism,* a seminal book on Joseph Smith that changed the pattern. Riley abandoned the search for larger significance. He narrowed the context for the Prophet to a purely American history and even more narrowly to Smith's psychology. In Riley's telling, Smith had no broader historical character than that of a bizarre, deformed offspring of Yankee culture.

Written as his doctoral thesis at Yale University, Riley's work was the most ingenious of the anti-Mormon books up to that point, inspiring a notable series of histories and biographies through the remainder of the century. Riley rejected the Spaulding theory of the Book of Mormon's composition, the ruling hypothesis in the earlier anti-Mormon histories. Those authors speculated that the Book of Mormon was not the work of Joseph Smith; he was too ignorant and crude to have produced such a complex work. The book was instead the reworking, probably by Sidney Rigdon, of a novel written by Dartmouth graduate Solomon Spaulding. Riley exploded this frail argument and looked for evidence that Smith wrote the book himself. Following Campbell's lead from seventy years before, Riley found in the Book of Mormon a bevy of American themes: anti-Masonry, anti-Catholicism, Methodism, attacks on infidelity, theories of Indian origins, anti-Calvinism, and Baptist doctrine—all ideas particular to the United States in Joseph Smith's time. Riley's work persuaded the Yale scholar George Trumbull Ladd, who wrote the preface, that Joseph Smith could not have emerged "under other conditions than those which actually surrounded him in the first third of the last century" in the United States. In other words, Joseph Smith was not only the product of America but of one particular moment in American history, the first third of the nineteenth century.[13]

Further narrowing the focus, Riley offered a psychological interpretation of Joseph Smith, finding the origins of Mormonism in Joseph's medical history. He diagnosed the Prophet as suffering from epilepsy and explained his visions as the result of seizures. Cultural history was not required to explain the visits of angels; they were the product of a diseased body. Adding the two together, immediate American influences and a psychological diagnosis, Riley believed he had fully accounted for the Mormon prophet. And he did not amount to much. At the end of the book, Riley asked, "Was He Demented or Merely Degenerate?" Joseph Smith was pretty much a freak and little more.[14]

The Riley model set the pattern for a significant tradition of Joseph Smith biographies into the twentieth century. Fawn Brodie, who was dependent on Riley for many of her ideas, adopted the same analytical structure. She found a psychological diagnosis for the Prophet in a personality type, the "impostor," which the psychoanalyst Phyllis Greenacre had discovered in her practice. According to Greenacre, the impostor suffers from a severely divided personality, one part being weak and the other, the impostor part, being fantastically strong. Brodie was more modest in her claims about the applicability to Joseph than Riley had been with epilepsy, but she thought it suggestive. Everything else about Joseph—his ideas, his revelations, and his translations—according to Brodie was "purely a Yankee product."[15] He had no history beyond his American environment and his own defective personality.

Dan Vogel's 2004 *Joseph Smith: The Making of a Prophet* stood in the same tradition: a sociopsychological diagnosis—in Vogel's case, family systems theory—along with American environmental influences explain Joseph Smith. Vogel argued that after the death of his older brother Alvin, Joseph became the family leader, replacing his failed father. His religion grew out of his search for a solution to a dysfunctional family's problems. Beyond that, everything else came from his American environment. No one has gone as far as Vogel in linking characters and events in the Book of Mormon to particular persons and happenings in Joseph Smith's immediate environment. *The Making of a Prophet* carried Riley's program to its ultimate realization in extreme detail.[16]

Like all of the books in the Riley tradition, Vogel's work diminishes Joseph Smith. By limiting the Prophet's cultural-historical horizon, all of the narrowly Americanist accounts strip the Prophet of grandeur and depth, even of the gothic horror of the religious fanatic. Brodie and Vogel will always be a part of the historiography of Joseph Smith, but they do not open new vistas for readers. They pile on more without going beyond Riley's original insight. By constricting Joseph Smith's historical horizon, they reduce him to a colorful fraud. They have no way of plumbing his depths or putting him in a broader perspective. Even Fawn Brodie, the biographer who valued Joseph Smith most out of the three, spoke of the "barrenness of his spiritual legacy."[17]

In my opinion, we have reached the end of the line for these purely nationalist studies. I expect that Joseph Smith's future biographers will swing back toward the nineteenth century's combination of American analysis and transnational histories of the Prophet, allowing Joseph Smith to escape a confining provinciality. The books that have most excited—and, in some instances, most irritated—historians in the last thirty years are the transnational histories of Joseph Smith by Jan Shipps, John Brooke, and Harold Bloom.

Shipps, a long-time student of Mormonism and a well-known insider-outsider, dazzled me with her brilliant analysis of early Mormonism in her 1985 study, *Mormonism: The Story of a New Religious Tradition.* Shipps's interpretation was exciting because she did not confine her study to the American environment. Approaching Mormonism from the perspective of religious studies, by its nature comparative, she drew parallels between the origins of Christianity and the emergence of Mormonism. Shipps saw Mormonism as departing from Christianity just as Christianity departed from Judaism. The idea was not solely hers; Brodie had suggested it in a few sentences much earlier. But Shipps expanded the hypothesis and revealed its reach. In her telling, Mormonism is much more than Yankee religion run amok. Mormonism is a global movement in the making that may eventually take its place alongside other global religions. Whether this is indeed the course Mormonism will follow remains to be seen, but Shipps's formulation compelled readers to look beyond the history of the United States.[18]

John Brooke's *The Refiner's Fire* reinforced the cosmopolitan outlook of Shipps's study. A cultural historian by training, Brooke placed Mormonism in the hermetic tradition, a Renaissance metaphysical practice linked to alchemy and magic, which he believes was conveyed to America by miners, counterfeiters, and Masons. In Brooke's telling, Smith was a miracle worker, a "magus," as the hermeticists called such people, who sought divinity by working upon nature and conducting emblematic divine weddings. The book had a mixed reception when it appeared in 1994. While exciting non-Mormon historians, it dumbfounded Mormons. The connections to hermeticism were so tenuous and the parallels so forced that Mormons thought the book must fall of its own weight. But Mormon objections notwithstanding, *The Refiner's Fire* broke through the nationalist boundaries that had constricted the views of other twentieth-century critical historians. Like Michael Quinn's *Early Mormonism and the Magic World View,* Brooke's reading of Joseph Smith traced his roots back to the Renaissance and before.[19] The favorable response to Brooke's work suggests that historians are prepared once more to go beyond national boundaries in the study of the Mormon Prophet, as in the study of so many other American subjects these days.

The Yale literary scholar Harold Bloom made the Prophet both more and less American by returning to the pattern of nineteenth-century historians in *The American Religion: The Emergence of the Post-Christian Nation*. Bloom thought of Smith as the premier example of what he called the American Religion, which emphasizes the individual's immediate access to God, but Bloom also found echoes of biblical antiquity in Smith's writings. Smith had an uncanny ability, Bloom thought, to recover ancient types, such as Enoch or Metatron, and to renew quests, such as the Kabbalistic search for the divine human, without instruction from his environment. "I can only attribute to his genius or daemon," Bloom wrote, "his uncanny recovery of elements in ancient Jewish theurgy that had ceased to be available either to normative Judaism or to Christianity, and that had survived only in esoteric traditions unlikely to have touched Smith directly."[20] By setting Smith against ancient religious traditions, Bloom discovered a Joseph Smith never fully seen before, a man in touch with religious currents from the deep past and, as Bloom said, a genius in religion making.[21]

Shipps, Brooke, and Bloom are not all admirers of Joseph Smith—Brooke condemns him, for example—but they each enlarge him and give him scope. Future historians of Joseph Smith will likely feel free to explore a much wider range of possible histories. Smith's American roots will continue to be investigated as they always have been, but national history will not confine our inquiries. The American history of Joseph Smith looks for causes: what led Joseph Smith to think as he did? Comparative, transnational histories explore the limits and capacities of the divine and human imagination: what is possible for humans to think and feel? Pursuing broader questions, future historians may compare Smith to the great mythmakers of history like Dante, Milton, Blake, and Nietzsche.[22] They may ask about his place among philosophers, reformers, politicians, and prophets. How does Smith look alongside religious figures such as Augustine, Luther, Gandhi, or Muhammad? We will no longer be bound by the tight historicist restrictions of the twentieth-century critical studies but look much farther afield for illumination of the Prophet. In my opinion, only by working in the larger field will we see his true dimensions.

The History Joseph Smith Assigned to Himself

To what history did Joseph attach himself? By the time he wrote his 1838 history, he had settled the question and was able to speak confidently about his early development. He smoothly blended his beginnings in Vermont and New York (his American origins) with his call to be a prophet, translator, and church founder (his biblical history). His development seemed easy and natural by then, but it may not have been so easy at the time. As I imagine Joseph Smith, the search for his own history was more arduous than he later let on. For a number of years, Joseph did not know who he was, that is, which history he belonged to. Not until he translated the Book of Mormon did his place in history become clear.

Judging from his own account, Joseph was less in control of his life than most believed. The way he told his story, things happened to him outside of his own initiative. He saw himself as a passive recipient of what he called "marvilous experience[s]" whose meanings were not clear at first.[23] Consider three of his early experiences: the First Vision, the discovery of the seer stones, and the command to translate the plates. These three constitute what Jan Shipps has called "the Prophet puzzle." In a 1974 essay, Shipps said historians must reconcile the apparently contradictory themes in Joseph's early years—his visionary life as a budding prophet versus his seerstone gazing as a young treasure-seeker.[24] I suggest this conflict may have been as much a puzzle to Joseph Smith as it has been to later historians.

Present-day Mormons can scarcely imagine Joseph's initial confusion about the First Vision's importance because we see so clearly in retrospect that the vision initiated Joseph's life as a prophet. What was he to make of the appearance of two heavenly beings when he was fourteen? Judging from his first written account, composed in 1832, he understood the vision primarily as a personal conversion. It was an event in the history of revivals. We must remember that Joseph was surrounded by incessant preaching for what was called the New Birth. The evangelical ministry's aim was to convict hearers of their sins, bring them to see their helplessness, and teach them to rely on Christ alone. Exposed to this kind of preaching, Joseph worried about his sins, perhaps concerned all the more because he was unable to undergo the usual emotional conversion. According to his 1832 account, he was, like the other revival subjects, concerned for "the wellfare of my immortal Soul," by which he meant he felt "convicted of my sins," the term used by revival preachers. In the vision, the first words he heard from the Lord assured Joseph "thy sins are forgiven thee."[25]

Coming out of the grove, Joseph had every reason to think that he had undergone a particularly dramatic New Birth experience, like hundreds of others in his neighborhood. As a sign of his confusion, his first reaction was to consult a minister to verify the validity of what happened. Why would a person who had just been informed that "those professors were all corrupt" immediately turn to a clergyman for guidance? He went because new converts customarily visited a minister. Because mere emotion might have overtaken them rather than the grace of God, the experience had to be checked out. In Joseph's case, the clergyman treated the story with contempt. He told Joseph his conversion was of the devil—that he was no better than all the other visionaries of his time who were visited by angels and carried into heaven to see Christ. According to the minister, the First Vision was not a true vision or a New Birth but an illusion. Such visions were common enough to anger clergymen, who saw them as counterfeit religion, diverting people from the serious business of acknowledging their sins and accepting Christ.

The minister's response left Joseph puzzled and frustrated. What was the vision? An expert in the field of religion had told him he was deluded. Was he merely one more misguided visionary? As late as 1838, when he wrote the story, he felt the frustration of a thwarted religious spirit. He was told to forget it, yet he knew what he had experienced. "I had actually seen a light," he wrote, "and in the midst of that light I saw two Personages, and they did in reality speak to me; and though I was hated and persecuted for saying that I had seen a vision, yet it was true" (Joseph Smith–History 1:25). He could not deny the vision's reality, but what did it mean? If not a conversion, as he had been told, what was it? He could not yet explain where it fit in the history of religion.

Two years later, in 1822, another marvel was thrust upon him. He discovered he had the ability to look into a stone and see things otherwise invisible to natural eyes. He had two seer stones, the origin of one being uncertain, the other found in a well. Martin Harris described the stone, as did David Whitmer and Emma and many others close to him. Apparently Joseph used the stone to find lost objects. He may have considered the knack an amusing diversion, but his father and others in the neighborhood wanted his help in finding lost treasure. For four or five years, they pressed him into service. Dan Vogel argues that Joseph planned to make a career out of treasure seeking, but I see him compelled by his cash-poor father and the enthusiasm of the money-digging neighbors into activities he did not enjoy. A year after finding the stone, Joseph was told by the angel to cut his ties with the treasure seekers, and three years later, even his father understood that Joseph was to use his powers for higher purposes.[26] Joseph knew his future did not lie with the treasure seekers, yet he had a gift for looking into a stone and seeing. Was the gift from God? Did it have a higher purpose? Was he a treasure seeker with a place in the history of magic, or something greater?

In 1823, Joseph Smith underwent the most perplexing experience of all. According to his own story, another heavenly visitor told him he was to translate an ancient record inscribed on gold plates. In this case, there were no conceivable precedents, no history of any kind to attach himself to. He had no committee of scholars assigned by King James to translate the Bible. He was not the learned Champollion cracking the Egyptian code on the Rosetta Stone. He was a poorly educated rural visionary who had never heard of gold plates with ancient histories inscribed on them or of partially literate young men translating. Where in sacred or secular history was there a precedent for an unlearned translator? Joseph was sailing in uncharted waters.

As he turned eighteen, these three marvelous experiences—the First Vision, the seer stones, and the command to translate—bestowed upon Joseph Smith an incomprehensible mixture of possible identities with only perplexing or indiscernible histories to explain them.[27] Groping his way and following the instructions of the angel, Joseph took possession of the plates in 1827 and began the baffling task of translating. In the early stages, the seer stone experience may have sustained him. His first reaction when he received the Urim and Thummim was to tell Joseph Knight, "They are marvelous; I can see anything."[28] Seeing lost objects in a stone had prepared him to look into the Urim and Thummim and see words. But still there was no history of unlearned translation, no known events to which he could attach himself, no way to secure an identity from past experience.

Joseph Smith must have been immensely relieved to hear about Martin Harris's visit to Charles Anthon. Joseph did not show much interest in the professor's opinion of the characters or the translation, but he was thrilled to recognize the fulfillment of a Bible prophecy. Someone—whether Harris or Joseph or someone else—discovered that Anthon's reply to Harris corresponded to a biblical prophecy. Joseph Smith's history explains how Anthon's response "I cannot read a sealed book" conformed to the prophecy in Isaiah 29 that says the unlearned would read a book the learned could not read (Joseph Smith–History 1:64–65). At last a tiny thread tied Joseph to the Bible. If the Bible prophesied his work, he had a history. His unlearned translation had been foreseen.

But it was the Book of Mormon itself, the book Joseph was translating, that finally clarified his identity. The Book of Mormon provided Joseph his long-sought history. Joseph must have been excited to translate Ammon's conversation with the Lamanite King Limhi about King Mosiah. When asked to translate the records of the Jaredites, Ammon said he had no such powers, but he knew someone who did. King Mosiah had an instrument, two stones, which he looked into and translated. Mosiah was a seer and a prophet also, and no greater gift than this existed, Ammon said (Mosiah 8:6–18). In Mosiah, Joseph found a kindred soul with a similar configuration of powers: seer stones, translation, and prophethood.

But the Book of Mormon offered more than Mosiah's example. It created a world history in which Joseph's set of powers played a critical part. One of the dominant historical structures in the Book of Mormon is the history of Israel. Nephi and Jacob rehearse Israel's story a half dozen times, and Christ repeats it during his visit to the Nephites. It is the story familiar from Isaiah and other Hebrew prophets: Israel covenanted with God; Israel has strayed from God; Israel will be forgiven and restored as God's favored people in the last days. The story is as persistent in the Book of Mormon as it is in the Bible.

The Book of Mormon, however, gives the familiar story a particular twist. The Israel of the Book of Mormon extends far beyond Israel in Palestine, the familiar homeland. The Book of Mormon speaks for scattered Israel, spread around the globe (1 Nephi 22:3–5). The Nephites' story begins with a departure from the Holy Land. Whereas the Israelites in the Bible always returned to the Promised Land, the Book of Mormon people headed for a new promised land, never to return. The Book of Mormon puts Israel on a world stage. It is a book about Israel in dispersion. Isaiah mentions Israel on the "isles of the sea" once; Nephi uses the term nine times.[29] Isaiah's "isles of the sea" phrase was assurance that God knew the dispersed Nephites, that they were still Israel, and that they had a place in God's plans, though far from their homeland. Later in the Book of Mormon, Christ says he will visit scattered Israel just as he visited the Nephites in America.[30] Overall, the Book of Mormon reorients biblical geography. It tells Israel's story from the margins and the isles of the sea, rather than from the heartland. The Book of Mormon is the story of Israel's diaspora.

And that is where Joseph Smith's particular configuration of gifts comes in. Scattered Israel kept records. According to the Book of Mormon, there is not one Bible but many bibles, each telling the story of a branch of Israel, as Mormon's history tells of the remnant of Jacob in the New World. All of these records are vital to the gathering of Israel and have to be translated. When the branches of Israel come together, so will their records.[31] The Book of Mormon even provides instruments for performing this vital task. Mosiah translated the records of the Jaredites, as the Book of Mormon says, "by the means of those two stones which were fastened into the two rims of a bow" (Mosiah 28:13). When the Lord gave the brother of Jared a vision written in a language no one understood, he also received "two stones" to seal up with the plates which "shall magnify to the eyes of men these things which ye shall write" (Ether 3:23–24).[32] The Book of Mormon's version of Israel's history calls for a translator who works with stones.[33]

Joseph stood at the center of this history of the world. He was to translate the records of Israel in America, which are in turn to assure the House of Israel everywhere "that they are not cast off forever" (title page, Book of Mormon). In translating the records, the puzzle of three disparate identities of his early life—visionary, seer, and translator—was resolved. As the revelation at the organization of the church said, "Behold, there shall be a record kept among you; and in it thou shalt be called a seer, a translator, a prophet" (Doctrine and Covenants 21:1).

The Book of Mormon gave what Harold Bloom would call a "strong reading" of scripture, an interpretation loyal to the original but decisive in its departures. The Book of Mormon turned Israel's story into global history. By striking out for the New World, the Book of Mormon prophets spread Israel across the earth. From that global perspective, a new set of phenomena resulted: scattered remnants, additional records, the requirement of translation, the need for translation instruments, and lastly, a prophet-translator. Joseph's seemingly haphazard collection of possible identities cohered into a providential design. His own revelation supplied him with a pertinent history, making him the ultimate self-made, or from his point of view, God-made man.

Once Joseph began translating the Book of Mormon his confidence soared. In 1828 after the first 116 pages were completed, he began writing revelations that would later comprise the Doctrine and Covenants. Initially it took courage to believe his own revelations, but by 1828 he believed the promptings of the Spirit. He trusted the inspired words enough to organize a church, send missionaries to find a site for the New Jerusalem, and call people to gather—all on the basis of his revelations. In 1831 according to one account, he strode into the Newel Whitney store in Kirtland, Ohio, and announced himself as Joseph the Prophet. It was a hard-won identity that he embraced confidently once the Book of Mormon revealed to him who he was.

As we address the meaning of Joseph Smith in the twenty-first century, such complex interweavings of experience, text, and history must figure in our narratives. Whatever we think about the origins of the Book of Mormon and Joseph Smith's revelations, all of us, critics and believers alike, must take into account the Prophet's self-understanding. Our stories of him must comprehend his story of himself—not an easy task. Could this uneducated, unpracticed, twenty-three-year-old have devised the whole intricate narrative on his own? New York farmers did not ordinarily come up with histories of scattered Israel and translating stones. It is doubtful that a purely American history of the Mormon prophet will explain him. His mind ranged far beyond his own time and place, and we will have to follow if we are to understand.[34] A small history will not account for such a large man.

Notes

1. Claudia L. Bushman, *America Discovers Columbus: How an Italian Explorer Became an American Hero* (Hanover, N.H.: University Press of New England, 1992).

2. Joseph Smith Jr., *General Joseph Smith's Appeal to the Green Mountain Boys* (Nauvoo, Ill.: Taylor and Woodruff, 1843), 3.

3. Leland A. Fetzer, "Tolstoy and Mormonism," *Dialogue* 6, no. 1 (Spring 1971): 13–29, throws into question the validity of the famous story. Tolstoy's question seems to have appeared only in a late, doctored version of the interview.

4. See Robert V. Remini, *Joseph Smith*, Penguin Lives Series (New York: Viking, 2002).

5. Fawn M. Brodie, *No Man Knows My History: The Life of Joseph Smith the Mormon Prophet*, 2d ed. (New York: Knopf, 1971), 69.

6. Josiah Quincy, *Figures of the Past from the Leaves of Old Journals* (Boston: Roberts Brothers, 1892), 376.

7. For example, George Q. Cannon, *Life of Joseph Smith the Prophet* (1888; repr., Salt Lake City: Deseret Book, 1986), 11–15.

8. Cannon, *Life of Joseph Smith the Prophet*, 25–34. Cannon traced Joseph Smith's American roots as well as situating him in the history of apostasy and restoration.

9. Alexander Campbell, *Delusion: An Analysis of the Book of Mormon; with an Examination of Its Internal and External Evidences, and a Refutation*

of Its Pretences to Divine Authority (Boston: Greene, 1832), 5–6; reprinted from Alexander Campbell, "Delusions," *Millennial Harbinger* 2 (February 1831): 85–96.

10. J. B. Turner, *Mormonism in All Ages; or, The Rise, Progress, and Causes of Mormonism; with the Biography of Its Author and Founder Joseph Smith, Junior* (New York: Platt and Peters, 1842), 65–109.

11. Dominique Colas, *Civil Society and Fanaticism: Conjoined Histories,* trans. Amy Jacobs (Stanford, Calif.: Stanford University Press, 1997). Colas treats fanaticism as a real threat, not as a stereotype, but his evidence points to the continuing fears. He also describes the danger of civil society overreacting as Luther did to the peasant uprisings.

12. Turner, *Mormonism in All Ages,* 13.

13. I. Woodbridge Riley, *The Founder of Mormonism: A Psychological Study of Joseph Smith, Jr.* (New York: Dodd, Mead, 1903), vi, 120–37, 141–65, 171–72, 367–95. On pp. 170–71, Riley offers a few examples of previous frauds as predecessors to Joseph Smith, but they are not central to his argument.

14. Riley, *The Founder of Mormonism,* 343–65. The emergence of psychological and sociological explanations for phenomena once considered moral and political is traced in Jeffrey P. Sklansky, *The Soul's Economy: Market Society and Selfhood in American Thought, 1820–1920* (Chapel Hill: University of North Carolina Press, 2002).

15. Brodie, *No Man Knows My History,* ix, 418–19.

16. Dan Vogel, *Joseph Smith: The Making of a Prophet* (Salt Lake City: Signature Books, 2004).

17. Brodie, *No Man Knows My History,* 403.

18. Jan Shipps, *Mormonism: The Story of a New Religious Tradition* (Chicago: University of Illinois, 1985), 65, 85, 148–49. Although treating American religions, Richard T. Hughes and C. Leonard Allen write from the same broad perspective in their chapter on Mormonism in *Illusions of Innocence: Protestant Primitivism in America, 1630–1875* (Chicago: University of Chicago Press, 1988), 133–52.

19. John L. Brooke, *The Refiner's Fire: The Making of Mormon Cosmology, 1644–1844* (New York: Cambridge University Press, 1994). Michael D. Quinn's *Early Mormonism and the Magic World View* (Salt Lake: Signature Books, 1987) blazed the path that Brooke later followed but emphasized magic more than alchemy.

20. Harold Bloom, *The American Religion: The Emergence of the Post-Christian Nation* (New York: Simon and Schuster, 1992), 101.

21. "He was an authentic religious genius, and surpassed all Americans, before or since, in the possession and expression of what could be called the religion-making imagination." Bloom, *The American Religion,* 96–97.

22. Bloom presages these broader comparisons in a comment about Joseph Smith's place among other American religious reformers. Many other religions have sprung up in America, Bloom observes, "but none of them has the imaginative vitality of Joseph Smith's revelation, a judgment one makes on the authority of a lifetime spent in apprehending the visions of great poets and original speculators" (*The American Religion*, 98).

23. Dean C. Jessee, ed. and comp., *The Personal Writings of Joseph Smith* (1984; repr., Salt Lake City: Deseret Book; Provo, Utah: Brigham Young University Press, 2002), 9.

24. Jan Shipps, "The Prophet Puzzle: Suggestions Leading toward a More Comprehensive Interpretation of Joseph Smith," *Journal of Mormon History* 1 (1974): 2–20.

25. Jessee, *Personal Writings*, 10, 11. A glancing reference to the First Vision in Doctrine and Covenants 20:5 also emphasizes forgiveness of sins.

26. Vogel, *Joseph Smith*, 35–43; Richard L. Bushman, *Joseph Smith and the Beginnings of Mormonsim* (Urbana: University of Illinois Press, 1984), 69–76.

27. Confusing as his situation was, he went ahead, supported only by his family. At first, they may have seen the plates as a buried treasure and Moroni as a guardian spirit. For a few years, the folk-magic culture may have provided a prop for Joseph's self-understanding, even while the angel was strictly instructing Joseph that he must leave treasure seeking behind.

28. Joseph Knight Sr., ca. 1847, published in Dean C. Jessee, "Joseph Knight's Recollection of Early Mormon History," *BYU Studies* 17, no. 1 (1976): 33–36, and in John W. Welch, "The Miraculous Translation of the Book of Mormon," in John W. Welch, ed., *Opening the Heavens: Accounts of Divine Manifestations, 1820–1844* (Provo, Utah: Brigham Young University Press, 2004), 168.

29. See Isaiah 24:15; 1 Nephi 19:10, 13, 16; 21:8; 22:4; 2 Nephi 10:8, 20, 21; 29:7.

30. See 3 Nephi 15:11–24; 16:1–3.

31. See 2 Nephi 29:8, 11–13; Alma 29:8.

32. See also Mosiah 8:13; Ether 4:5.

33. For a more elaborate explication of the themes in the preceding paragraphs, see Richard L. Bushman, "The Book of Mormon in Early Mormon History," in *Believing History: Latter-day Saint Essays*, ed. Reid L. Neilson and Jed Woodworth (New York: Columbia University Press, 2004), 65–78.

34. The task is complicated by the abundance of Joseph Smith's revelations. The Book of Mormon provided one history to which he could attach himself, but it was not the last word. As his life went on, further revelations created additional histories—the books of Moses and Abraham, sections 84 and 107 in the Doctrine and Covenants, and the extraordinary section 128. Joseph's histories multiplied until the end of his life, culminating according to many in the history of the intelligences in the King Follett discourse.

Biographical Reflections on the American Joseph Smith

Robert V. Remini

I have long thought that the importance and role of Joseph Smith in the history of religion in America has been muted more than necessary by the Latter-day Saint church. As his biographer, I was and remain very anxious that his contribution to American culture and religion in general be recognized and appreciated, both by Mormons and by non-Mormons.

The Proper Approach for Biographers of Religious Figures

First, I would like to make a few comments about what I think the proper approach of a historian should be in dealing with a subject such as the life of Joseph Smith. As I said in the preface of my biography of Smith,[1] the problem in writing on any religious figure, be it Christian, Jew, Muslim, Buddhist, Hindu, or whatever, is that believers see the person as somewhat sacred, and nonbelievers see him or her as strange or even fake. A historian's task, as I see it, is to maintain absolute impartiality in dealing with religious subjects, to study the evidence and try to present the facts in as objective a manner as possible.

Although not a Mormon, I have learned from my association with Joseph Smith to respect and admire what he accomplished. I was asked to write his biography in part because I was not affiliated with the church but presumably had a background to undertake the task since my principal field of research and writing is centered on the Jacksonian era—the years in which Smith grew to maturity, experienced visions, uncovered gold plates, translated the Book of Mormon, and organized The Church of Jesus Christ of Latter-day Saints.[2]

When initially asked to undertake this assignment, I wondered at its wisdom. After all, I am a historian of politics, not religion. More importantly, I wondered whether I could be impartial and could approach the subject objectively, as a historian should. I had wondered the same thing when I finished my biography of Andrew Jackson and began the study of Henry Clay, since Jackson and Clay were deadly enemies.[3] But in thinking about a life of the Prophet, I decided that I had no real prejudices against Mormons or their church, one way or the other. In fact, I was not aware of knowing a Mormon, and I did not understand what they were like. I finally decided that it might be interesting and instructive to investigate the subject and improve my knowledge of an important figure in American history and American religion. So I accepted the offer, believing I could bring to it the required objectivity.

I think a historian has an obligation to find, if possible, plausible, rational reasons to explain the controversial aspects of the subject's life and to leave theological speculation to experts in the field. For example, I know that many believe that the extraordinary conversion of thousands to the Christian church in the late ancient and early medieval periods was due to the guidance and help of the Holy Spirit. A historian, to my way of thinking, should not make any attempt to cite or infer divine influence when explaining the spread of Christianity. He should stick to his discipline and offer logical, intelligent, factual, and rational explanations for what happened.

Yes, Joseph Smith had visions, but were they divinely inspired? How can a historian possibly know? It is enough as a historian to lay out the facts and allow the evidence to speak for itself. If he decides on the basis of the evidence that the Prophet was divinely inspired and chooses to say so and explain why he has reached that decision, then, I think, he has laid down his historian's pen and has become an apologist.

At the same time, if a historian does not believe Joseph Smith's claims and sets out to prove that the Prophet was a fake, intent on deceiving the gullible for his own selfish purposes, as some have said, then the work is polemical and valueless as history. And I should also like to argue that a critical evaluation of Joseph Smith and his work is not necessarily the result of a conspiratorial effort to diminish Joseph's reputation or the value of his contribution to our culture. To be sure, some critical writers are hostile and anxious to discredit the Prophet. I do not deny that, but, as I say, their work is valueless as history.

I must admit that even before I began a serious study of Joseph Smith's life, I rather liked the man. I thought him a courageous and brave individual who achieved something quite remarkable. Moreover, he sacrificed his life for what he believed. As I studied him for several years, I came to admire him the more I got to know him. A biographer, I contend, should like his subject, and I do not doubt that this fact will color his work to some extent. I suppose someone has to write a biography of Josef Stalin and Adolph Hitler, but I could never do it.

A Very American Religion and Prophet

One of the first things I learned in my research on Joseph Smith was that Mormonism is a very American religion, more so than I originally understood. Moreover, I found Joseph Smith is a product of his environment, a product of his time and location. (I do not think anyone at anytime ever escapes the influence of his environment and the era in which he or she lives.) Remember that Americans of the early nineteenth century were far different from Americans of the early twenty-first century. The environment during the Prophet's lifetime was saturated with religious fervor. The Second Great Awakening generated a scalding religious ferocity unlike the religious response of any other period in American history. This nation was engulfed by the fires of repeated revivals in which itinerant preachers of little education but mesmerizing oratory reduced men and women to weeping supplicants, begging forgiveness of their sins and promising to reform their lives.

Joseph was born directly in the middle of this cauldron. As a teenager, he attended these revivals and, according to his own testimony, was deeply affected by them. He said he "wanted to get religion too, wanted to feel and shout like the rest." Unfortunately he "could feel nothing."[4] Remember, this was also a romantic age, and Joseph Smith was a romantic to his innermost fiber. So he turned to the scriptures for help, "believing as I was taught, that they contained the word of God."[5] And who taught him? Obviously his parents. He was born into a deeply religious family where he was indoctrinated into a life of daily prayer, dreams, visions, magic, and seer stones. This combination of religious turmoil surrounding him on the outside and the intense religious family upbringing at home produced a religious zealot.

So Joseph was a product of his time and family influence. But if Joseph is so American, why were Mormons rejected and persecuted? According to Richard Bushman, a localized view of Joseph Smith's history is too limiting; it cannot adequately address the question.[6] But the answer, I think, is simple: Americans are a violent people. We have a long history of killing those who are not like us or who disagree with us. And that turbulent history began from the arrival of the first Europeans on this continent. Whatever is different (and Joseph and Mormons certainly are different), whichever group does not conform to the approved norm for religious belief, and whatever Americans cannot or will not accept, they attack.

Bushman also asks why this American religion thrives in foreign lands. I think the answer is obvious. What is American has always been attractive to foreigners, starting with the fact that we dared to establish a republic and declare that all men are equal and have certain inalienable rights. In a sea of monarchies and dictatorships, we chose to experiment with a republican form of government that slowly evolved into a democracy. This experiment drew foreigners like Alexis de Tocqueville to these shores to investigate and report on them. Foreigners have been attracted not only to our American religion but also to our music, our movies, our computer technology, our lifestyle of jeans and fast foods and inane TV programs, and our many inventions—such as the light bulb, the telephone, the recording machine, the cell phone, the iPod, and on and on.

But why are people attracted to Mormonism, be they Americans or foreigners? My own view is that (other than a true religious conversion) people are attracted to what I call a Mormon culture, a culture that emphasizes the value and importance of the family, emphasizes helping each other and participating in community life. It is the genuine warmth of human relationships that is so attractive.

From the very beginning of Mormon history, Joseph, you will remember, sent missionaries abroad to spread the faith, and that in itself was very American. Remember the country had expanded from a hundred-mile ribbon along the Atlantic coastline in the seventeenth and eighteenth centuries to a nation that stretched three thousand miles to the Pacific Ocean. The era in which the Prophet lived, the Jacksonian Era, was a period in which Americans proclaimed their belief in Manifest Destiny. An article in *The Democratic Review* in 1845 provided its definition when the author said that other countries were "limiting our greatness and checking the fulfillment of our manifest destiny to overspread the continent allotted by Providence for the free development of our yearly multiplying millions."[7]

Notice, it is a right given us by Providence to bring enlightened government to the inhabitants of this continent. We are still doing it today in our attempts to bring democracy and freedom to the oppressed of this world. Is that so different from Joseph's efforts to spread the blessings of Mormonism to a deprived world? And this religion was attractive to foreigners by the very fact that it was American. What other elements "beyond the Yankee domain" are necessary? Focusing on Joseph Smith's origins in the United States is not limiting, as Bushman believes. Quite the opposite. Manifest Destiny is about expanding the vision and the goal of sharing our good fortune with others everywhere.

I frankly do not support the transnational concept in trying to explain Joseph Smith and who he was. Quite obviously, by founding a religion that has survived for almost two centuries, the Prophet did, in fact, place Mormonism in the great stream of the history of Christianity. Saying that does not mean this Yankee religion has run amok—or that it is confining. Mormonism has expanded, has been accepted, and has become part of the Christian tradition.

I might also remind you that in establishing his church Joseph Smith called its head a president and organized individual communities of Mormons into wards, the term used to describe political areas in Chicago. Both these designations are American concepts. Joseph claimed that the Garden of Eden was located in Missouri and that when Christ returns in the Second Coming, He will appear in the United States. Most particularly, Joseph Smith was assassinated. Even that is not unknown in America.

The command to translate an ancient record contained on gold plates also appeals to Americans. Americans have always wanted things written down in black and white. Starting with the Mayflower Compact when the Pilgrims first arrived and including the colonial charters, Americans sought legitimacy through the written word. We want documents to prove our right to exist as a free people. We want a written declaration of independence to set before the world the reasons we are breaking loose from the British Empire. We want articles of confederation and a written constitution to describe how we shall be governed. We want a clearly worded bill of rights so that we know the government is limited in what it can do. In the struggle to win passage of the Bill of Rights in the First Congress, Thomas Jefferson told James Madison that the American people deserved to have these clearly articulated rights added to the Constitution.[8] The American people had fought and won a revolution, and they wanted their principles of government validated by such a document. Joseph Smith is in the tradition of a nation committing one's beliefs and aspirations to writing. Jews have the Torah, Christians the Gospels, Moslems the Qur'an, and now Joseph Smith has provided his followers with the Book of Mormon.

The Book of Mormon is a typically American story, or at least one that Americans can easily appreciate. Here is the story of a people who left their homeland in search of a better life, crossed an ocean, and settled in a wilderness. It is the story of bringing the gospel to the Americas. It is a story that people of the Jacksonian age could easily relate to and understand because it is part of their own tradition. It explains where the Indians came from. It radiates the revivalist passion of the Second Great Awakening, the frontier culture and folklore, and the democratic impulses of the time.

What is truly remarkable—really miraculous—is the fact that this massive translation was completed in sixty working days by an uneducated but highly imaginative zealot steeped in the religious fervor of his age. As a writer, I find that feat absolutely incredible. Sixty days! Two months to produce a work running over six hundred pages and of such complexity and density. Unbelievable.

I frankly do not see why the experiences of the First Vision, the knack of looking into a stone and seeing things otherwise invisible to natural eyes, and a heavenly visitor informing him that he was to translate an ancient record on gold plates are necessarily, as Bushman puts it, "the puzzle of . . . disparate identities."[9] They are all part of who Joseph Smith was and became as he grew to manhood in a world saturated with religious enthusiasm. Because of his family background and the background of the Burned-over District of New York, he was prepared well in advance to undergo this contact with the divine. As for peering through stones and seeing things otherwise invisible to natural eyes, that was quite commonplace. A Palmyra newspaper reported that many men and women "became marvelous wise" in using seer stones by which "they saw all the wonders of nature, including of course, ample stores of silver and gold."[10] Joseph's father used them, as did his mother on occasion. Joseph later said that "every man who lived on the earth was entitled to a seerstone, and should have one, but they are kept from them in consequence of their wickedness."[11]

The Need to Plumb for Meaning

Rather than looking to a transnational explanation, both Mormon and non-Mormon historians need to seek a deeper understanding of Joseph Smith himself. I am not sure we have come to grips and plumbed the meaning of all the events that shaped his life—especially his young life. How did other things besides environment and family inform his life? For example, when Joseph was a boy, he endured a surgical operation that must have been excruciating. There was no anesthesia, and the doctors cut open the child's leg and removed part of the bone, drilling one side of the bone and then the other, using whatever primitive surgical instruments were available at the time. Surely such a shock to the system of young Joseph must have been so traumatic that it affected his personality. But how? Historians are not psychologists or psychiatrists, but they need to raise the question. We know that during these agonizing days he was carried around the house by his mother and later used crutches and walked with a limp. To further his recovery, he was sent to the home of an uncle, Jesse Smith, who lived in Salem, Massachusetts. What was it like to be separated from his family for nearly a year while he recovered? It is virtually impossible to state just what emotional and psychological scars he carried into adulthood, but surely this traumatic event and the agony he endured had an enormous influence on the kind of person he became and the career he chose to pursue.

Is there more to be learned about Joseph's youth? I think so. The following incident is only one of the events in Joseph's young life that has not been thoroughly explored to my knowledge. When he was eleven years old and the family moved from Norwich to Palmyra, New York, the guide taking the family to their new location made Joseph walk miles each day through the snow, despite his lameness, according to his mother. Joseph later remembered suffering the "most excruciating weariness & pain." Then when Joseph was left behind to ride on another sleigh and tried to gain a place in the sleigh, he was knocked down, he said, and left "to wallow in my blood until a stranger came along, picked me up, & carried me to the Town of Palmyra."[12]

How did these events affect his personality? His character? His sense of his own worth? The very fact that he remembered them as a mature man and wrote about them so graphically is an intriguing clue, I think.

Because of his fragile condition during these early years in Palmyra, Joseph could not help with the daily chores assigned to his brothers and sisters and came increasingly under the influence of his strong-willed, deeply religious mother. We know from her testimony that he was a "remarkably quiet" boy and so highly emotional that he would break down in tears at the slightest provocation.[13] He turned inward and not surprisingly became concerned about "the wellfare of my immortal Soul."[14] Revivals were going on all around him; his father had visions or dreams, which were related to the family, and his mother served as a driving force in the development of his religious and moral convictions. Added to these religious influences at home was the cruel way the world outside treated him—the many incidents in which he was made a victim of those who wished to do him harm. What was there about Joseph that attracted violence? And reverence?

Joseph tells us that in his youth and at the height of the harassment he regularly suffered by both the "religious and irreligious;"[15] he endured "all kinds of temptations . . . and . . . frequently fell into many foolish errors; and he displayed the weakness of youth, and the foibles of human nature . . . offensive in the sight of God" (Joseph Smith–History 1:28). What sins were these? What errors? Joseph does not say, except for the mention of levity and an association with "jovial company" (Joseph Smith–History 1:28). Were there other actions that really were "offensive in the sight of God?" All I am saying is that we need to know more about his youth and the forces and experiences that molded him.

Joseph Smith once said that "no man knows my history."[16] We still do not know him completely, but we must keep trying. There is still much to learn.

Notes

1. Robert V. Remini, *Joseph Smith*, Penguin Lives Series (New York: Viking, 2002).

2. But even after reading the Book of Mormon, researching both primary and secondary sources and completing this biography, I wish to state at the outset that I do not qualify as a scholar of Mormonism.

3. Robert V. Remini, *Andrew Jackson* (New York: HarperPerennial, 1999); Remini, *Henry Clay: A Statesman for the Union* (New York: W. W. Norton, 1991).

4. Larry E. Dahl and Donald Q. Cannon, eds., *Encyclopedia of Joseph Smith's Teachings* (Salt Lake City: Deseret Book, 2000).

5. Dean C. Jessee, ed. and comp., *Personal Writings of Joseph Smith* (1984; repr., Salt Lake City: Deseret Book; Provo, Utah: Brigham Young University Press, 2002), 10.

6. Richard L. Bushman, "Joseph Smith's Many Histories," in this volume, 9.

7. "Annexation," *The United States Magazine, and Democratic Review* 17, no. 85 (July–August 1845): 5; Bushman, "Joseph Smith's Many Histories."

8. Thomas Jefferson, Letter to James Madison, December 20, 1787, in *The Papers of Thomas Jefferson* (Princeton: Princeton University Press, 1955), 12:440.

9. Bushman, "Joseph Smith's Many Histories," 17.

10. "Golden Bible," *The Reflector* 2, no. 12 (February 1, 1831): 69.

11. *Manuscript History of Brigham Young*, December 27, 1841, Church Archives, The Church of Jesus Christ of Latter-day Saints, Salt Lake City.

12. Dean C. Jessee, ed., *The Papers of Joseph Smith*, 2 vols. (Salt Lake City: Deseret Book, 1989–92), 1:268–69.

13. Lucy Mack Smith, *Biographical Sketches of Joseph Smith the Prophet* (Liverpool: Richards, 1853), 73.

14. Jessee, *Personal Writings of Joseph Smith*, 10.

15. *Times and Seasons* 3 (November 1841–October 1842): 749.

16. Joseph Smith Jr., *History of The Church of Jesus Christ of Latter-day Saints*, ed. B. H. Roberts, 2d ed., rev., 7 vols. (Salt Lake City: Deseret Book, 1971), 6:317.

Joseph Smith as an American Restorationist

Richard T. Hughes

Richard Bushman's wonderfully expansive paper "Joseph Smith's Many Histories" reminds us in forceful ways of the historical complexity that helped create the Mormon Prophet, Joseph Smith. Bushman also reminds us that while historical complexity is embedded in history, it embeds itself as well in the hearts and minds of human beings who discover the various realities of history and then appropriate those realities for their own purposes. As an illustration of this point, Bushman tells the story of Christopher Columbus—how his standing as the grandfather of the United States was neither acknowledged nor celebrated until after 1776.[1]

A second Columbus anecdote serves to introduce further the point of seeing Joseph Smith in the context of the biblical "restorationism." A few years ago at Pepperdine University, where I teach, Christopher Columbus came very close to being baptized into the history of the American restorationist traditions. Two great restoration movements—movements that sought to restore the purity of the Christian faith—emerged on the American frontier in the early nineteenth century. One was led by Joseph Smith; the other was led by Alexander Campbell. These two movements shared much in common, and one of those commonalities was adult baptism by immersion for the forgiveness of sins. Pepperdine is an institution intimately related to the restoration efforts of Alexander Campbell, and in this tradition, as well as in that of the Latter-day Saints, baptism by immersion for the forgiveness of sins is valued no less today than it was two hundred years ago.

Some years ago, a donor presented Pepperdine with a statue of Christopher Columbus. This was no ordinary statue. It was a statue of Columbus extending his right arm to its full length and pointing. But pointing to what? The Pepperdine administration installed the Columbus statue on a precipice overlooking the Pacific Ocean, so on our campus, at least, Columbus points to water—indeed, to vast expanses of water.

About a year after the Columbus statue was erected, a friend of mine was visiting Pepperdine for the very first time. Upon seeing the statue, she wryly commented what a fine thing it might be to hang a sign on that outstretched, pointing arm of Columbus, a sign that would read, in the words of the Ethiopian eunuch, "See, here is water; what doth hinder me to be baptized?" (Acts 8:36). That struck me as a splendid suggestion, one that might alter once again the way that Columbus is perceived. But so far no one has mustered the courage to hang that sign on Columbus's extended arm.

This incident invites us to explore in greater depth the commonalities that tied Joseph Smith to Alexander Campbell, and vice versa. Bushman points out that Alexander Campbell in many ways fathered the non-Mormon perspective on Joseph Smith—a perspective that viewed Smith as a charlatan, a fraud, a fanatic, and, above all, as someone shaped entirely by his own provincial world. Indeed, Alexander Campbell viewed Joseph Smith as purely and simply a "product of his [local] American environment."[2] As Bushman points out, Campbell claimed that Smith, "through his stone spectacles, wrote on the plates of Nephi, in his Book of Mormon, every error and almost every truth discussed in New York for the last ten years."[3] This perspective found proponents in a host of critics ranging from J. B. Turner to I. Woodbridge Riley to Fawn Brodie and most recently to Dan Vogel.

Thus, Bushman argues that in the non-Mormon view America created Joseph Smith. He notes that Mormons, on the other hand, have "linked Joseph to the history of biblical prophets . . . [and have] assigned him the historical role of restoring the pure gospel after a long period of apostasy . . . [and] preparing the world for the Second Coming of Christ." According to Bushman, therefore, Joseph has an additional history, extending beyond the United States and "back to the New Testament and the loss of Christ's original gospel."[4]

I quite agree that Joseph has an additional history that extends beyond the United States. But first I want to explore the explicitly American dimensions of Joseph Smith. Indeed, to juxtapose an American Joseph with a gospel Joseph may be too simple. For the gospel Joseph that Bushman describes—the Joseph who "restor[ed] the pure gospel after a long period of apostasy . . . [and] prepar[ed] the world for the Second Coming of Christ"—was himself a product of two histories. This gospel Joseph was a product of the transnational biblical witness, to be sure. But the gospel Joseph was also a product of powerful forces in American life in the early nineteenth century.

I mean precisely this: that the restoration vision which so thoroughly informed the work of Joseph Smith flourished in antebellum America in ways that it has seldom flourished at any other place or any other time in the past two thousand years.

I understand that the restoration vision is a venerable vision that emerged as early as the second century with Irenaeus. It emerged again in the Middle Ages with sectarian movements that sought to recover the heart of New Testament Christianity. It emerged in the early sixteenth century with the Anabaptists and later in that century with the Puritans. But in America in the early nineteenth century, the restoration vision flourished as never before. More than this, virtually every restoration movement of that time imagined that by restoring the primitive church, or some feature of the primitive church, they were helping to usher in the Millennium or, as Bushman puts it in his paper, they thought they were "preparing the world for the Second Coming of Jesus Christ." One thinks, in this context, not only of Joseph Smith, but also of Alexander Campbell, who firmly believed that "just in so far as the ancient order of things, or the religion of the New Testament, is restored, just so far has the Millennium commenced."[5] This is the great commonality that Alexander Campbell shared with Joseph Smith, in spite of the fact that Campbell thought Joseph a fraud and an imposter and a product not of inspiration but of his local environment in New York State. Indeed, for some thirty-five years, Alexander Campbell edited a journal devoted to what he called the "restoration of the ancient order of things" but bearing the title *The Millennial Harbinger*.[6]

One could argue, as I did in the *Journal of Mormon History* in 1993, that while Joseph Smith and Alexander Campbell were both committed to the restoration of the ancient order of things, what divided them was the way they envisioned the task of restoration. Joseph was essentially a romantic, informed by the spirit of American Romanticism.[7] He therefore wrote and spoke about how God, in the days of prophets and apostles, spoke directly to humankind. In those days, he said, the heavens were opened. But apostasy reared its head and the heavens closed and God no longer spoke to men and women as he did in the golden age of the saints. Joseph viewed himself, therefore, as God's chosen vessel, commissioned to usher in a restoration of that golden age of direct revelation, and in that restoration, God once again would speak to humankind, just as he had in the days of old.

On the other hand, Alexander Campbell was a child of the eighteenth-century Enlightenment. He had no use for the romantic notion that God might speak to men and women through dreams and revelations. For him, God spoke only through a book that rational people could read and understand in rational ways. And only on the basis of a rational approach to a rational text could one possibly hope to restore the glories of the ancient church. At least that was Campbell's claim, and from this highly rational perspective, he imagined Smith both a fraud and a charlatan.

Joseph Smith and Alexander Campbell, therefore, clearly shared a vision of the restoration of the ancient order of things, but they parted company on how that vision should be understood and implemented.

Even more important is the fact that these two restorationists—Smith and Campbell—led the two most successful new religious movements in America in the early nineteenth century. The question we must ask is this: why did so many Americans find the gospel of the restored church and the gospel of the coming Millennium so incredibly attractive?

In nineteenth-century America, Joseph Smith and Alexander Campbell were not the only ones who advocated the restoration of the ancient faith, nor were they the only ones who claimed that the restoration of the ancient church would usher in the Millennium—the final golden age. One finds the very same perspective, the very same conviction that restoration leads to millennium, in the Shakers and even in John Humphrey Noyes's Oneida Community.

The Shakers believed that what stood at the core of the ancient church was sexual purity. After all, had Paul not advised the early Christians to remain celibate, even as he was celibate? And so the Shakers thought that if they could recover the purity of the ancient church in that respect, they would herald the Second Coming of Christ. This is precisely why the official name of the Shakers was the United Society of Believers in Christ's Second Appearing, or Millennial Church.

It is important to realize that in England Mother Ann Lee was able to win only a handful of converts to the gospel of a restored, celibate church. Once in America, however, she won to her cause not tens or hundreds but thousands. And once again, we must ask the question, what was it about the gospel of the restored church that Americans found so compelling?

John Humphrey Noyes and his followers in the Oneida Community also thought of themselves as restoring the heart and soul of New Testament Christianity. But Noyes defined the golden age of the church in terms precisely opposite those embraced by the Shakers. If the Shakers thought the essence of biblical Christianity consisted in celibacy, Noyes thought the core of biblical Christianity consisted in the rejection of selfish thoughts and selfish ways. And for Noyes, what could be more selfish than monogamous marriage? And so, in his attempt to restore biblical religion, he brought together men and women who were prepared to renounce the selfishness of the marriage bed and to practice instead what Noyes described as "complex marriage"—a euphemism, really, for what amounted to free love. But we should not allow the shocking nature of Noyes's experiment to obscure the fact that Noyes viewed himself, first and foremost, as a biblical restorationist.

Noyes never claimed that this restoration would usher in the final millennial age. Instead, he believed that the Millennium had already come in AD 70, and the possibility of millennial perfection, he argued, was precisely what allowed him and his followers to embrace the restoration of a selfless society, centered on the practice of complex marriage. So even in John Humphrey Noyes, one finds the close connection—even the interdependence—of the restoration and millennial motifs, even as one finds that same interdependence in Joseph Smith, Alexander Campbell, and the Shakers.

John Humphrey Noyes never attracted converts by the thousands as Joseph Smith, Alexander Campbell, and the Shakers did. But the fact that he attracted hundreds to his community of restored, selfless perfection is once again a tribute to the enormous popularity of the restoration vision in antebellum America.

The question we must ask ourselves now is, why? And how can we account for the popularity of the restoration vision in early nineteenth-century America? The restoration vision—especially the notion that a restoration of a golden age of the past would herald the Millennium or the golden age of the future—was an important theme built into the heart and soul of American culture in the early nineteenth century.

Where, for example, do we find the notion of restoration in the broader American culture of that period? We need look no further than the Declaration of Independence and the "self-evident" truths it proclaims. Those truths were self-evident because they were grounded, not in human history or human invention, but in nature, in the way things were meant to be, and were based on the original design one finds in the Garden of Eden. No wonder Thomas Paine announced that "the case and circumstances of America present themselves as in the beginning of the world." Or again, he wrote that when we view America "we are brought at once to the point of seeing government begin, as if we had lived in the beginning of time. The real volume, not of history, but of facts, is directly before us, not mutilated by contrivance, or the errors of tradition."[8]

But if Americans in the nineteenth century thought their nation was a restoration of the principles of nature, grounded in Eden at the dawn of time, they also imagined that this same nation, precisely because it had restored those truths, would usher in a final golden age for all humankind. For example, Lyman Beecher, a contemporary of Joseph Smith and a prominent evangelical preacher, claimed in 1827 that America

> will throw its beams beyond the waves; it will shine into darkness there and be comprehended; it will awaken desire and hope and effort, and produce revolutions and overturnings, until the world is free.
>
> . . . Then will the trumpet of Jubilee sound, and earth's debased millions will leap from the dust, and shake off their chains, and cry, "Hosanna to the Son of David."[9]

The great seal of the United States makes precisely the same point. There, an unfinished pyramid grows from arid desert sands. Inscribed on the pyramid's base is that notable date, 1776. Clearly, the pyramid represents the new nation. The barren desert terrain, above which the pyramid towers and from which it seems to grow, signifies all human history prior to 1776. For all their glories and achievements, past civilizations were essentially barren compared to the glories that would mark the new American state. The pyramid is unfinished since other nations have not yet emulated the American example and thrown off the yoke of tyranny. But as the American example penetrates the dark places of the world and as nation after nation and tribe after tribe rise up and reject the rule of tyrants, the world will become increasingly free, and when the world is free, the Millennium will have dawned. God clearly approves of this vision since above the pyramid we find his eye and, above that eye, the Latin phrase *annuity coeptis*, "He has smiled on our beginnings." And beneath the pyramid stands the most critical phrase of all, *novus ordo seclorum*, "a new order of the ages."

That is precisely what America was—a new order of the ages. But in a very real sense, it was also the most ancient nation of all, for it had sunk its deepest root into the beginning of time when the world came fresh from the hand of God.

What I am saying is simply this, that in the early nineteenth century, popular American culture thrived on the cosmic rhythm of restoration and millennium. And these are the very themes that informed not only Joseph Smith and his Latter-day Saints but a host of other new religions as well, including Alexander Campbell's Churches of Christ, Ann Lee's Shakers, and John Humphrey Noyes's Oneida Community.

This suggests that when I. Woodbridge Riley claimed that Joseph's Book of Mormon embodied popular American themes like "anti-Masonry, anti-Catholicism, Methodism, attacks on infidelity, theories of Indian origins, anti-Calvinism, and Baptist doctrine,"[10] he missed the most important theme of all, and that was the cosmic rhythm of restoration and millennium that defined both the nation and most of the nation's new religions.

In making this argument, I have no doubt come across as a reductionist with a vengeance, as the typical non-Mormon who wants to argue that "America created Joseph Smith." But in my view, there is far more to Joseph than this. For as Bushman has argued so eloquently, Joseph has a history that extends beyond the United States. That history, in my view, is preeminently the biblical saga.

In the first place, it would be hard to celebrate the cosmic rhythm of restoration and millennium apart from the biblical vision where those themes are most deeply rooted. And second, Joseph clearly draws on the biblical vision in ways that dwarf every other nineteenth-century American preacher or would-be prophet. For Joseph refused to confine himself to the New Testament or the Old Testament or to certain sections of the Bible that he found most useful. Instead, Joseph ranged throughout the Bible and drew from it all. What I wrote almost twenty years ago of early Mormons is also true of Joseph—indeed, is preeminently true of Joseph:

> Unwilling therefore to confine themselves to a single book or to a single sacred epoch as did traditional restorationists . . . [e]arly Mormons sought "the restoration of all things." Like bees sucking nectar first from this flower and then from the next, early Mormons moved at ease from the primitive church to Moses to the prophets to Abraham to Adam and finally to the coming millennium.[11]

Here is the history that, in Bushman's words, extends beyond the United States "back to the New Testament."[12] For this is a cosmic history that shaped the Prophet in cosmic ways. But even as that cosmic, biblical history shaped the Prophet in cosmic ways, it did so in a profoundly American context. In this way, Joseph Smith emerges as the dialectical prophet, the man with one foot in American culture and the other in biblical culture, and the man who fused the two in a profound act of creative genius. Bushman is exactly right: Joseph is American, but any attempt to understand Joseph exclusively in terms of his American setting is bound to fail.

Notes

1. Richard Bushman, "Joseph Smith's Many Histories," in this volume, 3.

2. Bushman, "Joseph Smith's Many Histories," 5.

3. Fawn M. Brodie, *No Man Knows My History: The Life of Joseph Smith the Mormon Prophet,* 2d ed. (New York: Knopf, 1971), 69, quoted in Bushman, "Joseph Smith's Many Histories," 5.

4. Bushman, "Joseph Smith's Many Histories," 6.

5. Alexander Campbell, "A Restoration of the Ancient Order of Things. No. I," *Christian Baptist* 2, no. 7 (February 7, 1825): 128.

6. Alexander Campbell, "Preface," *Millennial Harbinger* (January 3, 1831): 5.

7. Richard T. Hughes, "Tanner Lecture: Two Restoration Traditions: Mormons and Churches of Christ in the Nineteenth Century," *Journal of Mormon History* 19 (Spring 1993): 34–51.

8. Thomas Paine, "Rights of Man," in *The Complete Writings of Thomas Paine,* ed. Philip S. Foner, 2 vols. (New York: Citadel Press, 1945), 1:376.

9. Lyman Beecher, "The Memory of Our Fathers," in *Nationalism and Religion in America,* ed. Winthrop S. Hudson (New York: Harper and Row, 1970), 104–5.

10. Bushman, "Joseph Smith's Many Histories," 8.

11. Richard T. Hughes and C. Leonard Allen, *Illusions of Innocence: Protestant Primitivism in America, 1630–1875* (Chicago: University of Chicago Press, 1988), 146.

12. Bushman, "Joseph Smith's Many Histories," 6.

Attempting to Situate Joseph Smith

Grant Underwood

Undergirding Richard Bushman's insightful paper is a profound recognition (and a reminder) that histories are the creations of authors, not photographs of the past. Every aspect of writing a history, from the selection of sources to the interpretation of those sources bears the imprint of the author. The profoundly precarious and contingent character of all reconstructions of the past led Roland Barthes to quip that biography is "a novel that dare not speak its name."[1] Clearly, this is an overstatement, but it does warn us away from an unhealthy critical complacency when engaging in studying written histories.

Bushman draws attention to the fact that there are as many histories of Joseph Smith as there are authors, and he highlights representative types from J. B. Turner to Harold Bloom. In the end, some biographies are more detailed or more illuminating than others, but none has captured the man in his fullness. Moreover, Bushman is the first to admit that his long-awaited biography *Joseph Smith: Rough Stone Rolling*, though more comprehensive and nuanced than other studies, is still Bushman's Joseph just as we already have Brooke's Joseph and Brodie's Joseph.[2]

Bushman draws a contrast between authors who place Joseph solely within an American setting and those who link him to what

Bushman calls "transnational histories." Bushman argues that it is the transnational history that made Smith significant. "I am advocating global perspectives," he writes, "I think they are the only way to highlight the nature of Joseph Smith's achievement. If we tie him down to upstate rural New York, we will miss the expansiveness of his thinking, like explaining Shakespeare from the small town mentality of Stratford."[3] Bushman's stimulating comments need to be engaged further on at least two levels—in terms of content and methodology.

Additional Situational Histories

To Bushman's list of histories that have been attached to Joseph Smith, one may highlight several additional contexts that could yield important insights. How, for instance, does Joseph Smith's socioeconomic vision of Zion fit within the international history of utopian theorists and intentional communities around the world?[4] Or, how do his views on marriage and family look when compared with the many forms of familial organization found in world civilizations and societies?[5] And what about his notion of religious "restoration," which, as Richard Hughes has argued, places him in a long line of biblical primitivists in many countries committed to reclaiming the ancient faith and reforming their churches to match the scriptural pattern?[6]

Consider, for example, the complexity of the latter perspective. At the heart of Smith's primitivism lay the expectation of restoring the vital, charismatic Christianity he believed existed during New Testament times. Prophetic charismata had been officially squelched in the second Christian century in response to the outbreak of the Montanist prophecy.[7] The ecclesiastical establishment at the time redefined the biblical promise that the Spirit would lead into all truth. Christian theologians decided that the Spirit had uniquely led the original apostles into all truth as they composed the books of the New Testament and that the Spirit would lead subsequent generations of Christians to that same truth—but only through the apostles' writings rather than through direct, personal communications from God.[8] As Tertullian quipped, by this interpretation, "The Holy Spirit was chased into a book," and certain Christians have been trying to free it ever since.[9]

While Joseph Smith may have been among the most successful in seeking to revive a charismatic Christianity, he was not alone in this pursuit. Recent scholarship has documented an astonishingly rich presence of prophets and prophetic religion along the periphery of Anglo-American Christianity in the century before Smith. Historian Susan Juster has identified more than three hundred "prophets" who raised their voices and recorded their visions during this period.[10]

Here is another history that may be attached to the Mormon founder. Douglas Winiarski writes that this extensive "visionary culture" has been discovered among groups as diverse as the "English Methodists, New Light Scots-Irish Presbyterians, German sectarians, and African slaves," and their sons and daughters were prophesying and seeing visions "in the marshlands of Nova Scotia, the northern New England hill country, the 'Burned-Over District' of upstate New York, and the borderlands of Kentucky and Ohio."[11] By Joseph Smith's day, charismatic experience had clearly overflowed the dikes of denominational religion. As historian Gordon Wood states, "The disintegration of older structures of authority released torrents of popular religiosity into public life."[12] Far from being silenced by the onrush of the Enlightenment, "God had more prophets, tongues, and oracles than ever before," notes Leigh Schmidt; "thus, the . . . predicament actually became as much one of God's loquacity as God's hush."[13] "More and more people," explains Juster, "were seeing and speaking to God directly, without the mediating influence of preachers or churches, and all [the ministers] could do about it was scoff."[14]

Bushman has rightly pointed out that the problem with Joseph Smith's account of his first vision was that it struck local churchmen as merely the latest example in the long and lamentable history of prophetic activity they had come to denounce under the rubric of "enthusiasm." And Smith's encounter with Moroni recalls cleric Charles Woodmason's mocking description of a woman "highly celebrated for her extraordinary Illuminations, Visions and Communications," who told "of an Angel coming to visit her in the Night thro' the Roof of her Cabbin—In flames of Fire too!"[15] Yet all the fulminations of the clerical establishment could not change the fact that for many Christians, as Shaker prophet Ann Lee is reported to have declared,

God's work in these "latter days," was to be *"a strange work . . . even a marvellous work and a wonder."*[16]

Lee's comment points to still another history in which the prophet can be situated—the history of millenarianism. A religion is said to be millenarian when its

> basic source of energy and momentum [derive] from its sense of being the chosen people of God living in the final days of history. This self-understanding—which lies at the heart of all millenarian movements and distinguishes them from all other forms of religious expression—must be seen as the source of that explosive and transformative power which is characteristic of both early Christianity and early Mormonism.[17]

At times, millenarianism can be quite apocalyptic, threatening the spiritually effete religious establishment with imminent destruction and promising ultimate vindication for the beleaguered faithful. A world in the grip of sin can hardly be expected to yield to the entreaties of the righteous. Only God can set things aright, and such divine intervention is expected to come dramatically, even cataclysmically, and soon to introduce the millennial age.[18]

Smith's early writings exhibit just such an apocalyptic sensibility. In a letter to his followers in Colesville, New York, in August 1830, he wrote:

> Be not faint, the day of your deliverance is not far distant, for the judgements of the Lord are already abroad in the earth, and the cold hand of death, will soon pass through your neighborhood, and sweep away some of your most bitter enemies, for . . . the earth will soon be reaped—that is, the wicked must soon be destroyed from off the face of the earth, for the Lord hath spoken it . . . for the day is fast hastening on when the restoration of all things shall be fulfilled. . . . Then shall come to pass that the lion shall lie down with the lamb &c.[19]

In an open letter to the public in 1833, Smith told the American people, "Distruction to the eye of the spiritual beholder seems to be writen by the finger of an invisable hand in Large capitals upon almost evry thing we behold." For this reason, "I declare unto you the warning which the Lord has commanded me to declare unto this generation . . .

Repent ye Repent, ye and imbrace the everlasting Covenant and flee to Zion before the overflowing scourge overtake you."[20]

In time, Smith's sense of the immediacy of the Apocalypse moderated. Setbacks such as the Saints' expulsion from their Missouri Zion as well as an increasing awareness of how much they themselves had to do to build the Kingdom of God on earth before Christ returned deepened the Mormon prophet's understanding of God's timetable for human history. Especially after an encounter with followers of William Miller, who calculated that the Second Coming would occur about the year 1843, the Prophet's expectation of an imminent Advent of Christ diminished.[21]

In the latter part of his paper, Bushman turns to the "Prophet puzzle" posed by Jan Shipps and explores Smith's own efforts to find suitable histories to explain the experiences he had personally witnessed. Only through the Book of Mormon, Bushman suggests, was the young prophet able to find a history that solved the conundrum of his identity as visionary, seer, and translator. Today, other histories are available that articulate a compatibility between involvement with folk magic and religious visions. More than ever, the old Enlightenment dichotomy between magic and religion that used to underwrite critiques of the Prophet is now seen to artificially separate what has long been intermingled in most human societies.[22] The great Hebrew prophet Samuel, for instance, was sought for his seeric ability to locate lost donkeys as well as to proclaim the will of Yahweh (1 Samuel 9:1–10). And the use of divinatory aids to revelation, including seer stones and mineral rods, is not uncommon in the history of prophecy.[23] Among certain groups, however, most notably ancient Israel, scholars have noted that as substantive, written prophecies began to dominate, the formerly sanctioned divinatory devices became less common and even illegitimate.[24] Similarly, Joseph Smith's youthful seeric prowess in locating lost objects or discovering treasure was, in time, overshadowed by his more transcendent ability to bring forth God's works "out of obscurity and out of darkness," and his history was told accordingly.[25]

With regard to the Book of Mormon, Bushman points out that there was no precedent for Joseph's role as unlearned translator of an ancient record other than the account provided in the book itself of the translator-seer King Mosiah. This is certainly true for the world Smith knew, but Bushman's invitation to situate Joseph in broader, transnational histories, beyond the borders of the United States and even beyond a Judeo-Christian heritage, enables us to discover some interesting parallels. In the Nyingma tradition of Tibetan Buddhism, for instance, a fundamental source of religious teaching is the *termas* (treasures). Termas include sacred texts composed anciently, primarily by the great Guru Rinpoche (Padmasambhava), and hidden by him in various secret locations to be discovered at a later date. Termas can be located and interpreted only by a special class of spiritually enlightened adepts (bodishattvas) known as *tertons* (treasure finders). Only tertons can reveal these texts because they are written in the cryptic language of the *Dakini* (supernatural beings).[26]

Placing these histories side by side, Smith looks like an American terton-seer translating ancient texts written in cryptic Reformed Egyptian by the great prophets of the past, Mormon and Moroni. The prophets' purpose for writing, as it had been for Guru Rinpoche, included keeping the faith on track by making clear the fundamental "plain and precious" principles of the tradition. Further, it is interesting to note that some of the Tibetan termas are called "mind treasures" because they are "not physically discovered but are revealed through the mind of the terton."[27] This phraseology recalls the prophecies of Enoch or the parchment of John revealed by Joseph Smith. What is interesting here is not to preposterously argue for any organic connection between Joseph Smith and Tibetan Buddhism but to notice the similar mechanisms for authorizing a religious text and to ponder the social and intellectual dynamics that make them effective.

Joseph, of course, was reared in the biblically saturated culture of the Second Great Awakening and found in the Bible his most meaningful links to other histories. In several of his revelations, for instance, he is likened to Moses or identified as an apostle of Jesus Christ.[28] Throughout his life he unvaryingly affirmed his status as God's spokesman. While deciding the legitimacy of this claim is beyond the methods of academia, Joseph would be pleased to know that scholars today do not rule it out as a theoretical possibility. Some

Christian historians, such as the evangelical scholar George Marsden, insist that history, "when viewed without a proper awareness of the spiritual forces involved, 'is as confusing as a football game in which half the players are invisible' [quoting Richard Lovelace]." While the only possible realm of examination and analysis for an academic methodology remains the visible, natural world,

> it would be a mistake to assume that such [an approach] is incompatible with, or even antagonistic to, a view of history in which God as revealed in Scripture is the dominant force, and in which other unseen spiritual forces are contending . . . which we understand only imperfectly and whose true dimensions we only occasionally glimpse.[29]

Methodological Cautions about Comparative Histories

Marsden's comments provide a convenient segue into a discussion of methodological concerns. Bushman wants to tap the promise of comparative history and I agree, but religious devotees are sometimes skittish about comparative analysis because it seems to rob their particular religion of its uniqueness. They assume that uniqueness is prime evidence of their faith's divine origin. Such thinking, however, confuses a religion's character with its source. Similarity and difference are descriptive categories; they say nothing necessarily about origin. Properly pursued, comparative analysis is useful in drawing attention to larger processes of human behavioral and intellectual development. Comparisons can identify the commonalities of human nature that may be at work across cultures or make the distinguishing aspects of religious belief and practice stand out in bold relief. And, of course, pointing out similarities, like translating from one language to another, facilitates understanding, since, in one sense, all knowledge is analogical.[30]

However, comparisons can be overdone. What Samuel Sandmel, in a famous 1961 presidential address before the Society of Biblical Literature, called "parallelomania" has given comparative analysis a bad name. The sins of parallelomania are exaggerated similarities and the inappropriate inferences drawn from them about the source and derivation of ideas.[31] Conceptual parallels do not prove intellectual provenance. Twenty years ago in the introduction to *Joseph Smith and the Beginnings of Mormonism,* Bushman wisely wrote:

> In the first stages of composition this book was titled "The Origins of Mormonism." The word "Origins" was dropped when the actual complexities of identifying the sources of Mormon belief and experience bared themselves. An attempt to trace all the images, ideas, language, and emotional structure of a movement as elaborate as Mormonism became more evidently elusive and futile as the work went on.[32]

Inappropriate parallels are often a function of not knowing both sides of the comparison equally well. "Two passages may sound the same in splendid isolation from their context, but when seen in context [they] reflect difference rather than similarity," explains Sandmel. What is crucial is the "genuine comprehension of the tone, texture, and import of a literature."[33] Through the mistaken practice of parallelomania, notes New Testament scholar David Flusser, "we could easily construct a whole gospel from ancient Jewish writings without using a single word that originated with Jesus."[34]

At times, parallelomania has been a problem in Joseph Smith studies as well. Was Joseph Smith (per Brooke) really a Renaissance magus redivivus? Is Mormonism (per Emerson) really an afterclap of Puritanism? Is the Book of Mormon (per Brodie or Vogel) just thinly veiled autobiography?[35] Sometimes similarities can be so imaginative, they are imaginary. At least when Harold Bloom likens Smith's Nauvoo doctrines to the Jewish kabbalah, he is doing so comparatively, not genetically.[36]

As has been noted, what is too often lacking in these comparisons is an adequate immersion in both the extant Smith sources and those on the other side. Mormon historians tend to know Smith well but do not command the comparative sources. Non-Mormon scholars know their own fields but sometimes misstep because they lack a deep and contextualized grasp of Smith. As a result, superficial or wrongheaded comparisons are regularly made. The Mormon doctrine of deification is just one example. Upon close examination, divinization in Smith's thought looks quite different than what is taught in the kabbalah or hermetic mysticism. To believe that a resurrected, glorified human being with body of flesh and bones may eventually become a separate, autonomous god is something qualitatively distinct from believing that perfect creatures can be mystically united with and/or reabsorbed by a transcendent, wholly other Creator, or that such perfection is achievable in the present state as it was for mystic Nat Smith (no relation of Joseph Smith), who "wore a cap with the word GOD inscribed on its front."[37]

Intellectual historians emphasize that one can grasp the full meaning of an idea only by carefully recreating the religious idiom or culture from which it emerges. In doing transnational comparisons or studies of *longue duree*, we must ever keep our feet firmly planted in Joseph Smith's own time. Ideas are not things that move unchanged in and out of minds across the decades or across cultures. Careful attention must be paid to the immediate communities of discourse in which Joseph Smith participated in order to disclose the repertoire of possible meanings for his words. In one of Smith's revelations, God explains that the divine messages "were given unto my servants in their weakness, after the manner of their language, that they might come to understanding" (Doctrine and Covenants 1:24). The more the cultural as well as verbal language of Joseph Smith is understood in all its depth and breadth, the more nuanced and compelling will be the comparative histories that are attached to the prophet.

Joseph Smith once quipped that "no man knows my history."[38] Although present studies on Joseph Smith situating him in various contexts constitute the mere tip of a huge and growing iceberg of Joseph Smith scholarship, his history—or, in truth, the multiple histories that illuminate the Mormon prophet—will continue to enrich our understanding of his life and thought.

Notes

1. Roland Barthes, quoted in *Difference in View: Women and Modernism*, ed. Gabriele Griffin (London: Taylor and Francis, 1994), 41.

2. Richard Lyman Bushman, *Joseph Smith: Rough Stone Rolling* (New York: Knopf, 2005); John L. Brooke, *The Refiner's Fire: The Making of Mormon*

Cosmology: 1644–1844 (Cambridge: Cambridge University Press, 1994); Fawn M. Brodie, *No Man Knows My History: The Life of Joseph Smith* (New York: Knopf, 1945).

3. Richard Bushman, memo to author, April 22, 2005.

4. For broad historical context, see Frank E. Manuel, *Utopian Thought in the Western World* (Cambridge: Belknap, 1979); Roland Schaer and others, *Utopia: The Search for the Ideal Society in the Western World* (New York: Oxford University Press, 2000). U.S. communitarian history is reviewed in Robert P. Sutton, *Communal Utopias and the American Experience: Secular Communities, 1824–2000* (Westport, Conn.: Praeger, 2004); and Sutton, *Communal Utopias and the American Experience: Religious Communities, 1732–2000* (Westport, Conn.: Praeger, 2003). The ideals and activities of contemporary intentional communities are covered in *Communities: A Journal of Cooperative Living.*

5. One may find access to the vast literature on this subject by consulting Gwen J. Broude, *Marriage, Family, and Relationships: A Cross-Cultural Encyclopedia* (Santa Barbara, Calif.: ABC-CLIO, 1994). See also Stephanie Coontz, *Marriage: A History* (New York: Viking, 2005); G. Robina Quale, *A History of Marriage Systems* (New York: Greenwood Press, 1988).

6. Richard T. Hughes, ed., *The American Quest for the Primitive Church* (Urbana: University of Illinois Press, 1988); and Richard T. Hughes and C. Leonard Allen, *Illusions of Innocence: Protestant Primitivism in America, 1630–1875* (Chicago: University of Chicago Press, 1988), 133–52.

7. David E. Aune, *Prophecy in Early Christianity and the Ancient Mediterranean World* (Grand Rapids, Mich.: Eerdmans, 1983).

8. On Montanism, see Dennis E. Groh, "Montanism," in *Encyclopedia of Early Christianity*, ed. Everett Ferguson (New York: Garland, 1990), 622–23; and Christine Trevett, *Montanism: Gender, Authority and the New Prophecy* (New York: Cambridge University Press, 1996).

9. Quoted in Bruce L. Shelley, *Church History in Plain Language* (Waco, Tex.: Word Books, 1982), 80. On Tertullian and Montanism generally, see Timothy David Barnes, *Tertullian: A Historical and Literary Study* (Oxford: Clarendon Press, 1985), and Cecil M. Robeck Jr., "Prophetic Gifts in the Writings of Tertullian," in *Prophecy in Carthage: Perpetua, Tertullian, and Cyprian* (Cleveland: Pilgrim Press, 1992), 95–145.

10. Susan Juster, *Doomsayers: Anglo-American Prophecy in the Age of Revolution* (Philadelphia: University of Pennsylvania Press, 2003). "The total figure," comments Juster, "surely underrepresents the actual number by a considerable margin; it is based on a survey of published sources (pamphlets, broadsides, newspapers, literary journals, and evangelical memoirs), sources which do not capture the full range of unorthodox religious activity but only those individuals and practices thought noteworthy by churchmen and the educated elite," 64.

11. Douglas L. Winiarski, "Souls Filled with Ravishing Transport: Heavenly Visions and the Radical Awakening in New England," *William and Mary Quarterly* 61, no. 1, 3d ser. (January 2004): 41. See also Ann Kirschner, "'Tending to Edify, Astonish, and Instruct': Published Narratives of Spiritual Dreams and Visions in the Early Republic," *Early American Studies* 1, no. 1 (Spring 2003): 198–229.

12. Gordon S. Wood, "Evangelical America and Early Mormonism," *New York History* 61, no. 4 (October 1980): 368.

13. Leigh Eric Schmidt, *Hearing Things: Religion, Illusion, and the American Enlightenment* (Cambridge: Harvard University Press, 2000), 11, quoted in Juster, *Doomsayers*, 23.

14. Juster, *Doomsayers*, 23.

15. Richard J. Hooker, ed., *The Carolina Backcountry on the Eve of the Revolution: The Journal and Other Writings of Charles Woodmason, Anglican Itinerant* (Chapel Hill: University of North Carolina Press, 1969), 104.

16. Benjamin Seth Youngs, *The Testimony of Christ's Second Appearing: Containing a General Statement of All Things Pertaining to the Faith and Practice of the Church of God in This Latter-day* (Albany: Hosford, 1810), 9, quoted in Juster, *Doomsayers*, 54.

17. John G. Gager, "Early Mormonism and Early Christianity: Some Parallels and Their Consequences for the Study of New Religions," *Journal of Mormon History* 9 (1982): 56.

18. An excellent synthesis of the several-thousand-year history of apocalypticism is Bernard McGinn, John J. Collins, and Stephen J. Stein, *Encylopedia of Apocalypticism*, 3 vols. (New York: Continuum, 1998).

19. Joseph Smith and John Whitmer to Beloved in the Lord, August 20, 1830, copied in Newel Knight, "Autobiography," 132–34, original manuscript in possession of Robert Allen, Salem, Utah.

20. Joseph Smith to N. C. Saxton, editor of the *American Revivalist, and Rochester Observer*, January 4, 1833, reproduced in Dean C. Jessee, ed. and comp., *The Personal Writings of Joseph Smith* (1984; repr., Salt Lake City: Deseret Book; Provo, Utah: Brigham Young University Press, 2002), 297–98.

21. Grant Underwood, *Millenarian World of Early Mormonism* (Urbana: University of Illinois Press, 1993), 112–26.

22. Classic studies include James G. Frazer, *The Golden Bough: A Study in Magic and Religion*, abridged ed. (New York: Macmillan, 1958), and Keith Thomas, *Religion and the Decline of Magic* (New York: Scribner, 1971). For a contemporary reflection, see Randall Styers, *Making Magic: Religion, Magic, and Science in the Modern World* (New York: Oxford University Press, 2004).

23. Convenient historical summaries can be found in Ronald W. Walker, "The Persisting Idea of American Treasure Hunting," *BYU Studies* 24 (Fall 1984, actually published in 1986): 429–59, and D. Michael Quinn, *Early Mormonism and the Magic World View* (Salt Lake City: Signature Books, 1987), 1–52.

24. Scott B. Noegel and Brannon M. Wheeler, *Historical Dictionary of Prophets in Islam and Judaism* (Lanham, Md.: Scarecrow Press, 2002).

25. The quote is from the "preface" to Smith's compilation of his revelations known as the Doctrine and Covenants. See Doctrine and Covenants 1:30. The sentence's argument echoes Bushman's interpretation first laid out in *Joseph Smith and the Beginnings of Mormonism* (Urbana: University of Illinois Press, 1984), 69–80.

26. Yeshe Tsogyal, *The Lotus-Born: The Life Story of Padmasambhava* (Hong Kong: Rangjung Yeshe Publications, 2004); Sogyal Rinpoche, *The Tibetan Book of Living and Dying* (New York: HarperCollins, 1993); and Rebecca McClen Novick, *Fundamentals of Tibetan Buddhism* (Freedom, Calif.: Crossing Press, 1999).

27. Novick, *Fundmentals of Tibetan Buddhism*, 180.

28. See Doctrine and Covenants 28:2; 107:91; 21:1. For a broader discussion of Smith's relationship with the Bible, see Philip L. Barlow, *Mormons and the Bible: The Place of the Latter-day Saints in American Religion* (New York: Oxford University Press, 1991), 3–73.

29. George M. Marsden, *Fundamentalism and American Culture: The Shaping of Twentieth-Century Evangelicalism, 1870–1925* (New York: Oxford University Press, 1980), 229.

30. A good overview of the comparative enterprise is William E. Paden, "Comparative Religion," in *Encyclopedia of Religion*, ed. Lindsay Jones, 2d ed., 15 vols. (Detroit: Thomson Gale, 2005): 3:1877–81.

31. Samuel Sandmel, "Parallelomania," *Journal of Biblical Literature* 81 (1962): 1–13.

32. Bushman, *Joseph Smith and the Beginnings of Mormonism*, 3.

33. Sandmel, "Parallelomania," 2, 9.

34. David Flusser, "Sanders' *Jesus and Judaism*," *Jewish Quarterly Review* 76, no. 3 (January 1986): 249.

35. Brooke, *Refiner's Fire*; Brodie, *No Man Knows My History*; Dan Vogel, *Joseph Smith: The Making of a Mormon Prophet* (Salt Lake City: Signature Books, 2004).

36. Harold Bloom, *The American Religion: The Emergence of the Post-Christian Nation* (New York: Simon and Schuster, 1992), 79–128.

37. Brooke, *Refiner's Fire*, 56.

38. Andrew F. Ehat and Lyndon W. Cook, *The Words of Joseph Smith: The Contemporary Accounts of the Nauvoo Discourses of the Prophet Joseph*, Religious Studies Monograph Series, no. 6 (Provo, Utah: Religious Studies Center, Brigham Young University, 1980), 355.

Part 2

Joseph Smith and the Recovery of Past Worlds

A lmost beyond measure, Joseph Smith was spiritually and intellectually occupied with the past. He worked insatiably from
1828 to 1835 on his translations of the Book of Mormon, the Book
of Moses, the Old and New Testaments, and the Book of Abraham.
He drew great knowledge and strength from the revelations received
by past prophets and patriarchs, and he sought to see as they had
seen and to know as they had known. In considering Joseph Smith's
recovery of past worlds, the following chapters address several questions. What are modern scholars to make of Joseph Smith's efforts to
recover past worlds? In what ways were ideas, figures, and practices
from the past important to him? What was his intention in bringing
to pass the restoration of all things? Joseph Smith's encounters with
the past not only permeated his teachings about past worlds but also
informed such matters as his current understandings of faith, priesthood, church organization, temple worship, and the family.

Joseph Smith:
Prophecy, Process, and Plenitude

Terryl L. Givens

Joseph Smith was an explorer, a discoverer, and a revealer of past worlds. He described an ancient America replete with elaborate detail and daring specificity, rooted and grounded in what he claimed were concrete, palpable artifacts. He recuperated texts of Adam, Abraham, Enoch, and Moses to resurrect and reconstitute a series of past patriarchal ages, not as mere shadows and types of things to come, but as dispensations of gospel fullness equaling, and in some cases surpassing, present plenitude. And he revealed an infinitely receding premortal past—not of the largely mythic Platonic variety and not a mere Wordsworthian, sentimental intimation—but a fully formed realm of human intelligences, divine parents, and heavenly councils.

My topic focuses first on this process of recovery, not its products. That will lead me to say a few things about the cumulative meaning for Joseph Smith of the past, of the worlds he discovered.

One of the great challenges in dealing with Joseph Smith, historically, has been the difficulty of meeting him on his own terms. More than anything else, Joseph labored to free himself from the burdens of theological convention, intellectual decorum, and—perhaps most especially—the phobia of trespassing across sacred boundaries. Although several attempts have been made to situate Joseph with respect to the paradigm shift of the early nineteenth century that we call Romanticism, these efforts have still failed to fully appreciate Joseph and to meet him in the context of what we could call Romantic discourse. From Jean Jacques Rousseau's meandering "Reveries" to Samuel Coleridge's "Kubla Khan" and other partial dream-visions, to Schlegel's literary magazine, *Athenaeum Fragments*, the entire era was dominated (in literature but also in music and even landscape) by images of the remnant, the fragment, the ruin, the shard. Such indications of tentativeness, of searching exploration, or of residual hints and vestiges reaffirmed the Romantics in their refusal to ever see writing as final, utterance as complete, or discursive thought as definitive. Systematization is, in this regard, stultifying, deadening, and almost always derivative. "I must create my own system," insisted the mercurial William Blake, "or be enslaved by another man's."[1] The dynamic, active, ongoing *process* of creating meaning is primary to the Romantics—not the finality or polish of the final product.

Like Blake, Joseph Smith almost always put himself in an agonistic, if not antagonistic, relationship to all prior systems. Consistent with other Romantic thinkers from Malthus to Hegel to Darwin, Joseph believed that struggle, opposition, and contestation are not just the essence of personal probation and growth but also describe an intellectual dynamic that moves us ahead in our quest for understanding. "I am like a huge, rough stone rolling down from a high mountain," Joseph said, "and the only polishing I get is when some corner gets rubbed off by coming in contact with something else, striking with accelerated force against religious bigotry, priestcraft, . . . the authority of perjured executives . . . and corrupt men and women."[2] These words are not a description just of his character development, but also a delineation of his intellectual modus operandi—exploring the limits, challenging conventional categories, and engaging dynamically with the boundaries, all in the interest of productive provocation. Or as he said more simply, shortly before his death, "'By proving contraries,' truth is made manifest."[3]

Let me illustrate this epistemology in the case of Joseph Smith. Joseph paid as much attention to the process of true religion as to the content. I have argued elsewhere that the Book of Mormon is the prime instance of this.[4] The history of that scripture's reception clearly demonstrates that the Book of Mormon was both valued and reviled for the same reason: not its content, but its dramatic enactment of the principle of continuing revelation and an open canon.

I think it is clear that Joseph considered this process, not the particulars revealed thereby, as the cardinal contribution of his calling. So did his closest associates. On New Year's Day 1844, Parley P. Pratt published Mormonism's first piece of fiction in the *New York Herald*. It was a comic dialogue entitled "Joseph Smith and the Devil." In this humorous but earnest piece, the devil insists to the Prophet Joseph that contrary to popular beliefs, he, the devil, really is in favor of "all creeds, systems and forms of Christianity, of whatever name and nature; so long as they leave out that abominable doctrine which caused me so much trouble in former times, and which, after slumbering for ages, you have again revived; I mean the doctrine of direct communication with God."[5]

Certainly what Joseph revealed was important—and frequently revolutionary. A quick overview of his teachings on God and man, for instance, shows not just eruptions of novelty, but a thoroughgoing endeavor to overturn the most sacred tenets of cultural Christianity. He summarily repudiated the God of the creeds by preaching a deity who has a body, parts, and passions. Then he—almost cursorily—evaluated, dismissed, and reconceptualized answers to the three great questions of human existence. First, where do we come from? St. Augustine asked the question, "Did my infancy follow some earlier age of life? Before I was in my mother's womb, was I anywhere? Was I anyone?"[6] But Augustine gave it up as a great unknown. Second, what is our nature and purpose? "What could be worse pride," Augustine asks in bitter self-reproach, "than the incredible folly in which I asserted that I was by nature what You are?"[7] Contrast this with Joseph's emphasis on innocence, freedom, agency, accountability, liberty—these are the words that filled Joseph's mind, while other religionists were painting a portrait of "utter depravity," "corrupted nature," inherited guilt, predestination, and determinism. Not just Christendom, but as Louis Menand writes, "almost every nineteenth-century system of [Western] thought" was haunted by fatalism, mechanical or materialist determinism.[8] Third, where are we going? In reference to the final judgment, Joseph writes in the "Olive Leaf" revelation, "And they who remain shall also be quickened; nevertheless, they shall return again to their own place, to enjoy that which they are willing to receive, because they were not willing to enjoy that which they might have received" (Doctrine and Covenants 88:32). The question he poses to the human family is, what are we willing to receive? The divine potential of human destiny is limited only by our own unwillingness to receive the infinite opportunities God lays before us—even godhood itself.

Human acceptance of the serpent's invitation to "be as gods" (Genesis 3:5), according to the commentators, was the primal instance of human sinfulness. This audacity was likewise the most heinous of all human evils in Dante's catalog of evil. So profoundly wrong was it, his angelic guide explained, that "man, in his limits, could not recompense: / for no obedience, no humility, / he offered later could have been so deep / that it could match the heights he meant to reach / through disobedience."[9] As one of Dante's editors paraphrases, "Only the act of infinite humility whereby Christ became incarnate and suffered the Passion, could compensate for the infinite presumptuousness of man."[10] This fearsome presumption is what motivated an entire tradition of indignation. Jonathan Edwards, echoing Dante's horror, found "human rebellion against such perfection [holiness that was infinitely beyond human standards] so infinitely evil as to warrant eternal punishment."[11] Only Lucifer's attempted emulation of deity ("I will be like the most High" [Isaiah 14:14]) can equal, even as it foreshadowed, such titanic insolence.

I rehearse these specific examples, not to establish a basis for appraisal or a historical context, but to emphasize their common denominator: the ongoing elaboration of theological positions that stood in dramatic juxtaposition—in audacious or brash or blasphemous opposition some would say—to the status quo. Joseph knew that it was this collapse of sacred distance, the enunciation of the forbidden, the articulation of the ineffable, the concretization of the abstract, and the invasion of sacred space, that characterized both the bane and boon of his calling. In a letter to his attorney, Mr. Butterfield, he wrote,

> I stated that the most prominent difference in sentiment between the Latter-day Saints and sectarians was, that the latter were all circumscribed by some peculiar creed, which deprived its members the privilege of believing anything not contained therein, whereas

the Latter-day Saints have no creed, but are ready to believe all true principles that exist, as they are made manifest from time to time.[12]

This resistance to formal creeds, to a closed canon, and to conventional opinion are all so many versions of resistance to finality, to fixity, or what he called "circumscription"—being bound and hemmed in by orthodoxy. Elsewhere, he declared that "the first and fundamental principle of our holy religion" is to be free "to embrace all, and every item of truth, without limitation or without being circumscribed or prohibited by the creeds or superstitious notions of men, or by the dominations of one another."[13]

But Joseph also recognized that the agonistic nature of his thinking was beyond the capacity of even his followers to fully absorb:

> But there has been a great difficulty in getting anything into the heads of this generation. It has been like splitting hemlock knots with a corn-dodger for a wedge, and a pumpkin for a beetle. Even the Saints are slow to understand.
>
> I have tried for a number of years to get the minds of the Saints prepared to receive the things of God; but we frequently see some of them, after suffering all they have for the work of God, will fly to pieces like glass as soon as anything comes that is contrary to their traditions: they cannot stand the fire at all.[14]

At other times and places Joseph similarly hinted that he was constrained by a world, and even a following, that was unwilling, or incapable, of countenancing his ever-growing audacity, heterodoxy, and innovation.

To one of his friends, he lamented that "he did not enjoy the right vouchsafed to every American citizen—that of free speech. He said that when he ventured to give his private opinion on any subject of importance, his words were often garbled and their meaning twisted, and then given out as the word of the Lord because they came from him."[15] His insistence that his pronouncements did not always carry prophetic weight was not just a safety net or convenient means of prudent retreat. It meant that the process, the ongoing, dynamic engagement, the exploring, questing, and provoking dialectical encounter with tradition, with boundaries, and with normative thinking should not be trammeled or impeded with clerks and scribes looking for a final word, interrupting a productive process of reflection, contestation, and creation. Sometimes, it would appear, he merely wanted the privilege of thinking out loud, but that is difficult when surrounded by court stenographers with their sharpened pencils. I imagine, in this regard, he would have seconded the memorable protest of Virginia Woolf: "I should never be able to fulfill what is, I understand, the first duty of a lecturer—to hand you after an hour's discourse a nugget of pure truth to wrap up between the pages of your notebooks and keep on the mantel-piece for ever."[16]

A study of Joseph Smith seems to always come back to the dynamics of the revelatory process, rather than the finality of a polished product; the structure of his thinking, rather than the end result of his thought. One of these dynamics in particular has enormous repercussions for a philosophy of history and for Joseph's recovery of both past and future worlds. I am referring to Joseph's integration of the divine into the historical, and the historical into the divine, a process that could be said to have begun when he experienced his first epiphany in the woods of upstate New York. Of course, any personal encounter with God represents a collapse of sacred distance, an intersection of the transcendent, the heavenly, and the divine, with the personal, the earthly, and the human. But Joseph inaugurated a pattern that would increasingly intensify the collapse of those two domains, creating in the process a radical reconceptualization of sacred history. As he translated the Book of Mormon, he found several things about the experience to be the subjects of ancient holy writ, including his own role in the process, the commencing rise of the restored church, and even the particulars of his friend Martin Harris's visit to Columbia professor Charles Anthon. Scriptural mythology became historical script. When he reached the account of Christ's visit to the Nephites inhabiting ancient America, the episode recontextualized the Incarnation itself. That divine condescension into mortality—the primary miracle of Christian history whereby the full eruption of the divine into human history is a unique event, producing a spate of mythic reverberations—became in Joseph Smith's expanding vision only one of an extensive series of historical iterations, evidence of the complete and literal interfusion of the human by the divine.

This development pushes us in a direction opposite the dominant trend of modernity described by the religious scholar Wilfred Cantwell Smith. "With the relatively recent rise in Western consciousness . . . of the new sense of history," he writes, "and the (consequent?) careful and rigorous distinction between history and myth, . . . what happened by and large was that the West opted for history and rejected myth." Regarding a scriptural event like the earth's creation, for example, he writes, "We may recognize now that the problem . . . [is] the notion that one is dealing here with historical time, rather than mythical time."[17] But with Joseph, *all we have* is historical time—but it is transformed into a dimension that extends infinitely in both directions.

Joseph understood the prophetic role in ways that furthered this project. We have been raised to believe that archaeologists and textual scholars recover history and the determinate and earthy past, while the future—eschatology in particular—is the province of prophets and visionaries. The Day of Judgment and millennial events are the stuff of faith and shadow. But from the day Joseph relied upon prophetic authority and sacred artifacts to recover the words and deeds of Nephi, a sixth-century-BC Israelite who migrated to the western hemisphere and founded a civilization, he elided the enormous psychological and experiential distance that separated the down-to-earth world from the metaphysical.

C. S. Lewis has suggested the enormous psychological investment we have in maintaining the fundamental distinction of separating the human and the divine and hints at the crisis their conflation would occasion:

> [When] the distinction between natural and supernatural . . . [breaks] down, . . . one realise[s] how great a comfort it had been—how it had eased the burden of intolerable strangeness which this universe imposes on us by dividing it into two halves and encouraging the mind never to think of both in the same context. What price we may have paid for this comfort in the way of false security and accepted confusion of thought is another matter.[18]

Joseph Smith did not allow us such comfortable dichotomizing.

I want to move in another direction now and discuss the totality of his thought—conceived not exactly as system, for he was not a systematic thinker, and he does not present us with enough materials to fashion a comprehensive theology. But I think we can nonetheless say something about what all of his thinking and revealing and speculating was tending toward. If we trace out briefly the evolution of Joseph's prophetic career, we can mark a decisive turn sometime in 1830. When he went to that grove as a fourteen-year-old youth, he was only asking a private question in a personal prayer. And what he found was, he thought, a revelation of purely personal significance. As he said to his mother, "I have learned for myself that [such and such a church] is not true" (Joseph Smith–History 1:20). He had no clear intimation of future projects and heavenly callings. It was not until he was seventeen that he tells of an angel of light appearing in his room, telling him that God had a work for him to do. That work, as he soon learned, was the translation of the Book of Mormon. It would appear as he labored on that project that he still did not dream of any greater calling or mission. It was not until March 1829, just a few months before he finished that considerable task, that the Lord first mentioned to Joseph, "the beginning of the rising up and the coming forth of [his] church out of the wilderness" (Doctrine and Covenants 5:14).

Accordingly in April 1830, Joseph complied with that directive and organized a church. But even then he did not know that this church was not just another restorationist congregation with a few dozen members and a new revelation. He had yet to learn that this church, so called, was to become much more. And so it was that in December after that humble meeting of six men and onlookers in Fayette, Joseph was commanded to gather his followers and actually "assemble together at the Ohio" (Doctrine and Covenants 37:3). Thus it came to pass that the "little flock" (Doctrine and Covenants 6:34) was now set on the path to become a people, the kingdom of God on earth, the rock cut without hand from a mountain that would roll forth and fill the earth.

But as his religious sphere of influence grew, so did his revelatory scope. Joseph Smith initially conceived of the Book of Mormon as "a record of a fallen people" (Doctrine and Covenants 20:9). It was presented to the world, in the first generation of the church especially, as a history of the American Indian. Its status as sacred scripture depended, first, on the fact that it was written by ancient prophets as sacred history, and second, on the fact that it bore the modern traces of the sacred, manifest through its miraculous transmission and translation. Its relationship to the Bible evolved and continues to do so. Originally, the Book of Mormon derived much of its authoritative weight *from* the Bible. But at the same time, of course, the elevation of the Book of Mormon to scriptural status challenges the supremacy, the uniqueness, and most importantly, the sufficiency of the Bible. The implications of that realignment deserve a second look. The principle of *sola scriptura* (the Bible as the only and sufficient ground for authority) is clearly undermined by the Book of Mormon. But that heretical affront to the Bible's status—to the Bible's function as source and guarantor of orthodoxy—may have distracted many from exploring how, in Joseph's mind, that process of dethronement and realignment finished playing out.

As a youth of seventeen, when visited by the angel Moroni, Joseph recorded that the heavenly messenger in his room was quoting to him passages from the Old Testament but "with a little variation from the way [they read] in our Bibles" (Joseph Smith–History 1:36). True, as all discussions of this episode suggest, at this point Joseph would have become aware of the imperfection or fallibility of the King James Version. But I wonder if another seed was planted at this time, suggesting to his mind not just the deficiency of the known biblical text but also the possibility of an unknown text, one cited casually by heavenly messengers. Clearly, it would seem the angel was quoting something, of which the Bible was apparently an imperfect version or derivation.

Conventional notions of a Christian apostasy—or falling away from Christian truth—began with the premise that Christ had established his true church in Palestine, only to have errors and corruptions creep in with the passage of time. In the course of the Reformation, the question was only how far those corruptions extended and how drastic the required remedies were.[19] But in the course of measuring current institutions against past incarnations of truth, those of a more liberal disposition asked how much a just God might have revealed to the ancients. Some posited that foreshadowing and fragments of the true gospel were evident among a variety of peoples scattered through time. Jonathan Edwards, like many of the Church Fathers, believed that God had in fact imparted to several ancient peoples essential gospel truths that were subsequently lost. Much earlier, Augustine expressed a version of this idea when he wrote in his *Retractions*, "What is now called Christian religion has existed among the ancients, and was not absent from the beginning of the human race."[20] While smatterings of eternal principles emerged in the religions and philosophies of antiquity, adherents of this line of reasoning held that only the Bible represented the full and complete account of God's revelation. (Speaking of the Jews, for instance, a commentator contemporary with Edwards wrote that "we have the gospel as well as they [had], and in greater purity."[21])

Prisca theologia (ancient wisdom), as this doctrine has been labeled, or "fulfillment theology" as variations of the doctrine are called in recent formulations, were useful both to account for prevalent archetypes (such as animal sacrifice and the idea of a divine incarnation) that could otherwise impugn the uniqueness and hence the validity of Christian doctrines and to assert God's justice and mercy in dispensing truth to Christian, Jew, and pagan alike. But whereas previous thinkers had emphasized the fragmentary nature of prior revelation and its final consummation in modern scripture, Joseph pushed the principle of *prisca theologia* in the other direction. "From what we can draw from the Scriptures relative to the teaching of heaven," he said, "we are induced to think that much instruction has been given to man since the beginning *which we do not possess now*."[22]

Joseph's production of the Book of Mormon was the most conspicuous embodiment of this challenge to biblical sufficiency; the new scripture itself hammered home the message of God's word as endlessly iterated and endlessly proliferating. As God declared in Nephi's account, "I shall speak unto the Jews and they shall write it; and I shall also speak unto the Nephites and they shall write it; and I shall also speak unto the other tribes of the house of Israel . . . and they shall write it; and I shall also speak unto all nations of the earth and they shall write it" (2 Nephi 29:12). But before Joseph even finished the translation, a most enigmatic revelation suggested that Joseph's paradigm was undergoing another dramatic revision. In April 1829, he produced "a translated version of the record made on parchment" by John the Beloved (Doctrine and Covenants 7, section heading). No matter that Joseph never claimed to have the parchment itself, or that the content of the record was not theologically significant (except insofar as it turned the *myth* of John's reputed immortality into the *history* of John's immortality). It was, again, what this fragmentary puzzle piece was suggestive of: the incompleteness of the biblical record and the corresponding totality of something that Joseph was moving toward.

Mere months after publishing the Book of Mormon, Joseph even more emphatically reversed the Christian arrow of time, with its consummation in a totalizing biblical revelation and Christian dispensation, when he recast the Mosaic narrative of Adam as one in which the patriarch of the human race was the first Christian proselyte. God himself, Joseph wrote in this restoration of ancient scripture,

> called upon our father Adam by his own voice, saying: . . . If thou wilt turn unto me, . . . and repent of all thy transgressions, and be baptized . . . in the name of mine Only Begotten Son, . . . which is Jesus Christ, the only name which shall be given under heaven, whereby salvation shall come unto the children of men, ye shall receive the gift of the Holy Ghost. (Moses 6:51–52)

This Book of Moses was unlike anything Joseph had until then produced. In contrast to the Book of Mormon, it was not rooted in a recovered ancient record. And unlike his many other revelations, it was not God speaking to his heart and mind. It was a verbal facsimile, but of what original? At this same moment in time, Joseph embarked upon a translation of the Old Testament, and later the New, but it was a translation again without any original to which he had access. He used no ancient manuscripts. Two years later, he received an elaborate revelation long honored with the simple designation "the Vision," which detailed the kingdoms of glory in the hereafter. It was, Joseph wrote significantly of the document he dictated, "a transcript from the records of the eternal world."[23] One year later, in a similar manner, Joseph recorded an excerpt of quotations from a first-person account written by John—yet another record that Joseph quotes from that he did not possess himself (Doctrine and Covenants 93:6–17).

A few years later, Joseph pushed the temporal parameters of the gospel even further back when he recounted in the writings of Abraham the foundational events that occurred in the Great

Council in Heaven—a scriptural production apparently inspired by, but apparently not translated directly from, ancient papyri. The particulars of these Abrahamic writings—like the recuperated Genesis material, including an account of Enoch, and also the Zenos parable from the Book of Mormon and missing writings of the apostle John—need to be evaluated on their own terms, but it is simply the grand project, the intimated master blueprint, that constitutes a major idea in its own right. The cumulative weight of these experiences seems to have created in Joseph's mind a major paradigm shift, a wholesale inversion of the traditional model of biblical fullness and *prisca theologia*. Rather than finding in the pagans and ancients foreshadowing and tantalizing hints of God's revelation, which would culminate in the Christian canon, Joseph worked, with growing momentum, backwards and outwards. He gradually conceived of his objective as nothing less than to point us in the direction—through the assemblage of the myriad worlds he revealed—of a gospel plenitude that transcended, preceded, and subsumed any and all earthly incarnations, the Bible included. This vision or intimation of what I would call an "Ur-Text" induced him to transgress linguistic, religious, and other boundaries in its pursuit.[24]

This text was not only immanent in Joseph's thought; it is in fact a powerful and prominent image in the scriptural canon itself. Only eleven verses into the Book of Mormon, Lehi is bidden by Christ to take a book and read, from which book he then reads and sees "many great and marvelous things" (1 Nephi 1:14), which give him a knowledge of the future, horror at human wickedness, and rejoicing in God's mercy. Likewise Ezekiel is given a book, which he is commanded to eat (Ezekiel 2:8–10) as is John the Revelator (Revelation 10). Joseph's enterprise thus takes literally the implications of these scriptural images. Since those books precede, rather than follow from, the canonical record, Joseph works backwards in quest of the wholeness they represent.

In this context, one begins to see why Joseph's thoughts appear undisciplined and unsystematic. His major project was not the correction or enunciation of particular theological principles but the complete reconceptualization of the scope and sweep of gospel parameters themselves. The burden that he bequeathed to posterity was an array of remarkable, tantalizing texts with consistent themes, motifs, and patterns that emerge in a whole series of entire worlds recovered from the past: premortal realms, councils in heaven, Nephite and Jaredite civilizations, an Adamic gospel dispensation, Enoch's life and ministry, Mosaic epiphanies, and weeping Gods. One searches for a vocabulary adequate to such endlessly proliferating layers of time and being, beckoning us to imagine a totality that they all share.

The remaining question is: how do the particulars of Joseph's past worlds hold up? If his collapse of the sacred into the temporal is to succeed, if we are to see his project as truly historical rather than as simply mythic, then ultimately, the worlds of the Nephites and Jaredites and of Enoch, like the words of Adam and Abraham and Moses and John that he recovered, cannot resist examination as the historical records they purport to be.

Only now, with the passage of two hundred years or more, may we have enough distance from the career of Joseph Smith to adequately assess his contributions. This is not alone because of the advantages of hindsight and historical perspective or of the development of critical tools and disciplinary sophistication adequate to the task. These are all important aids. But in the case of Joseph Smith, one simply has to step back from a canvas as large as the one he painted.

Notes

1. William Blake, *Jerusalem* (London: Allen and Unwin, 1964).

2. Joseph Smith Jr., *History of The Church of Jesus Christ of Latter-day Saints*, ed. B. H. Roberts, 2d ed., rev., 7 vols. (Salt Lake City: Deseret Book, 1971), 5:401 (hereafter cited as *History of the Church*).

3. *History of the Church*, 6:428.

4. Terryl L. Givens, *By the Hand of Mormon: The American Scripture That Launched a New World Religion* (New York: Oxford University Press, 2003). See especially pages 66–82.

5. Parley P. Pratt, "A Dialogue Between Joseph Smith and the Devil," *New York Herald* (January 1, 1844), reprinted in Richard H. Cracroft and Neal E. Lambert, *A Believing People: Literature of the Latter-day Saints* (Provo, Utah: Brigham Young University Press, 1974), 34.

6. Augustine, *Confessions*, trans. F. J. Sheed, rev. ed. (Indianapolis: Hackett, 1993), 1:vi.

7. Augustine, *Confessions*, 4:xv.

8. Louis Menand, *The Metaphysical Club* (New York: Farrar, Straus and Giroux, 2001), 371.

9. Dante Alighieri, *Paradiso*, trans. Allen Mandelbaum (New York: Bantam, 1984), Canto 7:97–101.

10. Dante, *Paradiso*, 335.

11. George M. Marsden, *Jonathan Edwards: A Life* (New Haven: Yale University Press, 2003), 112.

12. *History of the Church*, 5:215.

13. Dean C. Jessee, ed. and comp., *The Personal Writings of Joseph Smith* (1984; repr., Salt Lake City: Deseret Book; Provo, Utah: Brigham Young University Press, 2002), 458.

14. *History of the Church*, 6:184–85.

15. Hyrum L. Andrus and Helen Mae Andrus, *They Knew the Prophet: Personal Accounts from over 100 People Who Knew Joseph Smith* (American Fork, Utah: Covenant Communications, 2004), 140.

16. Virginia Woolf, *A Room of One's Own* (New York: Harcourt, Brace, Jovanovich, 1989), 4.

17. Wilfred Cantwell Smith, "The Study of Religion and the Study of the Bible," in *Rethinking Scripture: Essays from a Comparative Perspective*, ed. Miriam Levering (Albany: State University of New York Press, 1989), 26.

18. C. S. Lewis, *Perelandra* (New York: Macmillan, 1965), 11.

19. It became imperative, for instance, "to distinguish between corrupt Churches & false Churches," since, as the non-separating Puritans would argue, "the corruption of a thing doth not nullify a thing." Francis J. Bremer, *John Winthrop: America's Forgotten Founding Father* (New York: Oxford University Press, 2003), 199.

20. Augustine, *Retractions*, 1.13, cited in Gerald R. McDermott, "Jonathan Edwards, John Henry Newman, and Non-Christian Religions," paper delivered at the American Society of Church History Meeting, Yale University, New Haven, Conn., March 31, 2001.

21. *Matthew Henry's Commentary* (Grand Rapids, Mich.: Zondervan, 1961), 1914. The glossed verse is Hebrews 4:2. A board of non-Conformist ministers wrote the commentary on the epistles after Henry's death in 1714.

22. Joseph Fielding Smith, comp., *Teachings of the Prophet Joseph Smith* (Salt Lake City: Deseret Book, 1976), 61, emphasis added.

23. *History of the Church*, 1:252.

24. Hugh Nibley has used this term in the context of temple rituals, when he referred to "a God-given Urtext which has come down to the present day in many more or less corrupt forms." See his "What Is a Temple?" in *The Prophetic Book of Mormon*, volume 8 of the Collected Works of Hugh Nibley (Salt Lake City: Deseret Book; Provo, Utah: Foundation for Ancient Research and Mormon Studies [FARMS], 1989), 215.

Joseph Smith and Preexilic Israelite Religion

Margaret Barker

Terryl Givens has set Joseph Smith in the religious and cultural context of his time and raised many important issues. I should like to take a few of these issues and set them in another context, that of preexilic Jerusalem. I am not a scholar of Mormon texts and traditions. I am a biblical scholar specializing in the Old Testament, and until some Mormon scholars made contact with me a few years ago, I would never have considered using Mormon texts and traditions as part of my work. Since that initial contact I have had many good and fruitful exchanges and have begun to look at these texts very closely. I am still, however, very much an amateur in this area. What I offer can only be the reactions of an Old Testament scholar: are the revelations to Joseph Smith consistent with the situation in Jerusalem in about 600 BCE? Do the revelations to Joseph Smith fit in that context, the reign of King Zedekiah, who is mentioned at the beginning of the First Book of Nephi, which begins in the "first year of the reign of Zedekiah" (1 Nephi 1:4)? Zedekiah was installed as king in Jerusalem in 597 BCE.

A Dynamic World of Divine Revelation

Givens raises the companion questions of open canon, ongoing revelation, and prophetic preeminence.[1] As far as we know, there was no idea of a closed canon in 600 BCE, and ongoing revelation from the prophets was accepted in that day, even if what the prophets said was sometimes very uncomfortable.

One generation before Zedekiah there had been the great upheaval in the reign of King Josiah, something now regarded as the turning point in the history of Jerusalem and its religion. The events are usually described as King Josiah's "reform," the assumption being that everything he did was good and that the biblical texts describing the reform are an accurate and objective account. Other ancient texts had a very different view of Josiah and his work, but since they were eventually not included in the Bible, they are not often considered when the Bible is taught today. Yet here is our first warning: if some of the wickedness in Jerusalem mentioned in the First Book of Nephi (1 Nephi 1:13) included parts of Josiah's temple purges, we should expect to find information relevant to the Mormon tradition in texts outside the Bible. And we do. Moreover, the biblical texts themselves take on new significance if we no longer assume that everyone agreed with Josiah's purge. Jeremiah, a contemporary of King Josiah, has many passages that seem to criticize what has just happened in the city.[2]

Perhaps reflecting these ancient disagreements, some books mentioned in the Old Testament are now lost. 1 Chronicles 29:29, for example, cites as sources for the history of King David the Chronicles of Samuel the seer, the Chronicles of Nathan the prophet, and the Chronicles of Gad the seer. There are several more examples of lost books. Some books found among the Dead Sea Scrolls are clearly sacred texts, but we did not know about them previously. Even the biblical texts found among the Dead Sea Scrolls have significantly different wording from the Masoretic Hebrew text in several places, reminding me of Joseph Smith's vision, when Moroni spoke the words of Malachi but "with a little variation" (Joseph Smith–History 1:36). It can come as a shock to traditional Christians to discover that there were different versions of the Old Testament text in the time of Jesus. We cannot know for certain which Bible Jesus knew, neither the books he regarded as scripture nor the precise text of those books.

It seemed to me, as I began to look at the revelatory traditions of the Latter-day Saints, that Latter-day Saint scholars might have more in common with the more radical elements in contemporary biblical scholarship than with the strictly traditional and conservative people. Bearing this in mind, consider another of Givens's points.

Givens spoke of the scandal that Joseph Smith claimed "direct communication with God."[3] We now recognize that King Josiah enabled a particular group to dominate the religious scene in Jerusalem about 620 BCE: the Deuteronomists. Josiah's purge was driven by their ideals, and their scribes influenced much of the form of the Old Testament we have today, especially the history in 1 and 2 Kings. The Deuteronomists denied that anyone had a vision of the Lord (Deuteronomy 4:12), they denied that anyone had revelations from heaven, and they insisted the Ten Commandments were all that was necessary (Deuteronomy 30:8, 11–14). Nothing more was to be added to them (Deuteronomy 5:22). Prophecies were genuine only if they had already been fulfilled and had no more power (Deuteronomy 18:21–22). The Deuteronomists had no place for angels, and so they did not use the title "Lord of Hosts." These were the minds that eventually led to the closed canon of scripture and the cessation of prophecy. But the prophets *did* have visions of the Lord and the angels, they *did* speak in the name of the Lord, and their unfulfilled prophecies *were* carefully preserved. Not everyone shared the views of the Deuteronomists, but the writings of these other people are often outside the Bible.

The Deuteronomists wrote the history of the kings in Jerusalem, compiling it from written sources about ancient kings and heroes, much as we might compile a history today. Other ancient texts, however, give a different picture of how history was written. Past, present, and future were revealed to prophetic figures. Those three sources mentioned in 1 Chronicles were all prophets: Samuel the seer, Nathan the prophet, and Gad the seer. We find prophetic history also in the Book of Jubilees, parts of which were found among the Dead Sea Scrolls some fifty years ago. The full text of the book had been rediscovered in Ethiopia and published at the end of the nineteenth century, but the Scrolls fragments confirmed that it was an ancient book.[4] Jubilees describes how the past and the future were revealed to Moses on Sinai and how he was told to write down what he learned (Jubilees 1:4–5).[5] Enoch—of whom I will say more later—saw all the history of his people, past, present, and future, in dream-visions (1 Enoch 83–93). The Christians said that Jesus had revealed the past, the present, and the future,[6] and the Book of Revelation did not reveal only the future. If prophets revealed the past as well as the future, the revelation of history to Joseph Smith is not out of character.

Another enigmatic history in 1 Enoch, known as the Apocalypse of Weeks, implies that Josiah's purge was a disaster. This history makes no mention of the Exodus. How was it possible to have such a history? For the Deuteronomists, the story of Moses leading the Exodus from Egypt was the defining event of their history. In the centuries after Josiah's purge, and after the demise of the monarchy in Jerusalem, legends surrounding Moses made Moses more and more like the ancient kings. By the time of Jesus, even the Egyptian Jew Philo could describe Moses as the God and King of his people.[7] But the people who considered Josiah's legalistic reforms to be a disaster could not also have considered Moses a dominant figure. For many years scholars have suspected that the account of Moses on Sinai receiving the Ten Commandments had been merged with memories of Solomon's Temple, and that a temple ritual when the anointed king brought divine revelation from heaven had been blended with the Moses on Sinai story.[8]

The Apocalypse of Weeks describes how an unnamed person received the "law for all generations" whilst there were "visions of the holy and righteous." Was this perhaps a temple vision scene, where a "God and King" figure received revelation in heaven among the angels and brought it to earth, the same figure later absorbed into Moses? There are many places where memories of the old temple ritual survive; for example, the Son of Man figure and the holy ones in Daniel 7. I wondered about such incidents when I first read Lehi's vision of the open heaven, the angels, and a radiant figure descending to give Lehi a book (1 Nephi 1:8–12).

Most of the summaries of history in the Old Testament focus on Moses and the Exodus but omit the Sinai story. In other words, they are the exact opposite of the Apocalypse of Weeks. Scholars have suspected for some time that Sinai and Exodus were originally distinct traditions, joined only after the destruction of the first temple, with Exodus predominating. The earliest fusion in the Bible is in Nehemiah 9:9–15, a document from the fifth century BCE. The final form of the Pentateuch may have been compiled even later by people who emphasized Moses and the Exodus rather than temple tradition.[9]

For others, though, a different history of Jerusalem had been summarized in Enoch's Apocalypse of Weeks (1 Enoch 93)—a vision of history given to Enoch by angels and learned from heavenly tablets. It described Noah, Abraham, the lawgiving, the temple, the disaster in the temple just before it was destroyed, and the scattering of the chosen people. Try to imagine how these different groups might have reacted to discovering their history rewritten, supplemented by the history of their Lord appearing in Egypt and rescuing some people there, or how they might have reacted to Ezekiel's claim that the Lord had appeared to his people in Babylon. In the course of time, all these accounts have been absorbed into the tradition of ongoing revelation. The authors of the Apocalypse of Weeks, however, saw the people who rebuilt Jerusalem and wrote the biblical histories as apostates, even though we consider those histories as the norm. The Apocalypse of Weeks, that tiny fragment of ancient history in 1 Enoch, is almost forgotten, or considered rather strange.

While this dynamic world of prophets and revelations is consonant with the picture presented in the Book of Mormon, we may compare that situation with the crisis that has now engulfed biblical scholarship: archaeology simply does not give supporting evidence for a great deal of the "history" in the Old Testament. Scholars are asking themselves: What are we reading? Whose Bible is this?[10] When was it written? Is the Old Testament older than its earliest written deposits found among the Dead Sea Scrolls? And why are some of those different from the Old Testament as we have known it?

An Inviting World of Deification

Let us now consider another of Givens's points: the question of human beings becoming divine and accepting the serpent's invitation to "be as gods."[11] In the later Old Testament tradition, wanting to be as the gods was indeed a sin, but how might such an invitation have been viewed in 600 BCE?

The familiar story of Adam and Eve is the reworking of an older story, after memories of the loss of Eden and the loss of the original temple had merged. The tree that had been originally intended for human food was the tree of life, and the perfumed oil of that tree was to have been used to anoint humans and make them like the angels, sons of God.[12] This was the tradition of the ancient priests, who thought of themselves as angels, messengers from heaven (Malachi 2:7). The tree of life gave wisdom (Proverbs 3:13–18) and eternal life (Genesis 3:22); but the human pair disobeyed and chose knowledge that could be used for good or evil. Only then did they discover that they were barred from the tree of life.

The prophet Ezekiel, who also lived in Jerusalem in 600 BCE, said that the anointed one in Eden became mortal and died because wisdom and perfection had been abused for the sake of power and splendor (Ezekiel 28:11–19). Satan's deception in Eden was to imply that both the tree of life and the tree of the knowledge of good and evil had the same benefit, both made humans like the angels. It was the disobedience that was the problem,[13] not the state they aspired to, and they had to be barred from eternal life because they had disobeyed. In the Book of Revelation, this is reversed: the faithful Christian is promised access again to the tree of life (Revelation 2:7), which meant access to the angel state. It was not the aspiration but the attitude that was wrong.[14] In 600 BCE the sin would have been pride and disobedience, not the wish to be angels and sons of God.[15] When Isaiah described the sins of Jerusalem, he emphasized pride, rebellion, and the abuse of knowledge. These themes are strongly reflected in the Book of Mormon (1 Nephi 8:36; 12:18; 22:15; 2 Nephi 26:20; 28:15). All these failings are equated with the sins of fallen angels, not with the breaking of the Ten Commandments.[16]

This correction invites us to reexamine a related assumption, that the books in the Old Testament are older than the ancient Israelite books not in the Old Testament. The Enoch texts must be late, it is assumed, because they are not in the Bible. Last year I published a commentary on Isaiah that showed that the original Isaiah of Jerusalem knew the Enoch traditions but was not much concerned with Moses. Instead, Isaiah's world was the world of Enoch's angels.[17] Other scholars are now exploring the possibility that Enoch traditions underlie some of the older stories in Genesis. Enoch traditions could have been very important in 600 BCE, just as the revelation to Joseph Smith implies (1 Nephi 1:8–11; 8:5; 11:14; Jacob 7:5–7; Omni 1:25; Mosiah 3:2; Mosiah 27:11).

The emphasis placed on Enoch's writings should not surprise us, as the Enoch traditions show clearly that human beings who continue their lives on earth can become angels. In the coded language of Enoch's dream-visions, animals represent human beings and "men" are angels. Noah, we read, was born a bull and became a man after an angel taught him a secret (1 Enoch 89:1), and in the Apocalypse of Weeks there are three "men": Noah, Abraham, and possibly Isaiah, but the text is enigmatic (1 Enoch 93:4, 5, 8). The Enoch books are clearly in the same tradition as the Bible, yet there is no quotation from the Bible in them. Those who preserved the Enoch traditions may have had different scriptures.

Isaiah, who prophesied in the years before 700 BCE, spoke also of a female figure and her son and also of a great tree that had been cut down but had sacred seed surviving in the stump (Isaiah 6:9–13). His contemporary, the prophet Micah, spoke of a woman in travail who had gone out of the city but would give birth to the great Shepherd of Israel (Micah 4:10; 5:3–4). Who was this Mother? What was the great tree? Piecing together other contemporary evidence, we could conclude that she was Wisdom, the one whom Josiah eventually purged from the temple but whose symbol, the tree of life, had also been removed in the time of Isaiah (2 Kings 18:4) and later replaced. In the time of Josiah, her tree—the Asherah, the menorah—was finally removed from the temple, burned, beaten to dust, and cast on the common graves (2 Kings 23:6). It was utterly desecrated. Why such hatred? Hostility to Wisdom was a hallmark of the Deuteronomists, and due to their influence, the Mother and her tree have been almost forgotten—but not in the Book of Mormon.

Her son was the Lord.[18] We can deduce this from the Dead Sea Scrolls version of Isaiah's Immanuel prophecy: "Ask a sign," said the prophet, "from *the mother* of the LORD your God.[19] . . . Behold the Virgin shall conceive and bear a son and call his name Immanuel" (Isaiah 7:10–14). And angels attended her, the Host of heaven whom the Deuteronomists tried to obscure. Each time the Lady was driven from the temple, so too were the angels, the holy ones, a word very similar to the word for prostitutes, which is how it is often translated.[20] The divine Son, the priest of the order of Melchizedek, was born in the glory of these "holy ones," or so it seems. Psalm 110 is an enigmatic text, but it seems to describe the birth of an angel priest after the order of Melchizedek in the Holy of Holies of the temple, which represented heaven, which evokes related ideas in Alma 13:1–16 in the Book of Mormon.

White Fruit and a Guiding Rod

The tree of life made one happy, according to the Book of Proverbs (Proverbs 3:18), but for detailed descriptions of the tree we have to rely on the noncanonical texts. Enoch described it as perfumed, with fruit like grapes (1 Enoch 32:5), and a text discovered in Egypt in 1945 described the tree as beautiful, fiery, and with fruit like white grapes.[21] I do not know of any other source that describes the fruit as *white* grapes. Imagine my surprise when I read the account of Lehi's vision of the tree whose *white fruit* made one happy, and the interpretation that the Virgin in Nazareth was the mother of the Son of God after the manner of the flesh (1 Nephi 11:14–23).[22] This is the Heavenly Mother, represented by the tree of life, and then Mary and her Son on earth. This revelation to Joseph Smith was the ancient Wisdom symbolism, intact, and almost certainly as it was known in 600 BCE.

Consider as well the mysterious rod of iron in this Book of Mormon vision (1 Nephi 8:20; 11:25). In the Bible, the rod of iron is mentioned four times as the rod of the Messiah. Each mention in the King James Version says the Messiah uses the rod to "break" the nations (Psalm 2:9) or to "rule" them (Revelation 2:27; 12:5; 19:15). The ancient Greek translation (the Septuagint) is significantly different; it understood the Hebrew word in Psalm 2:9 to mean "shepherd" and it reads, "He will shepherd them with a rod of iron." The two Hebrew verbs for "break" and "shepherd, pasture, tend, lead" look very similar and in some forms are identical. The Greek text of the Book of Revelation actually uses the word "shepherd," *poimanei*, of the Messiah and his iron rod, so the English versions here are not accurate. The holy child who was taken up to heaven (Revelation 12:5) was to "shepherd the nations with a rod of iron." The King James Version of Micah 7:14 translates this same word as "*Feed* thy people with thy rod," where "guide" would be a better translation. Psalm 78:72 has, "He *fed* them . . . and guided them," where the parallelism of Hebrew poetry would expect the two verbs to have a similar meaning: "He *led* them . . . he guided them." Lehi's vision has the iron rod *guiding* people to the great tree—the older and probably the original understanding of the word.[23]

Forgotten Memories of the Temple

There can also be no doubt that teachings from the time of the first temple have been lost, or rather, are now to be found only in texts outside the Bible. Jewish tradition says that all the sacred texts were lost when Jerusalem was destroyed and that Ezra the scribe restored them, inspired by God Most High to dictate ninety-four books (2 Esdras 14). Only twenty-four of them could be revealed; the rest were to be kept secret. This story may refer to the destruction of Jerusalem in 597 BCE or to the second destruction in 70 CE; either way, it was recognized that the original scriptures had been lost and that only a fraction of those restored became the public canon. Justin Martyr, a Christian writer in the middle of the second century CE, claimed that the Jews had been altering the scriptures.[24] An Aramaic document from the same period, known as the Scroll of Fasting,[25] lists the anniversaries of great events in the second temple period as days on which it was forbidden to fast. On the third of Tishri it was forbidden to fast because "the memory of the documents was removed" or "the memory was removed from the documents." Some records had been destroyed, and this was a cause for celebration. It would be interesting to know what these were!

The Book of 1 Enoch records that lying words had been written, perverting the eternal covenant. Sinners had altered the truth as they made copies, made fabrications, and written books in their own name (1 Enoch 98:14–99:2; 104:10–11). The Qur'an also tells of people who had altered the meaning of texts (2:75), had composed texts they claimed as scripture (2:79), and had accepted only part of the sacred text (2:85). One passage describes how some of the people of the Book threw it away and chose instead to follow evil teaching from Babylon (2:101–2). This could easily be describing the people who returned from Babylon and built the second temple, people whom Enoch called the apostate generation. There are many similar references in the Qur'an, for example, to people who look for allegorical and hidden meanings rather than the plain meaning of the text (3:7) and who twist the words of scripture (4:46).[26] The Qur'an also mentions the Book of Abraham and the Book of Moses, described as "the Books of the earliest (Revelation)" (53:36–37; 87:18–19).[27] These were prophecies in Arabia in the seventh century CE. They resonate with the words of Nephi about "plain and precious things taken away from the book" (1 Nephi 13:28), as well as Joseph Smith's revelation of texts called the Book of Moses and the Book of Abraham.

Along the same lines, the extraordinary similarity between the History of the Rechabites (the Narrative of Zosimus) and the story of Lehi leaving Jerusalem has already been studied by Mormon scholars.[28] This ancient text, which survives in Greek, Syriac, and Ethiopic, tells the story of some people who left Jerusalem about 600 BCE and went to live in a blessed land. They did not drink wine. They were called the sons of Rechab, which could mean that he was their ancestor, or it could be the Hebrew way of saying they were temple servants, priests who served the divine throne.[29] In their blessed land, angels had announced to them the incarnation of the Word of God from the Holy Virgin who is the Mother of God.[30] Nobody can explain this text. The Jerusalem Talmud, compiled in Palestine perhaps early in the fifth century CE, remembers a similar tradition: that a large number of priests fought with the Babylonians against Jerusalem after Josiah's purges and later went to live in Arabia, the country into which Lehi and his family departed.[31]

Jehovah and Jesus

Givens spoke of Joseph Smith's "thoroughgoing endeavor to overturn the most sacred tenets of cultural Christianity,"[32] and one of these must be the identity of Yahweh (Jehovah), the Lord, who appears in the Old Testament as the God of Israel. New Testament scholars agonize over why the first Christians applied Yahweh texts to Jesus. And how, they ask, could all of the early Christian teachers have found Jesus in the Old Testament? When I wrote a book setting out all this rather obvious evidence,[33] it was regarded as strange and hopelessly radical. Another example: the Jerusalem Bible, the translation prepared by the Roman Catholic Church, leaves the name Yahweh in the Old Testament, instead of using the customary form, the Lord, and then has "the Lord" in the New Testament. With one editorial decision, they broke the link between the Old Testament and the New and obscured the fundamental proclamation of the first Christians: Jesus is the Lord, Jesus is Yahweh. A third example: the new English translation of the Targum, the Aramaic version of the Old Testament, does not use the term Messiah in the Psalms when translating the Hebrew word *msyh,* which means Messiah. The reason given is, "It does not seem appropriate to use words like Messiah and 'messianic'" in connection with the Hebrew text of the Old Testament.[34]

It was my challenge to assumptions such as these, which simply ignore the evidence of both the Hebrew Bible and of early Christian writings, that led to my first contact with Mormon scholars. The original temple tradition was that Yahweh, the Lord, was the Son of God Most High, and present on earth as the Messiah. This means that the older religion in Israel would have taught about the Messiah. Thus finding Christ in the Old Testament is exactly what we should expect, though obscured by incorrect reading of the scriptures. This is, I suggest, one aspect of the restoration of "the plain and precious things, which have been taken away from them" (1 Nephi 13:40).

The Jehovah of the Old Testament is the Christ of the Book of Mormon (Mosiah 3:8; 3 Nephi 15:5).

Yearning for the Temple

With the destruction of Jerusalem shortly after 600 BCE, the greatest loss was without doubt the temple, its angels, and everything they represented. There can also be no doubt that the central theme of Jesus' teaching was the restoration of the true temple and what it meant.[35] He was proclaimed as the Melchizedek priest (Hebrews 7)—the expected Messiah described in the Melchizedek text found among the Dead Sea Scrolls (11 Q Melch).[36] But what had happened to the Melchizedek priesthood? One of the great moments in my own journey of discovery was reading an article published in 1980,[37] showing that the religion of Abraham must have survived until the time of King Josiah because that was part of what he purged from his kingdom. In 600 BCE, the religion of Abraham was not just a distant memory. This suggests that the Melchizedek priesthood also survived until the time of Josiah, who was associated with the monarchy, as Psalm 110 makes clear. It was superseded in Jerusalem by the Aaronic priesthood very much later than we often suppose. It is likely that Aaron's family came to prominence in Jerusalem only when Moses did, as a result of King Josiah's changes around 600 BCE. We must remember that it was the Deuteronomists who wrote the major history of these times.

There were long memories of the lost temple. In the time of the Messiah, it was said, the true temple would be restored: the Spirit, the fire, the cherubim, and the ark, but also the anointing oil and the menorah.[38] This is strange, because there *was* a seven-branched lamp in the second temple—but maybe it did not represent what the original had represented. It was not the tree of life. Down until the times of the New Testament, the era of Melchizedek was linked to memories of the temple, the Spirit, the fire, the anointing oil, and the lamp representing the tree of life. It should not go unnoticed that these memories are also linked to coming of the Messiah in the texts of the Book of Mormon.

Notes

1. See Terryl L. Givens, "Joseph Smith: Prophecy, Process, and Plenitude," in this volume, 56–57, 59.

2. Private communication with Kevin Christensen about his work in progress.

3. Givens, "Joseph Smith: Prophecy, Process, and Plenitude," 57.

4. An edition was published in 1895. There are fragments of Greek and Latin text also, the Latin published in 1861. Details in *The Old Testament Pseudepigrapha*, ed. James H. Charlesworth, 2 vols. (Garden City, N.Y.: Doubleday, 1983–85), 2:41–42.

5. The Apocalypse of Abraham, which has survived only in Old Slavonic, even though a Hebrew original is likely, describes Abraham seeing all history in a vision.

6. Clement of Alexandria, *Miscellanies* 6.7.

7. Philo, *Moses* 1:158.

8. Sigmund Mowinckel, *Le Décalogue* (Paris: Félix Alcan, 1927).

9. See Gerhard von Rad, *The Problem of Hexateuch and Other Essays*, trans. E. W. Trueman Dicken (New York: McGraw-Hill, 1966).

10. See Philip R. Davies, *In Search of "Ancient Israel"* (Sheffield, England: JSOT Press, 1992).

11. Givens, "Joseph Smith: Prophecy, Process, and Plenitude," 58, citing Genesis 3:5.

12. See Margaret Barker, *The Great High Priest: The Temple Roots of Christian Liturgy* (New York: Clark, 2003), 129–36.

13. Cf. Isaiah 1:12; 14:12–21, the Lord's judgments on pride.

14. John Milton, *Paradise Lost* 5:519–43, captured this well; the human pair would be happy like the angels only for as long as they were obedient like the angels.

15. It is interesting that the Targum to the Psalms renders the Hebrew "begotten" with the Aramaic "anointed;" the anointed ones were remembered as sons of God—angels.

16. See Margaret Barker, *The Older Testament* (London: SPCK, 1987), 128–32.

17. In James D. G. Dunn, ed., *Eerdmans Commentary on the Bible* (Grand Rapids, Mich.: Eerdmans, 2003).

18. Barker, *The Great High Priest*, 229–61.

19. 1Q Isaa has 'm, "mother," where the Masoretic Text has cm, "with."

20. Cf. 1 Kings 15:12–13; 2 Kings 23:6–7.

21. *On the Origin of the World*, in *The Nag Hammadi Library in English*, ed. James M. Robinson (New York: Harper and Row, 1977), 2.5.110, page 169.

22. Discussed by Daniel C. Peterson, "Nephi and His Asherah," *Journal of Book of Mormon Studies* 9, no. 2 (2000): 16–25.

23. See Margaret Barker, *The Revelation of Jesus Christ* (New York: Clark, 2000), 305–6.

24. Justin Martyr, *Dialogue with Trypho* (Washington, D.C.: Catholic University of America Press, 2003), 71.

25. Text in Joseph A. Fitzmyer and Daniel J. Harrington, *A Manual of Palestinian Aramaic Texts* (Rome: Biblical Institute Press, 1978), 185–87.

26. See also: 1 Enoch 3:48; 3:79; 3:81; 4:54; 4:113; 5:110.

27. *The Holy Qur'an*, translation and commentary by Abdullah Yusuf 'Ali (Birmingham, England: IPCI, Islamic Vision, 1934), capitalization and parentheses in this source. By the Books of Moses, the text means "apparently not the Pentateuch, or the Tawrat [Torah], but some other book or books now lost," 1570 n. 5110. Note 5111 on the same page states, "No original Book of Abraham is now extant." See also 1846 n. 6094, "No Book of Abraham has come down to us. . . . There is a book in Greek, which has been translated by Mr. G. H. Box, called The Testament of Abraham."

28. John W. Welch, "The Narrative of Zosimus (History of the Rechabites) and the Book of Mormon," in *Book of Mormon Authorship Revisited*, ed. Noel B. Reynolds (Provo, Utah: Foundation for Ancient Research and Mormon Studies [FARMS], 1997), 323–74; Jeffrey P. Thompson and John W. Welch, "The Rechabites: A Model Group in Lehi's World," in *Glimpses of Lehi's Jerusalem*, ed. John W. Welch, David Rolf Seely, and Jo Ann Seely (Provo, Utah: FARMS, 2004), 611–24.

29. The throne was in the form of a chariot, 1 Chronicles 28:18; and *recheb*, one word for chariot, is identical in written form with *rechab*.

30. *History of the Rechabites* 12:8–9, in Charlesworth, *Old Testament Pseudepigrapha*, 2:457.

31. *Jerushalmi Ta'anit* 4:5.

32. Givens, "Joseph Smith: Prophecy, Process, and Plenitude," 57.

33. Margaret Barker, *The Great Angel: A Study of Israel's Second God* (Louisville: Westminster, 1992).

34. David M. Stec, *The Targum of Psalms*, in The Aramaic Bible, vol. 16 (Collegeville, Minnesota: Liturgical Press, 2004), 30.

35. See Margaret Barker, *Temple Theology: An Introduction* (London: SPCK, 2004).

36. See Barker, *The Great High Priest*, 34–41.

37. John Van Seters, "The Religion of the Patriarchs in Genesis," *Biblica* 61 (1980): 220–33.

38. *Numbers Rabbah* 15.10; Babylonian Talmud, *Horayoth* 12a.

Archaeological Trends and Book of Mormon Origins

John E. Clark

Had circumstances permitted a marked grave for the slain prophet, a fitting headstone could have read, "By Joseph Smith, Junior, Author and Proprietor." Such an epitaph, taken from the title page of the Book of Mormon, captures the enduring bond between the man and the book, and also the controversy which coalesced around both with the book's publication and the organization of The Church of Jesus Christ of Latter-day Saints[1] in 1830. In the ensuing and continuing "war of words" (Joseph Smith–History 1:10) and prejudice, redemption may hang on the single preposition "by." What hand did Joseph[2] have in producing the book?

Joseph claimed he translated by the power of God an ancient record inscribed on golden plates entrusted to him by an American angel. His account of the origin of the Book of Mormon is, to understate the obvious, outrageously incredible. One critique dubbed it "knavery on two sticks."[3] Or is it? Are Joseph's claims truth or nonsense? How can one know? This question implicates classic antitheses between science and religion, reason and faith. I consider both faith and reason here in evaluating competing explanations of the book. When confronted with the book, most people reject it because of its cover story. Sterling M. McMurrin, a former Latter-day Saint, said critically, "You don't get books from angels and translate them by miracles."⁴ Others excommunicate the angels and pull the book back down to earth. Joseph Smith, they argue, wrote the book from his galloping imagination, aided and abetted by scraps of truth and speculation rifled from others. From this skeptical view, the book is a fiction, fraud, hoax. There are other explanations, but the never-ending quarrel is between the book as hoax and the book as history. Born of a miracle or a hoax, and father to another, the book commands serious attention from believers and skeptics alike. An over-riding question in Book of Mormon scholarship is: did Joseph Smith write or translate the book?⁵

Any fair understanding of Joseph Smith must derive from a plausible explanation of the Book of Mormon, and both science and reason can and should be involved in the evaluation. Because the book makes claims about American prehistory, archaeology has long been implicated in assessments of the book's credentials as ancient history, and, by direct implication, of the veracity, sanity, or honesty of Joseph Smith. I revisit issues of archaeology and the Book of Mormon here in addressing the character of Joseph Smith. Archaeology shows that almost everyone involved in the running quarrel over Joseph and his book have misrepresented and misunderstood both.

"By Joseph Smith . . . ":
Rival Hypotheses of the Book of Mormon

For Mormons, Joseph Smith is a prophet, seer, and revelator, and the Book of Mormon is the word of God. Detractors ridicule both as blasphemous frauds. There is no secure middle ground between positions, but there is one spectacular point of agreement. Champions on both sides see the Book of Mormon as the key to Joseph Smith's claim to be a prophet. Divergent views on the origin of the book lead to different supposed authors; in each case the deduced person thought to be responsible for the book remains incomplete. Surprisingly, both friends and foes have diminished Joseph and the Book of Mormon in the same way—by exaggerating his abilities. Considerable as his abilities were, Joseph Smith was neither superman nor superbrain.

Critics see Joseph Smith as author of a romantic fiction, the Book of Mormon, and in so doing they distort both the man and the book beyond belief. They see the book as a logical product of its 1820s intellectual environment, combined with Joseph Smith's native intelligence and deceitful propensities.[6]

Most Mormons fall into a more subtle error that also inflates Joseph's talents; they confuse translation with authorship. They presume that Joseph Smith knew the contents of the book as if he were its real author, and they accord him perfect knowledge of the text. This presumption removes from discussion the most compelling evidence of the book's authenticity—Joseph's unfamiliarity with its contents. To put the matter clearly: Joseph Smith did not fully understand the Book of Mormon. I propose that he transmitted to readers an ancient book that he neither imagined nor wrote.

One thing all readers share with Joseph is a partial understanding of the book's complexities. Indeed, many things about the book were simply unknowable in 1830. Over the last sixty years, Hugh Nibley, John Sorenson, and other scholars have shown the Book of Mormon to be "truer" than Joseph Smith or any of his contemporaries could know.[7] Consequently, what Joseph Smith knew and understood about the book ought to be research questions rather than presumptions. Thanks in large part to his critics, it is becoming clear that Joseph Smith did not fully understand the geography, scope, historical scale, literary form, or cultural content of the book.

For example, early Mormons believed Book of Mormon lands stretched throughout all of North and South America, a presumption clearly at odds with the book itself (fig. 1a).[8] The book speaks specifically only of a limited land about the size of Pennsylvania. In 1842, after reading about ancient cities in Central America, Joseph speculated that Book of Mormon lands were located there (fig. 1b).[9] I derive two lessons from his speculation: First, Joseph did not know exactly where Book of Mormon lands were; second, he considered their location an important question addressable through scholarship. The book makes hundreds of claims about ancient peoples in the Americas. It has always been clear to people on both sides of the controversy that antiquities could be, and should be, used to corroborate or destroy the book's pedigree.

The rival hypotheses about the book's origins implicate four knowledge worlds of diverse content and undetermined relationship: the ancient world, the nineteenth-century world, the twenty-first-century

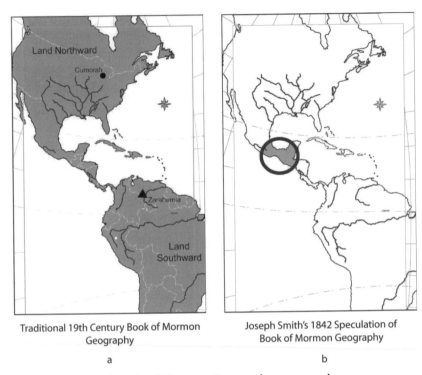

Traditional 19th Century Book of Mormon Geography

Joseph Smith's 1842 Speculation of Book of Mormon Geography

a

b

Figure 1. Views of Book of Mormon Geography compared.

world, and the Book of Mormon world. Environmental or natural-istic explanations see the book as a hoax tethered to its nineteenth-century background. Thus, all details mentioned in the book should conform to knowledge and speculations available to Joseph Smith before the book was written in 1829. Mormon explanations see the book as history and situate it in the ancient world. These opposed views will play out differently through time because knowledge of the past has increased since Joseph Smith's day and will continue to do so. These gains in knowledge should allow us to identify the stronger hypothesis. Noel Reynolds puts the matter this way:

> While a book might conceivably be made to look authentic by matching the standard knowledge at the time of its production, it would gradually become less persuasive as more and more is learned about the times it claims to describe. On the other hand, truly authentic ancient documents would continue to look ancient, even in light of new discoveries and new expectations.[10]

What should this trend look like? If the Book of Mormon was part of the ancient world, more and more details ought to be confirmed as scholarship learns more about the past. Therefore, if the book is history, one would expect confirmations of the book's claims to increase as modern scholarship reveals more about the ancient world and the Book of Mormon's part of that world.[11]

The Book of Mormon has been discussed and dissected now for 175 years, but only during the last fifty has American archaeology been capable of addressing issues of history and generating reliable facts. In this paper, I will marshal recent facts from archaeology to evaluate the trends in seeing the Book of Mormon as hoax or as history. Past quarreling has ranged over hundreds of topics. Rather than attempting a comprehensive review, I will focus on evidence of place, time, and population that was unknowable in 1829.

"Where in the World?": Finding a Place for the Book of Mormon

A major turning point in Book of Mormon studies came with the realization that early Mormons had missed or misunderstood salient facts of geography, history, and culture embedded in its narrative. The book describes a small place. This insight has shifted the whole debate in recent years. Consider Reverend M. T. Lamb's criticisms in 1886:

> An ordinary school boy who had studied geography with any attention, should have been able to form a plot and locate cities and lands in a way to conform in the main to the physical conformations of the country. . . . Not one of the physical peculiarities of either of these western continents is alluded to except the existence of the large lakes and "many fountains of waters," in the northern part of the United States (the only portion of our country that our youthful prophet knew anything about). . . . The Book makes a large number of geographical statements that could not under any possible conditions or circumstances be true except upon some imaginary continent, of size and shape wholly unlike anything existing upon our world to-day, or that has ever existed since Noah's flood. The facts are, my good Mormon brother—that Book *has been proven a fraud beyond the possibility of question.*[12]

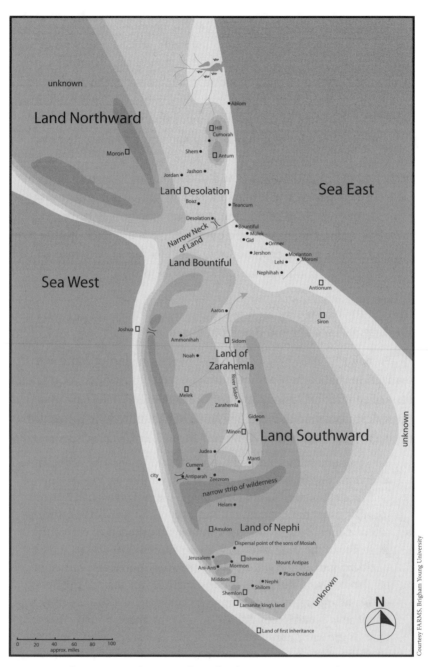

Figure 2. John Sorenson's internal Book of Mormon geography.

It should be clear that Reverend Lamb was precipitous in deploying geography to deliver the *coup de grace* to the Book of Mormon. The point is still being argued today, a century after his proclamation of the book's demise. If Book of Mormon geography does not rise to the standards of an "ordinary school boy," and if it bears no resemblance to obvious physical features, we should not expect to find any place for it in the Americas, but we do.

Book of Mormon geography is a complex topic that covers swaths of both the Old and New Worlds. Recent studies demonstrate that the book's description of Old World lands is precise, down to place names.[13] The New World geography is less crisp, but not less impressive. The book provides over seven hundred references to its geography and is consistent from beginning to end, allowing construction of an internal geography.[14] The book describes a narrow, hour-glass-shaped territory several hundred miles long that is sandwiched between eastern and western seas. John Sorenson has demonstrated that southern Mexico and northern Central America fit remarkably well the book's geography in overall size, configuration, and location of physical features. His proposal for Book of Mormon geography is illustrated in figure 2.

These highly credible Book of Mormon lands are tucked away where Joseph Smith never saw them and would never have found them. Contrary to Reverend Lamb and subsequent critics, the Book of Mormon does have a place in the Americas—just not a place in Joseph Smith's experience. Book of Mormon geography fits a corner of the Americas Joseph did not know. Therefore, the book's geography could not have derived from his personal experience. It follows that he dictated a book with complexities beyond his own comprehension.

"Finding the Time": The Book of Mormon as American Prehistory

After geographical considerations, the second major challenge for Book of Mormon correlations is history. Reverend Lamb found no support for the book's claims as he understood them in 1886.

> We have found that the entire ancient history of this western world
> is flatly against the claims in the Book of Mormon. . . . *The entire
> civilization of the Book of Mormon, its whole record from beginning
> to end is flatly contradicted by the civilization and the history of
> Central America.*[15]

Because current understandings of prehistory differ significantly from what was believed in Lamb's day, they provide an independent check for Book of Mormon claims. For present purposes,
the best place to search for histories matching those in the book is
Mesoamerica.

Peoples there had calendar systems. Evidence of these native
calendars is doubly interesting because Joseph Smith's critics have
accused him of plagiarizing books that contain information on
Hebrew and Aztec timekeeping, principally from Ethan Smith's *View
of the Hebrews* published in 1825.[16] Similarities between Amerindian
and Hebrew months were taken long ago as evidence that American
Indians descended from the Lost Ten Tribes,[17] another idea Joseph
supposedly pilfered. Neither accusation holds up. Timekeeping in
the Book of Mormon differs from descriptions available in 1829 of
Hebrew and Indian lunar counts. Of greater interest, some peculiar
details in the book correspond to Maya time-cycles discovered nearly
sixty years after the book's publication.[18]

As the consummate recordkeepers in Mesoamerica, the Maya
erected numerous stone monuments in their cities that recorded the
time elapsed since 3114 BC, their year zero. Maya calculations were
based on counting by twenties instead of our practice of counting by
tens. The major cycle of Maya time was a four-hundred-year period
called a *baktun*. The Book of Mormon records several references to a
significant four-hundred-year prophecy,[19] consistent with this idiosyncratic Mesoamerican calendar practice.

This similarity in recording time in Mesoamerica and Book of Mormon times is reinforced by each group's parallel narratives of sequential
civilizations. Historic similarities include time, place, and content.
Lamb relied on the best archaeology of his day to demonstrate a lack
of correspondence between Book of Mormon claims and American

antiquities. That was 1886; what about 2005? The top of figure 3 displays the broad histories of Book of Mormon cities. Jaredite culture started towards the end of the third millennium BC, and its first cities were built later. The Jaredites vanished from the Book of Mormon record about 500–400 BC. Nephites arrived on the scene about 580 BC and disappeared about AD 400. Figure 3 juxtaposes Book of Mormon claims with current facts about Mesoamerica, and the trend is quite remarkable.[20] The Olmecs featured on this chart were not identified as a real culture until 1942, and archaeologists did not know their true age until 1967.[21] If early critics cannot be faulted for failing to predict these discoveries, the Book of Mormon should not be denigrated for getting them right.

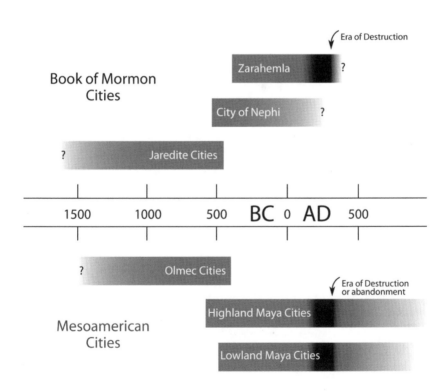

Figure 3. Comparative histories of Book of Mormon and Mesoamerican cities and civilizations.

"Spread upon All the Face of the Land": Populations in the Book of Mormon

One perplexing issue in the Book of Mormon is its population counts. The numbers in the book have always looked out of kilter with traditional readings of the reproductive potential of its founding groups. In 1834, E. D. Howe questioned how the Nephites had become so numerous in just forty years:

> He [Jacob, a first-generation Nephite] says that a hundredth part of the doings of these people could not be engraved on plates on the account of their having become so very numerous, . . . and all sprang from five or six females, in about forty years; . . . According to the most extravagant calculation, in point of increase among five or six females, the whole could not have amounted to more than about sixteen hundred.[22]

The close of the Nephite history is equally problematic in terms of the numbers, as aptly stated by Tyler Parsons in 1841:

> This Mormon bulletin or sword fight with the Lamanites sets Napoleon Bonaparte all in the shade. The battle of Waterloo or Trafalgar is not a circumstance to this. Here is 230,000 of God's people killed, but the 24 that General Mormon saved in his 10,000. The Mormons fought bravely, that's a fact. Mormon says he was wounded. He gives us no account of the loss of the Lamanites, the black sceptics. Probably the Lord was on their side, and of course, as in old times, they did not lose a man.[23]

Millions died in the final Jaredite wars, and at least half a million souls perished in the final Nephite and Lamanite battle, if one allows for Lamanite casualties. These statistics worry some analysts, but they should not. Estimating ancient populations is one of the most difficult tasks archaeologists undertake, and it may require another fifty years to reconstruct Mesoamerica's demographic history.[24] Enough is known, however, to address some claims about lands and peoples.

It is now known that the pan-American model of Book of Mormon geography was wrong and that the lands were actually small. A corollary of this insight is that the book does not describe all peoples on both continents. A further implication is even more important: Book of Mormon peoples who immigrated to the New World did not come to vacant lands.[25] Natives occupied American territories for millennia before Jaredites and Nephites arrived. The apparent rabbit-like population counts for early Nephites, therefore, are best explained by the Nephites' incorporation of natives. The book does not provide a clear account of such associations, but this is an issue of record keeping, not of biological reproduction. At the closing chapter of their history, the astronomical casualty numbers that set Napoleon "all in the shade" may also reflect reporting practices as much as body counts. It is worth remembering that we are dealing with ancient books and their reporting practices, and not with yesterday's newspaper. The Aztecs inflated their war numbers for the record; they described armies of 200,000 soldiers plus their support personnel,[26] the same size as Nephite armies.

Although archaeology does not currently allow an assessment of Book of Mormon population counts, it is important to recognize that Mesoamerica was the most densely populated spot in the Americas and had millions of inhabitants,[27] an order of magnitude that supports the general plausibility of Book of Mormon demography. Crude population profiles can be constructed for the Jaredites and the lowland Olmecs.[28] The Olmec population grows and falls in respectable parallel to that of the Jaredites' reported increase and demise. To summarize, in terms of its claims for lands, peoples, populations, and chronology, the Book of Mormon gets better than passing marks.

The Changing Face of Missing Evidence for the Book of Mormon

As a final check of the book's historical authenticity, I consider a long list of frequently voiced complaints. Standard arguments against the book concern things mentioned in the text not found archaeologically, such as gold plates. In past research, I considered sixty supposed blunders of the Book of Mormon as asserted by three popular nineteenth-century critics. I found that about 60 percent of those criticisms have been resolved in favor of the book.[29] This exercise was meant, however, only as an indicator of trends rather than as a valid, statistical sample of criticisms. Because I am now working with others to obtain a scientific sample of criticisms and a reliable statistic of the number of those that have been resolved, I will exclude the details of that preliminary study pending results of the broader analysis. A few comments on this ongoing research are appropriate here to establish the simple point of this paper: the Book of Mormon looks better with age.

This project will catalog every criticism of the Book of Mormon published in English from 1829 to 2004 related to historic details potentially verifiable through archaeology. We have already identified over 1,000 criticisms from 150 sources for the nineteenth century, and we anticipate uncovering another thousand more fresh complaints for the twentieth century. This means that the original sample of sixty was only about 3 percent of published criticisms, so the number of confirmations from that sample should not be taken as conclusively indicative of the whole. As far as we are able, we will assess the validity and current status of each criticism—whether each is an accurate and fair reading of the text, has been confirmed or not, or is in the process of being confirmed. This list and its documentation, which exceeds the scope of this publication, will be made available elsewhere. The final percentage of confirmed and unconfirmed items relating to Book of Mormon claims will never be a fixed number, of course, because new criticisms of the book are devised each year, and science continues to recover evidence for items mentioned in the book. We will always be dealing with a "ballpark" number indicative of a trend.

Many items mentioned in the Book of Mormon have not been and may never be verified through archaeology, but many have been. Verification is a one-way street in this instance. Positive and negative evidence do not count the same, as anyone tested for a serious medical condition knows. Given current means of verification, positive items are here to stay, but negative items may prove to be positive ones in hiding. "Missing" evidence focuses further research, but it lacks compelling logical force in arguments because it represents the absence of information rather than secure evidence.

It is in this light that we should consider many arguments against the Book of Mormon. The most frequently mentioned deficiencies of the book concern the lack of hard evidence in the New World for the right time periods of precious metals, Old World animals and plants, and Book of Mormon place names and personal names. These deficiencies of negative evidence persist, for the most part, but they should not distract attention from the scores of other unusual items mentioned in the book which have been confirmed through archaeology—nor from the possibility that missing evidence may someday be found.

The overall trend in the data over the past 175 years fits the expectations for the Book of Mormon as history rather than hoax. The Book of Mormon did not play well in Joseph Smith's lifetime as ancient American history; Mormon missionaries got the worst of most debates on the merits of physical evidence in the 1840s.[30] But that was decades before scientific archaeology appeared on the scene. Today, current science is more supportive because many claims made in the book have been substantiated. Given the number of complaints over the years and the range of evidence, quibbling over a point or two of fact will not alter this trend. As seen by science, the Book of Mormon is stronger today than it was in 1830, 1844, 1950, or even 2000, so I expect it will continue to become stronger in the future.

Claims in the book once thought absurd that have been confirmed in recent years include evidence in the Old World of steel swords and metal plates for the right time and place, and in the New World, a strain of domesticated barley, cement, military regalia, assorted weapons, Hebrew words, evidence of reading and writing, and multiple expectations for geography and history. Other probable items await full confirmation, including horses, Solomon-like temples, scimitars, large armies, a script that may qualify as reformed Egyptian, and the two hundred years of Nephite peace.[31] The absolute percentages of confirmed items will change, of course, but not likely the pattern. If the book were a hoax, we would not expect any more than about 1 percent of the items to be confirmed beyond random chance, but several hundred items supporting the book's historical validity have already been verified.

Evidences and Consequences

What do these myriad facts and observations add up to? They constitute a strong case that the Book of Mormon is an ancient Mesoamerican record, an authentic old book. This conclusion harbors multiple ironies, two worth touching on in closing. First, if the book is an ancient Mesoamerican record, most past arguments for and against it have been wrongheaded. Second, if the book is authentic history, most biographies of Joseph Smith are deficient.

Consider the book. For the first 120 years of debate, until 1950, assumptions made by both sides were self-defeating. Critics assumed the book could be, and should be, read as American fantasy and that its moorings could be recovered in early New York and in Joseph Smith's biography. If the book is a Mesoamerican record, however, it cannot be nineteenth-century fiction. The cultural worlds of ancient Mesoamerica and early New York are far enough apart that it ought to be simple to discover from which one the book came. The cultures described in the Book of Mormon fit much better in Mesoamerica than in New York for any century.

For their part, Mormons have traditionally assumed that the book pertained to all peoples in the New World. But if the book describes only four groups from Middle America, it is not a blanket history of all the Americas. Arguments raised by critics through the years demonstrated the insufficiency of the Book of Mormon as universal history and helped Mormon scholars realize they had been misreading the book and overgeneralizing its claims. The book is a regional rather than a continental record.

Now consider Joseph Smith. Friends and foes have used the book to take his measure. The view of the Book of Mormon as hoax distorts Joseph Smith beyond recognition and creates an impossible paradox, as follows.

Early arguments—made at a time when the Book of Mormon remained virtually unread—were greatly flawed by insisting on trumped-up slanders that dismissed Joseph Smith as a lazy liar with a host of even more serious flaws.[32] These *ad hominem* arguments left Joseph without sufficient skills to have written any book, let alone the Book of Mormon. Once the book's complexity became public knowledge, however, it became logically impossible for detractors to derive the book from Joseph Smith. The second round of argumentation imagined intelligent co-conspirators and a plagiarized text. This raised the book's authorial I.Q. but countered obvious facts that eventually leaked out and undermined the argument.[33] In the third and current round of reassessments, critical historians who returned Joseph Smith to his environment have identified over two hundred books from which Joseph could have cribbed an idea or two.[34] This would make the Book of Mormon something of a doctoral dissertation written by a slick, very well-read operator with photographic recall—but without the footnotes. Joseph has gone from being a fool to a genius or perhaps even more than that.[35] Ironically, it is Joseph's critics, not his supporters, who have lately been according him phenomenal powers in their attempts to explain the Book of Mormon through his biography.[36] Although an improvement over base slanders, this swing in opinion lacks credibility or logic, and it does nothing to resolve the Book of Mormon problem.

As Truman Madsen points out, a genius could no more have written the Book of Mormon than could a fool:

> How could any genius or set of geniuses in the nineteenth century concoct a book that is filled with stunning details, now confirmable, of the ancient cultures it claims to represent? By the use of Occam's razor and David Hume's rule that one only credits a "miraculous" explanation if alternatives are more miraculous, the simplest and least miraculous explanation is Joseph Smith's: he translated an ancient record.[37]

This is where archaeology intersects theology and history. The basic question to be resolved is this: What needs to be explained about Joseph Smith and the Book of Mormon? The most remarkable things about the book are *not* the intricate plots, myriad characters, rich settings, or textual consistencies. Ordinary novelists and movie-makers create elaborate fantasy worlds every year. The Book of Mormon separates itself from all fantasy and fiction in its *predictions about the past*. Accurate predictions of a then unknown past beg explanation. Emerging facts from archaeology, as shown, confirm a trend of unusual and specific details in the book that could not have been known in any book or language in 1829.[38]

The continuing challenge is to explain how these facts made their way into the Book of Mormon. The two most likely answers are that they either had to be conveyed to Joseph Smith through supernatural means, or he had to guess each one individually and sequentially at virtually impossible odds. Thus, explanations of the book will need to admit God or the Devil into the equation, or grant supranatural clairvoyance or abilities to Joseph Smith.

Latter-day Saints typically do not turn to extraordinary human abilities in explaining Joseph's role in bringing forth the book, because they see God as doing most of the work, with Joseph Smith as His human conveyance. That Mormons are currently running a distant second to Joseph's critics in praising his human abilities should give both parties pause. Accepting that Joseph translated a book beyond his and our comprehension is the beginning of wisdom. To understand Joseph Smith, all must take his limitations seriously.

As I see it, Joseph Smith did not write the Book of Mormon, it cannot be understood through recourse to his biography, and his biography cannot be recovered by studying the book. The scientific trend of archaeological evidence of its historic facticity indicates that the Book of Mormon is what Joseph Smith claimed it was—an ancient book. It follows that no amount of scrutiny of the book will ever betray Joseph's mind or heart because it is not mirrored in the text. It further follows that Joseph was neither a fool nor a genius, an imposter nor a liar. He was an honest man who told the truth about the book. The Book of Mormon is part of Joseph Smith's story but not the window to his soul. It vouchsafes his claim to prophetic status, not to literary genius. The book was a product of his activity and obedience, not of his imagination.

Notes

1. The Church was first called the Church of Christ when it was organized on April 6, 1830; the name was officially changed in 1838 to The Church of

Jesus Christ of Latter-day Saints (Doctrine and Covenants 115:3). Members of the Church were first called "Mormonites" by outsiders to identify them as believers in the Book of Mormon, and this was later shortened to "Mormons," among whom the preferred term of self-reference is "Saints" or "Latter-day Saints." Latter-day Saints do not consider the term "Mormon" derogatory, only insufficient and ambiguous. Jesus Christ is at the center of their worship, not Mormon, Joseph Smith, or any other prophet.

2. I follow the Latter-day Saint practice of referring to the prophet Joseph Smith Jr. by his first name rather than the distancing academic practice of referring to scholars by their patronym. This usage of the first name signals my affiliation with the community of believers and my lack of disinterested distance in the matters discussed.

3. Adrian Orr, *Mormonism Dissected, or, Knavery "On Two Sticks," Exposed* (Bethania, Penn.: Reuben Chambers, 1841).

4. Sterling M. McMurrin, quoted in Louis Midgley, "The Current Battle over the Book of Mormon: 'Is Modernity Itself Somehow Canonical?'" *Review of Books on the Book of Mormon* 6, no. 1 (1994): 204.

5. For legal reasons, Joseph Smith had to claim to be the "author or proprietor" of the Book of Mormon to obtain and maintain legal copyright, but it has always been clear that he claimed to have translated the book and not to have written it. For a discussion of these matters, see John W. Welch, ed., "Joseph Smith: 'Author and Proprietor,'" *Reexploring the Book of Mormon* (Salt Lake City: Deseret Book; Provo, Utah: Foundation for Ancient Research and Mormon Studies [FARMS], 1992), 154–57.

6. For popular critical stances towards Joseph Smith and the Book of Mormon, see John C. Bennett, *The History of the Saints, Or, An Exposé of Joe Smith and Mormonism* (Boston: Leland and Whiting, 1842); Fawn M. Brodie, *No Man Knows My History: The Life of Joseph Smith, the Mormon Prophet* (New York: Knopf, 1945); Eber D. Howe, *Mormonism Unvailed: or, A Faithful Account of That Singular Imposition and Delusion from Its Rise to the Present Time* (Painesville, Ohio: Howe, 1834); M. T. Lamb, *The Golden Bible or, The Book of Mormon: Is It from God?* (New York: Ward and Drummond, 1886); Brent Lee Metcalfe, ed., *New Approaches to the Book of Mormon: Explorations in Critical Methodology* (Salt Lake City: Signature Books, 1993); David Persuitte, *Joseph Smith and the Origins of the Book of Mormon* (Jefferson, N.C.: McFarland, 1985); Dan Vogel, *Indian Origins and the Book of Mormon: Religious Solutions from Columbus to Joseph Smith* (Salt Lake City: Signature Books, 1986); Dan Vogel, *Joseph Smith: The Making of a Prophet* (Salt Lake City: Signature Books, 2004); Dan Vogel and Brent Lee Metcalfe, eds., *American Apocrypha: Essays on the Book of Mormon* (Salt Lake City: Signature Books, 2002).

7. For popular favorable views of Joseph Smith and the Book of Mormon see the following: Hugh Nibley, *Lehi in the Desert and the World of the Jaredites*

(Salt Lake City: Bookcraft, 1952); Hugh Nibley, *Since Cumorah: The Book of Mormon in the Modern World* (Salt Lake City: Deseret Book, 1967); Hugh Nibley, *An Approach to the Book of Mormon*, 2d ed. (Salt Lake City: Deseret Book, 1976); John L. Sorenson, *An Ancient American Setting for the Book of Mormon* (Salt Lake City: Deseret Book; Provo, Utah: FARMS, 1985); John L. Sorenson, *Nephite Culture and Society: Collected Papers* (Salt Lake City: New Sage Books, 1997); John L. Sorenson, *Images of Ancient America: Visualizing Book of Mormon Life* (Provo, Utah: FARMS, 1998).

8. For good overviews of Book of Mormon geographies and related issues, see Sorenson, *An Ancient American Setting*; John L. Sorenson, *The Geography of Book of Mormon Events: A Source Book* (Provo, Utah: FARMS, 1992); John L. Sorenson, *Mormon's Map* (Provo, Utah: FARMS, 2000).

9. This claim is based on an editorial published in the *Times and Seasons*, attributed to Joseph Smith: "Since our 'Extract' was published from Mr. Stephens' 'Incidents of Travel,' & c. [*Times and Seasons* 3, no. 22 (September 15, 1842): 911–15] we have found another important fact relating to the truth of the Book of Mormon. Central America, or Guatimala [*sic*], is situated north of the Isthmus of Darien [Panama] and once embraced several hundred miles of territory from north to south.—The city of Zarahemla, burnt at the crucifixion of the Savior, and rebuilt afterwards, stood upon this land." *Times and Seasons* 3, no. 23 (October 1, 1842): 927.

Joseph Smith's personal authorship of this statement cannot be established with final certainty because it is unsigned. The basic facts attributing the statement and sentiments to him are summarized by V. Garth Norman, "Joseph Smith and the Beginning of Book of Mormon Archaeology," *Meridian Magazine* (2005): http://www.ldsmag.com/ideas/030930joseph.html.

Joseph Smith had assumed personal responsibility for the contents of the paper on March 15, 1842: "This paper commences my editorial career, I alone stand responsible for it, and shall do for all papers having my signature henceforward. I am not responsible for the publication, or arrangement of the former paper; the matter did not come under my supervision. Joseph Smith." *Times and Seasons* 3, no. 9 (March 15, 1842): 710. Joseph Smith turned editorial control over to John Taylor on November 15, 1842: "I beg leave to inform the subscribers of the Times and Seasons that it is impossible for me to fulfil the arduous duties of the editorial department any longer. The multiplicity of other business that daily devolves upon me, renders it impossible for me to do justice to a paper so widely circulated as the Times and Seasons. I have appointed Elder John Taylor, who is less encumbered and fully competent to assume the responsibilities of that office, and I doubt not but that he will give satisfaction to the patrons of the paper. As this number commences a new volume, it also commences his editorial career. Joseph Smith." *Times and Seasons* 4, no. 1 (November 15, 1842): 8.

This valedictory statement by Joseph Smith, and the statement following by John Taylor, are clear evidence that Joseph took his responsibility seriously and was responsible for the volumes under his editorship. Although it is hypothetically possible that someone else penned the statement, it is sufficiently clear that the sentiments expressed represented Joseph's views and are likely his own words.

10. Noel B. Reynolds, "The Logical Structure of the Authorship Debate," in *Book of Mormon Authorship Revisited: The Evidence for Ancient Origins*, ed. Noel B. Reynolds (Provo, Utah: FARMS, 1997), 98–99.

11. For an insightful evaluation of the environmental hypothesis of the Book of Mormon, see John Gee, "The Wrong Type of Book," in *Echoes and Evidences of the Book of Mormon*, ed. Donald W. Parry, Daniel C. Peterson, and John W. Welch (Provo, Utah: FARMS, 2002), 307–29.

12. Lamb, *The Golden Bible*, 308, 321. I quote extensively from this book, not because it is an easy target for polemics, but because he argued so carefully from the facts of the Book of Mormon and from the best archaeology available to him at the time. Thus, his book is a valuable time capsule of how arguments against the book have evolved through time necessitated by the changing facts of science.

13. See S. Kent Brown, "'The Place That Was Called Nahom': New Light from Ancient Yemen," *Journal of Book of Mormon Studies* 8, no. 1 (1999): 66–68; Warren P. Aston, "Newly Found Altars from Nahom," *Journal of Book of Mormon Studies* 10, no. 2 (2001): 56–61; S. Kent Brown, "New Light from Arabia on Lehi's Trail," *Echoes and Evidences of the Book of Mormon*, 55–125.

14. See note 8.

15. Lamb, *The Golden Bible*, 319, 289.

16. Ethan Smith, *View of the Hebrews or The Tribes of Israel in America*, 2d ed. (Poultney, Vt.: Smith and Shute, 1825).

17. James Adair, *Adair's History of the American Indians*, ed. Samuel Cole Williams (1775; repr., Johnson City, Tenn.: Watuaga, 1930), 77–83.

18. The classic statements on the Maya Calendar are: Sylvanus G. Morley, *An Introduction to the Study of Maya Hieroglyphics* (1915; repr., New York: Dover, 1975); J. Eric S. Thompson, *Maya Hieroglyphic Writing: An Introduction* (Norman: University of Oklahoma Press, 1960). Most introductory books on Mesoamerican archaeology cover the basics of the calendar. I recommend any edition of Michael D. Coe, *The Maya* (London: Thames and Hudson, 1966–2005). Ernst Wilhelm Förstemann is credited with discovering the principles of the Maya calendar in 1887; see his article repr. in Stephen Houston, Oswaldo Chinchilla Mazariegos, and David Stuart, *The Decipherment of Ancient Maya Writing* (Norman: University of Oklahoma Press, 2001).

19. See Alma 45:10, Helaman 13:9, 2 Nephi 26:9–10, Mormon 8:6, and Moroni 10:1.

20. Not all Mesoamerican cities followed the same historic trajectory, of course. The city histories shown in figure 3 represent the largest cities in their regions, El Mirador in the Maya Lowlands, Kaminaljuyú in the Guatemala highlands, Chiapa de Corzo in central Chiapas, Mexico, and La Venta in the Olmec heartland of Tabasco, Mexico. Summaries of these and other cities can be found in Susan Toby Evans and David L. Webster, eds., *Archaeology of Ancient Mexico and Central America: An Encyclopedia* (New York: Garland Publishing, 2001).

21. The precise dates for Olmec culture have not been determined to everyone's satisfaction. The culture achieved official recognition at the Second Round Table of the Sociedad Mexicana de Antropología, Olmecs and Mayas, held in Tuxtla Gutiérrez, Chiapas, Mexico, in 1942. A major controversy at the conference was the chronological placement of Olmec culture, with most Mexican scholars arguing for it being earlier than Maya culture. With the advent of radiocarbon dating in 1950, the Olmecs were soon dated to about 1000 BC at their principal site of La Venta, Tabasco. Subsequently, an even earlier Olmec city, San Lorenzo, was explored and dated to about 1200 BC. See Michael D. Coe, Richard A. Diehl, and Minze Stuiver, "Olmec Civilization, Veracruz, Mexico: Dating of the San Lorenzo Phase," *Science* 155, no. 3768 (March 17, 1967): 1399–401; for a recent synthesis of Olmec culture, see Richard A. Diehl, *The Olmecs: America's First Civilization* (New York: Thames and Hudson, 2004).

22. Howe, *Mormonism Unvailed*, 55–56.

23. Tyler Parsons, *Mormon Fanaticism Exposed: A Compendium of The Book of Mormon, or Joseph Smith's Golden Bible* (Boston: n. p., 1841), 26.

24. Estimating ancient populations is always only approximate even under the best of conditions. Good estimates require that archaeologists find or extrapolate through controlled sampling all the sites in a region, their sizes, the dates of their occupations, the size of each site during any given century, the number of occupied houses, house sizes, and the likely average of the number of persons per household per generation. This is a long string of "ifs," so archaeologists generally take precise estimates of population with considerable skepticism. Most estimates could be off by more than 100 percent, given the conditions for the preservation and/or recovery of evidence of ancient occupation. We are on slightly firmer ground in projecting general trends of high and low population densities for any time or place.

25. John L. Sorenson, "When Lehi's Party Arrived in the Land, Did They Find Others There?" *Journal of Book of Mormon Studies* 1, no. 1 (1992): 1–34, repr. in John L. Sorenson, *Nephite Culture and Society*.

26. Diego Durán, *The Aztecs: The History of the Indies of New Spain*, trans. Doris Heyden and Fernando Horcasitas (New York: Orion, 1964), 217.

27. An appreciation for the population history of North American can be obtained by comparing two recent synthetic treatments of its archaeology:

Brian M. Fagan, *Ancient North America: The Archaeology of a Continent*, 3rd ed. (New York: Thames and Hudson, 2000) and Susan Toby Evans, *Ancient Mexico and Central America: Archaeology and Culture History* (New York: Thames and Hudson, 2004).

28. The population profile for the Lowland Olmecs is based on data for the history of the two principal capitals in the area, San Lorenzo and La Venta, as well as some limited surveys around both capitals. I draw from the following sources: Michael D. Coe and Richard A. Diehl, *In the Land of the Olmec* (Austin: University of Texas Press, 1980); Ann Cyphers, "Reconstructing Olmec Life at San Lorenzo," in *Olmec Art of Ancient Mexico*, ed. Elizabeth P. Benson and Beatriz de la Fuente (Washington D.C.: National Gallery of Art, 1996), 61–71; Ann Cyphers, *Escultura Olmeca de San Lorenzo Tenochtitlán* (Mexico City: UNAM, 2004); Ann Cyphers, ed., *Población, Subsistencia y Medio Ambiente en San Lorenzo Tenochtitlán* (Mexico City: UNAM, 1997); Rebecca González Lauck, "La Venta: An Olmec Capital," in *Olmec Art of Ancient Mexico*, 73–82; Stacey C. Symonds and Roberto Lunagómez, "Settlement System and Population Development at San Lorenzo," in *Olmec to Aztec: Settlement Patterns in the Ancient Gulf Lowlands*, ed. Barbara L. Stark and Philip J. Arnold III (Tucson: University of Arizona Press, 1997), 144–73; Stacey C. Symonds, Ann Cyphers, and Roberto Lunagómez, *Asentamiento Prehispánico en San Lorenzo Tenochtitlán* (Mexico City: UNAM, 2002); Christopher von Nagy, "The Geoarchaeology of Settlement in the Grijalva Delta," in *Olmec to Aztec*, 253–77; Richard A. Diehl, *The Olmecs: America's First Civilization* (New York: Thames and Hudson, 2004).

29. The three sources I considered in my original sample of critiques were Howe, *Mormonism Unvailed*; Bennett, *The History of the Saints*; and Lamb, *The Golden Bible*; see note 6.

30. See Origen Bacheler, *Mormonism Exposed: Internally and Externally* (New York: 162 Nassau St., 1838); Orr, *Mormonism Dissected*; Parsons, *Mormon Fanaticism Exposed*; La Roy Sunderland, *Mormonism Exposed. In Which Is Shown the Monstrous Imposture, the Blasphemy, and the Wicked Tendency, of that Enormous Delusion, Advocated by a Professedly Religious Sect, Calling Themselves "Latter Day Saints"* (New York: Office of the N.Y. Watchman, 1842).

31. Documentation for all Book of Mormon claims is an ongoing process that has not been attempted systematically. Recent books published by FARMS list dozens of novel items. See Parry, Peterson, and Welch, *Echoes and Evidences of the Book of Mormon*; Noel B. Reynolds, ed., *Book of Mormon Authorship: New Light on Ancient Origins* (Provo, Utah: Religious Studies Center, 1982); Reynolds, *Book of Mormon Authorship Revisited*; John L. Sorenson and Melvin J. Thorne, eds., *Rediscovering the Book of Mormon* (Salt Lake City: Deseret Book; Provo, Utah: FARMS, 1991); John W. Welch and Melvin J. Thorne, eds., *Pressing Forward with the Book of Mormon: The FARMS Updates of the 1990s* (Provo,

Utah: FARMS, 1999); John W. Welch, ed., *Reexploring the Book of Mormon: The F.A.R.M.S. Updates* (Salt Lake City: Deseret Book; Provo, Utah: FARMS, 1992).

32. See Alexander Campbell, "Delusions," *Millennial Harbinger* (February 1831): 85–96; Howe, *Mormonism Unvailed*.

33. See John C. Bennett, *The History of the Saints*; Persuitte, *Joseph Smith and the Origins of the Book of Mormon*; Bacheler, *Mormonism Exposed*.

34. See Brodie, *No Man Knows My History*; Vogel, *Indian Origins and the Book of Mormon*; Vogel, *Joseph Smith: The Making of a Prophet*.

35. See Harold Bloom, *The American Religion: The Emergence of the Post-Christian Nation* (New York: Simon and Schuster, 1992).

36. Metcalf, *New Approaches to the Book of Mormon: Explorations in Critical Methodology*; Vogel and Metcalf, *American Apocrypha*; Vogel, *Indian Origins and the Book of Mormon*; Vogel, *Joseph Smith: The Making of a Prophet*.

37. Truman Madsen, "B. H. Roberts and the Book of Mormon," in *Book of Mormon Authorship*, 12.

38. See John L. Sorenson, "Viva Zapato! Hurray for the Shoe!" *Review of Books on the Book of Mormon* 6, no. 1 (1994): 297–361; Sorenson, "The Book of Mormon as a Mesoamerican Record," in *Book of Mormon Authorship Revisited*, 391–521.

Joseph Smith and the Past

John W. Welch

M y thoughts on Joseph Smith's interest in past worlds cluster into three sections. The first deals with the challenge of evaluating and assessing Joseph Smith's recoveries of texts or views from past worlds or civilizations. The second develops a list of ways in which the past functioned in Joseph Smith's process of continuing revelation. The third focuses on the dynamic link between the past and the present in Joseph Smith's concept of priesthood authority and its restoration.

The Challenge of Evaluation

I am drawn to Givens's remark that the texts which Joseph Smith presented as translations must submit to "examination as the historical records they purport to be."[1] In my experience, these texts lend themselves to examination in many ways better than most people realize. But others disagree. The questions that go begging here are: who will judge between these views, and on what basis can people determine if these translations are what they purport to be?

I have been involved in Book of Mormon research now for forty years. Recently, the field seems to be moving farther away from any agreement on certain basic issues, such as which bits of evidence are relevant, how evidence is to be weighed, and what amount of evidence is needed to prove or disprove a proposition. Full agreement on such evidentiary issues may still be lacking, but that does not excuse scholars from striving to state their evidence as clearly as possible and to seek to achieve such agreement.

Chiasmus may serve as an example. In 1967, I discovered a remarkable literary structure in Alma 36, which I see as one of the best examples of extended chiasmus anywhere in world literature.[2] I imagine that Joseph Smith would be quite amazed to be shown this phenomenon in the text of the Book of Mormon. While chiasmus is not an exclusively Hebraic style of writing, some biblical scholars have considered it to be highly characteristic of ancient Israelite literature. But opinions range from "chiasmus is solid evidence of the antiquity of the Book of Mormon," to "chiasmus proves absolutely nothing about anything in the Book of Mormon."[3] Which assessment is correct? Who is making sense? Who is credible, if anyone?

Participants in these opinion matches are often intransigently predisposed to their points of view—as often occurs in biblical or religious studies generally—with believers or proponents of certain theories on the one side and skeptics or those who are disaffected on the other. Inquirers who listen in on these in-group volleys must often wonder, what is really going on? And, judging by the recent publications of the Book of Mormon by both the University of Illinois Press and Doubleday,[4] it is clear that some people really want to know. But whose footnotes are reliable? Whose descriptions are not over- or understated?

Who can judge if the points made by Margaret Barker and others in glimpsing the world of Lehi's Jerusalem succeed in situating the Book of Mormon in preexilic Israel?[5] Who can judge if the naturalistic explanations for the Book of Mormon have fallen short? Who can confirm that the Gadianton robbers are much better understood in terms of ancient brigandage than nineteenth-century Masonry?[6] Who can judge what is anachronistic, when our knowledge is incomplete and when we do not have Nephi's or Benjamin's prophetic BCE originals but only an English translation of Mormon's much later AD abridgement? Who can authoritatively declare the Spaulding theory finally dead and give it a proper burial?[7]

Regarding the Book of Abraham, many details mentioned in that text have also turned out to be more widely attested than anyone had previously suspected. Forty elements found in the Book of Abraham but absent in the Bible are found in obscure Jewish and Islamic traditions about the early life of Abraham.[8] But who is to say if these forty points are significant?

Might one imagine a bureaucracy holding hearings on such questions? Impaneling officers in such a body would be far trickier than confirming Supreme Court nominees, and it is doubtful that such a process could ever be any less problematic than the Jesus Seminar has been. But, with Mormon Studies programs now being inaugurated in highly regarded universities, an unofficial peer panel may informally emerge. Yet, could such a panel of academicians be composed of highly informed but also disinterested observers? Not likely. Could they judge strengths and weaknesses according to disclosed assumptions and articulated criteria? Perhaps. Could they be methodologically savvy but not ideologically slavish? Could they produce responsible, cautious, written opinions? Or at least call preliminary attention to misleading statements and material omissions? That much one can hope for.

But then again, how will they determine what weight should be given to the book's complexity, profundity, and artistry, together with Joseph's lack of education, the testimonies of the Book of Mormon witnesses, and the rapidity of the dictation through which the book came forth? Chiasmus, for example, can be used as evidence of many things—from multiple authorship to meaningful composition.[9] Going beyond and rightly avoiding simplistic parallelomania,[10] the Book of Mormon's literary complexity is evidence that its texts were written in some way that normal dictation does not explain.

And who will finally say when enough evidence, one way or the other, has finally been heard? Many interesting things in support of the Book of Mormon have surfaced, but all the evidence still is not in yet. Pre-Columbian barley has been found;[11] will pre-Columbian

horses turn up next? The name of Alma has been found in Jewish
and other Near Eastern texts;[12] will other Book of Mormon names
also show up? While the authorship of some sections in the book of
Isaiah remains debated, the Hebrew of Isaiah 48:11 in the Great Isaiah
Scroll Dead Sea Scrolls (1Q Isaᵃ 14:32) has the verb in the first person,
"I shall not suffer my name to be polluted," which happens to agree
in this respect with the Book of Mormon's reading of that passage,
which differs from the King James.[13] Givens is correct that readers
must "step back from a canvas as large as the one [Joseph] painted,"[14]
but looking closely at minute details is important too.

Regarding the unusual practice of writing on metal, a tiny silver amulet scroll has recently been authenticated, giving tangible
evidence of Hebrew writing on metal from Lehi's Jerusalem.[15] Brass
plates found in central Italy contain ancient religious laws of the
Umbrians, written in their language but using the script of another
language (that of the Etruscans),[16] which seems to echo the linguistic
description of the plates of Laban. Doubled, sealed, witnessed bronze
Roman plates, bound together, with one part open and the other
part sealed, may be reminiscent of the configuration of the plates
of Mormon.[17] As Lehi's group traveled down the Arabian Peninsula,
the Book of Mormon says that they came to a place that was called
Nahom, where they turned east. An altar inscription from the seventh-
century BC has recently been discovered in Yemen very significantly
containing the name Nihm, linguistically close to the name Nahom,
just where the ancient frankincense trail turned east.[18]

What more may come along? Good science takes time. Much
careful work remains to be done. In the meantime, we will need to
wait for conclusive answers that now evade us. Indeed, in all matters
of faith, important evidence will always be lacking. The result will
always be a hung jury, as arguments can be made on both sides. These
are surely debatable subjects. One should not expect these exami-
nations to be any more conclusive than the inconclusively arrayed
approaches in biblical studies.

Would Joseph Smith be disappointed in this? Probably not. For
one thing, he expected something less than direct proof, to be sure.
He said, "It will be as it ever has been, the world will prove Joseph

Smith a true prophet by circumstantial evidence."[19] Conspicuous is his mention of circumstantial or indirect evidence. If evidence of all types were not such a complicated matter, many things in life, whether in historical studies, in the courtroom, or in religious persuasions, would be much simpler. But, this complexity itself allows evidence to combine with faith, precisely because evidence is both a product of data attractive to the mind and the result of human choices arising from values and beliefs.[20] Thus, while Joseph Smith would certainly welcome Givens's expected examination of these revealed records as the historical texts they claim to be, everyone will want to bear in mind in this process that Joseph knew the element of personal faith and prayer would still be required. When asked how the translation process occurred, he always answered with the words, "By the gift and power of God."[21]

Functions of the Past

Givens's main point, that we should focus more on process than on the product of Joseph Smith's thought, is well taken. Further development of this distinction will surely yield good academic insights. In particular, one will want to ask next, how did the recovery of the past function in Joseph's process of continuing revelation? He could, after all, have introduced the principle of continuing revelation only with respect to the present and the future; revelation need not have involved the past.

Indeed, the past meant many things and served many functions for Joseph Smith. He was captivated by the idea of past visions, lost scriptures, ancient covenants, vanished civilizations, and former dispensations of the gospel. And, more than captivated, he was liberated and expanded by what he saw in the past. He never explained how this all worked, but we should attempt to detect the dynamics that drove his process. Here are ten such dynamics:

1. For Joseph Smith, the past is inviting, for what has happened before can happen again. It opens doors for all. If Moses and God spoke with each other, face to face, "as a man speaketh unto his friend" (Exodus 33:11), then others could do likewise today. If in times past

God revealed his plans to his prophets (Amos 3:7), then God could do likewise again, as unsettling as it might seem.[22]

2. Joseph Smith certainly saw the past as instructive. On one occasion Joseph said that Jesus' "disciples, in days of old," were sorely afflicted because they "sought occasion against one another and forgave not one another in their hearts," and for this reason Joseph emphatically instructed his brethren "to forgive one another" absolutely (Doctrine and Covenants 64:8–10).

3. The past is pertinent to the present. For Joseph Smith, the words of past prophets were pertinent in the present precisely because he saw them as seeing this day. Not only had Isaiah seen the scholar who would say, "I cannot read a sealed book" (see Isaiah 29:11), but Jesus foresaw the Saints purchasing land in Missouri when he spoke of the man who found "a treasure hid in a field" and sold all that he had to buy it (Matthew 13:44). For Joseph, these were more epistemologically compelling than just historical attractions or "mythic reverberations."[23]

4. The past is personal. This is another aspect of his collapse of the distance between the heavenly and the earthly. Joseph Smith saw himself prefigured in the past, in what Jan Shipps describes as a "recapitulation process" of restoring many elements from the biblical past, such as the priesthood after the order of Melchizedek.[24] Whether he intentionally set out to recapitulate past events or simply realized after the fact what had happened, either way it was confirming that the past had reiterated itself in his life personally.

5. The past was better than the present, at least in certain ways. Joseph Smith yearned for the purity and goodness of the city of Enoch. Beyond that, he even revealed that "man was also in the beginning with God" (Doctrine and Covenants 93:29); a view of human origins does not get much better than that. But sometimes things devolve. Over time, religion had degenerated. This means that, for Joseph, evolution or agonistic struggle is not an iron law of improvement. Things get garbled. Apostasies occur. Civilizations die. Even at the euphoric dawn of a new American republic, Joseph Smith cried out sharp warnings from the past (as in Doctrine and Covenants 64:8–9).

6. The past is important. Another axiom in Joseph Smith's thought process was the realization that the losses of instructions and covenants which were "from the beginning" (Doctrine and Covenants 22:1) were serious losses. Without past knowledge—and, just as much, without records currently kept—rising generations are not just uninformed but are painfully lost, without a knowledge of the plan of salvation laid from the foundation of the earth.

7. Past truths are reaccessed through the spirit of revelation. The Book of Mormon states, "A seer can know of things which are past" (Mosiah 8:17). Quite remarkably, one usually thinks of a prophet as one who foresees the future; rarely have revelators also revealed the past. And, one might ponder, which is harder or more important: knowing the future or knowing the past?

8. Remembering is sacramental. Remembering is to the past as faith is to the future. Remembering the past covenants of the Lord and remembering progenitors were not just exercises in historiography for Joseph. Remembering is a stipulation required in covenants revealed by Joseph Smith (Mosiah 5:11–12; Doctrine and Covenants 20:77, 79).

9. The process seeks to recover whole worlds. Interestingly, as considerable research using numerous academic tools now shows, Joseph Smith's recovery of past worlds came complete with a large cast of individual characters, who act in various real-life settings, whose vocabularies are statistically and conceptually distinctive. These personalities are arrayed amidst multigenerational family feuds, well-crafted lineage histories, accurately sophisticated legal proceedings, military campaigns, guerrilla warfare, temple convocations, prophetic speech forms, and inspired world views. This completeness not only allowed Joseph and his followers to affirm these accounts but also to liken them ethically unto themselves (1 Nephi 19:23).

10. Ultimately, the goal for Joseph Smith was fullness. Above all, he sought expansively to embrace "all true principles," which must include things that have been, as well as things that are and will be. His goal was abundance, "wholeness" and "totalizing" "plenitude." Givens rightly uses such words,[25] for Joseph Smith strongly preferred

completeness over consistency, a distinction of profound importance in many ways. Over and over, his doctrines and attitudes relish fullness and multiplicity. Many words, traditionally singulars, appear as plurals in his teachings: he spoke of priesthoods, eternal lives, creations, worlds, degrees of glory, and even Gods.

Source of Authority

Finally, Joseph Smith claimed to get more from the past than information alone. Givens is not alone in speaking of the propositional content of Joseph's work, how he restored records from the past, how fragments of true gospel teachings were "scattered through time," and how "much instruction" given in the past had been lost.[26] All of that information was significant to Joseph, but the recovery of lost knowledge was not the vital force that impelled his grand project forward. In the minds of his followers, more potent than truth claims were Joseph Smith's power claims. Knowing of ancient orders is one thing; having the authority to revive those lost orders is something else.

Authority, of course, means different things to different traditions, as Richard Mouw has noted in *BYU Studies*.[27] To Evangelicals, the concept of authority is grounded in the words of the Bible as the authoritative source of truth. To Catholics, authority has to do with the right to speak as the "authentic organ to transmit and explain" God's revelations.[28] But for Joseph Smith, authority not only embraced the scriptures and the orthodox conveyance of interpretations, but also was rooted in actually conferred rights and powers to act and speak in the name of God. More than *words* from the past, Joseph relied upon *beings* from the past. Thus, he relied not only upon biblical *authority to recover the past*,[29] but upon *the past to recover authority*.

If we could ask Joseph Smith what he gained from the past, he would probably speak first and foremost of the restoration of divine keys, priesthood powers, and the authority to perform eternally binding ordinances according to the will of God and in the name of Jesus Christ, as is evident in his joyous listing of heavenly manifestations in Doctrine and Covenants 128:20–21. It would seem that nothing was more important to Joseph Smith's perception of his own mission than the recovery of lost priesthood authority.

Thus, the version of Malachi 4:5, as quoted by Moroni, is interesting, not just because it seems to reflect an unknown heavenly Ur-Text[30] or a lost textual variant,[31] but also because this version promises "Behold, I will reveal unto you the Priesthood, by the hand of Elijah" (Doctrine and Covenants 2:1), rather than just the familiar "Behold, I will send you Elijah." Thus, more than a visit, Joseph expected, apparently as early as 1823, the conferral of priesthood by the hand of an ancient prophet. Such a visitation goes beyond the normal visionary experience. Eventually, as Joseph Smith and others testified, came John the Baptist, Peter, James, John, Moses, Elijah, and others from Adam on down, as resurrected beings, not just to disclose knowledge of the past but to confer authority and to commit keys of all past dispensations "to introduce . . . the dispensation of the fullness of times, [as] it was known . . . by the ancient servants of God."[32]

Consistent with this concept of authority, records from the past, such as the Book of Mormon, were significant to Joseph Smith not only for the histories and doctrines they offered, but especially for the priesthood powers and procedures they warranted and directed. What immediately struck Joseph and Oliver Cowdery as they translated 3 Nephi was not the human pathos or the divine presence depicted there, but their sudden realization that "none had authority from God to administer the ordinances of the Gospel" as was given by Christ in two increments to the twelve in that Nephite account.[33] That realization drove the translator and scribe to the banks of Susquehanna River to seek that authority. The most immediate use made by Joseph Smith of the Book of Mormon was to implement its priesthood instructions.

The priesthood focus of the Book of Abraham is similar: how Abraham became "a High Priest" (Abraham 1:2), opposed false priests who had no "right of Priesthood" (1:27, 31), and entered into a covenant to bear the "Priesthood unto all nations" (2:9). Priesthood threads run through the Book of Abraham, his altar (3:17), prayers

(3:19), approaching the throne of God (3:10–11), the opening of his eyes (3:12), and his premortal calling (3:23). Above all, Joseph saw in the Egyptian facsimiles depictions of priests (Book of Abraham, Facsimile 1, fig. 3), priesthood (Facsimile 2, figs. 3, 7), powers (Facsimile 2, fig. 5), grand priesthood keywords (Facsimile 2, fig. 7), and presidency (Facsimile 3, fig. 1).

In addition to ancient records, visions of the past also served to direct Joseph Smith's use of priesthood authority. The Kirtland High Council Minutes in 1834 report that "the order of councils in ancient days [was] shown to [Joseph] by vision,"[34] in which he learned the distinctive order of a president serving with two counselors. This recovery from the past legitimized the use of that same order in the present. In good restorationist form, his desire was that "all things pertaining to [this] dispensation should be conducted precisely in accordance with the preceding dispensations,"[35] but his manner of implementing that program was certainly unprecedented.

It is sometimes remarked that the world's view of Joseph Smith is shaped by the world's view of America. But Joseph Smith's concept of lines of authority attaches him in one more way to the past, more than to his contemporaneous American surroundings. His claim of priesthood from John the Baptist links him more to the River Jordan than the Potomac or the Mississippi. His assertion of priesthood from Peter, James, and John links him more to the eastern Mediterranean than to eastern New York. The receipt of keys of Elijah, Moses, and Abraham links him more to Mount Carmel, Mount Sinai, and Mount Moriah than to Mount Vernon. And his vision of personally returning all priesthood keys eventually to Adam through the order of the antediluvian prophet Enoch links him more to all the world than to any single nation or people.

Thus to Joseph Smith, knowing the past was as important as knowing the present or the future, and revealing the details and instructions of the past in their antiquity and fullness was offered as a sign of his calling as a prophet. But, perhaps above anything else, he saw the past as a repository of divine powers. Recovering that authority has everything to do with what the past meant to the essential Joseph Smith.

Notes

1. Terryl L. Givens, "Joseph Smith: Prophecy, Process, and Plenitude," in this volume, 67.

2. For comparisons and analyses of chiasmus in several bodies of ancient literature, see John W. Welch and Daniel B. McKinlay, *Chiasmus Bibliography* (Provo, Utah: Research Press, 1999); John W. Welch, ed., *Chiasmus in Antiquity* (Hildesheim: Gerstenberg, 1981), with Alma 36 discussed on pages 206–7. See further, John W. Welch, "A Masterpiece: Alma 36," in *Rediscovering the Book of Mormon,* ed. John L. Sorenson and Melvin J. Thorne (Salt Lake City: Deseret Book, 1991), 114–31.

3. Comments such as these posted recently on blogs are not new. A degree of subjectivity, and hence a range of opinions, is inevitably involved in identifying and interpreting any meaningful feature of any literary composition, as I discuss in the introduction to *Chiasmus in Antiquity,* 13–15. Regarding chiasms defined in terms of thoughts and themes, David Noel Freedman in the preface to *Chiasmus in Antiquity,* 7, similarly stated, "A large subjective element enters into these discussions, and the presence or absence of chiasm on this level can become almost a voter's choice. Scholars, therefore, may range between separated areas of research in their approach to chiasm." For statistical evaluations of the objective features of these lengthy passages, however, see the methods employed and the results derived by Yehuda T. Radday, "Chiasmus in Hebrew Biblical Narrative," in *Chiasmus in Antiquity,* 50–115, and by Boyd F. Edwards and W. Farrell Edwards, "Does Chiasmus Appear in the Book of Mormon by Chance?" *BYU Studies* 43, no. 2 (2004): 103–30.

4. Grant Hardy, ed., *The Book of Mormon: A Reader's Edition* (Urbana: University of Illinois, 2003); *The Book of Mormon* (Garden City, N.Y.: Doubleday, 2004).

5. John W. Welch, David Rolph Seely, and Jo Ann H. Seely, eds., *Glimpses of Lehi's Jerusalem* (Provo, Utah: Foundation for Ancient Research and Mormon Studies [FARMS], 2004).

6. Regarding similarities between the Gadianton robbers and the complex phenomenon of ancient brigandage, see John W. Welch, *Reexploring the Book of Mormon* (Salt Lake City: Deseret Book, 1992), 248–49, and John W. Welch, "Legal and Social Perspectives on Robbers in First-Century Judea," in *Masada and the World of the New Testament,* ed. John F. Hall and John W. Welch (Provo, Utah: BYU Studies, 1997), 141–53.

7. For a candid assessment, see Lance D. Chase, "Spaulding Manuscript," in *Encyclopedia of Mormonism,* ed. Daniel H. Ludlow, 4 vols. (New York: Macmillan, 1992), 4:1402–3, concluding that "since 1946, no serious student of Mormonism has given the Spaulding Manuscript theory much credibility. In that year Fawn Brodie . . . dismissed the idea of any connection between Spaulding and Smith or their writings." Yet the notion lingers in some circles.

8. John A. Tvedtnes, Brian M. Hauglid and John Gee, comps., *Traditions about the Early Life of Abraham* (Provo, Utah: FARMS, 2001), 537–47.

9. For a discussion of these various prospects, see John W. Welch, "What Does Chiasmus in the Book of Mormon Prove?" in *Book of Mormon Authorship Revisited*, ed. Noel B. Reynolds (Provo, Utah: FARMS, 1997), 199–224.

10. In my essay "Criteria for Establishing the Presence of Chiasmus," *Journal of Book of Mormon Studies* 4, no. 2 (1995): 1–14, reprinted in McKinlay and Welch, *Chiasmus Bibliography*, I propose fifteen useful criteria.

11. John L. Sorenson and Robert F. Smith, "Barley in Ancient America," in *Reexploring the Book of Mormon*, 130–32.

12. Observed by Hugh W. Nibley in Yigael Yadin, *Bar-Kochba* (New York: Random House, 1971), plate on p. 177, and reviewed in *BYU Studies* 14 (Autumn 1973): 115–26, reprinted as chapter 15 in *The Prophetic Book of Mormon*, Collected Works of Hugh Nibley (Salt Lake City: Deseret Book; Provo, Utah: FARMS, 1989), 8:274–88. See further Paul Y. Hoskisson, "Alma as a Hebrew Name," *Journal of Book of Mormon Studies* 7, no. 1 (1998): 72–73; and Terrence L. Szink, "The Personal Name 'Alma' at Ebla," *Religious Educator* 1, no. 1 (2000): 53–56.

13. Donald W. Parry and Elisha Qimron, *A New Edition of the Great Isaiah Scroll (1QIsaa): Transcriptions and Photographs* (Leiden: Brill, 1998), 81. The original manuscript of this passage in 1 Nephi 20:11 was emended by Oliver Cowdery but also had the verb in the first person: "for how should I suffer my name to be polluted." See Royal Skousen, *The Original Manuscript of the Book of Mormon* (Provo, Utah: FARMS, 2001), 154–55; and Royal Skousen, *Analysis of Textual Variants of the Book of Mormon* (Provo, Utah: FARMS, 2004), 1:432–33.

14. Givens, "Joseph Smith: Prophecy, Process, and Plenitude," 67.

15. Gabriel Barkay, "Excavations at Ketef Hinnom in Jerusalem," in *Ancient Jerusalem Revealed*, ed. Hillel Geva (Jerusalem: Israel Exploration Society, 2000), 102–5; Dana M. Pike, "Israelite Inscriptions from the Time of Jeremiah and Lehi," in *Glimpses of Lehi's Jerusalem*, 213–15.

16. See Augusto Ancillotti and Romolo Cerri, *The Tables of Iguvium: Colour Photographs, Facsimiles, Transliterated Text, Translation and Comments* (Perugia, Italy: Jama Perugia, 1997).

17. John W. Welch, "Doubled, Sealed, Witnessed Documents: From the Ancient World to the Book of Mormon," in *Mormons, Scripture, and the Ancient World*, ed. Davis Bitton (Provo, Utah: FARMS, 1998), 391–444; the two Roman bronze plates from Mainz, Germany, are discussed on pages 398–99.

18. See Andrey Korotayev, *Ancient Yemen: Some General Trends of Evolution of the Sabaic Language and Sabaean Culture*, Journal of Semitic Studies Supplement 5 (Oxford: Oxford University Press, 1995), 81–83; S. Kent Brown, "New Light from Arabia on Lehi's Trail," in *Echoes and Evidences*, 81–82.

19. Joseph Fielding Smith, comp., *Teachings of the Prophet Joseph Smith* (Salt Lake City: Deseret Book, 1976), 267.

20. John W. Welch, "The Power of Evidence in the Nurturing of Faith," in *Echoes and Evidences,* 30–42.

21. John W. Welch, "The Miraculous Translation of the Book of Mormon: Documenting the Translation Chronology," in *Opening the Heavens: Accounts of Divine Manifestations, 1820–1844,* ed. John W. Welch (Provo, Utah: Brigham Young University Press, 2005), 121–29.

22. Givens, "Joseph Smith: Prophecy, Process, and Plenitude," 57, 59–60.

23. Givens, "Joseph Smith: Prophecy, Process, and Plenitude," 60.

24. Jan Shipps, *Mormonism: The Story of a New Religious Tradition* (Chicago: University of Illinois, 1985), 58.

25. Givens, "Joseph Smith: Prophecy, Process, and Plenitude," 65, 66.

26. Givens, "Joseph Smith: Prophecy, Process, and Plenitude," 63, 64.

27. Richard Mouw, "What Does God Think of America? Some Challenges from Evangelicals and Mormons," *BYU Studies* 43, no. 4 (2004): 10–12.

28. See Jean Bainvel cited in David L. Paulsen, "Joseph Smith Challenges the Theological World," 183.

29. As Givens points out in "Joseph Smith: Prophecy, Process, and Plenitude," 61.

30. Givens, "Joseph Smith: Prophecy, Process, and Plenitude," 66.

31. Margaret Barker, "Joseph Smith and Preeexilic Israelite Religion," in this volume, 70.

32. John Taylor in *Journal of Discourses,* 26 vols. (Liverpool: F. D. Richards, 1855–86), 21:94, April 13, 1879.

33. Oliver Cowdery, "Letter VII," *Messenger and Advocate* 1 (October 1834): 14–16; quoted in Joseph Smith–History, note on p. 59.

34. Kirtland High Council Minutes, February 17, 1834, Church Archives, The Church of Jesus Christ of Latter-day Saints, Salt Lake City.

35. Joseph Smith Jr., *History of The Church of Jesus Christ of Latter-day Saints,* ed. B. H. Roberts, 2d ed., rev., 7 vols. (Salt Lake City: Deseret Book, 1971), 4:204.

The Worlds of Joseph Smith Gallery Display

A display of books, manuscripts, photographs, and artifacts was assembled to accompany "The Worlds of Joseph Smith" conference at the Library of Congress. Twelve items in this display came from collections in the Library of Congress; three from the Library-Archives of the Community of Christ in Independence, Missouri; two from the L. Tom Perry Special Collections at Brigham Young University in Provo, Utah; and thirteen from the LDS Church History Library, Archives, and Museum of Church History and Art in Salt Lake City.

The display was organized by James H. Hutson, Director of the Manuscript Division of the Library of Congress, and by John W. Welch, Editor in Chief of *BYU Studies*. They were assisted by Larry Draper, Kristi Bell, and others at BYU, and also by Steve L. Olsen, Glenn N. Rowe, and several others on the staff of the LDS Church Historian's office. The display was finalized and mounted in the foyer and display cases of the Coolidge Auditorium by the Library's Exhibition Office.

The captions were researched and written by John Welch, with assistance from Steven C. Harper, document editor for *BYU Studies*; the texts were then edited by the Exhibition Office. The captions that appear here are lengthened from the labels that were used in the display cases. Among other additions, quotations have been expanded and further sources have been supplied, drawing attention especially to relevant articles in *BYU Studies* and to works authored by presenters at this conference.

Courtesy Community of Christ Library-Archives, Independence, Missouri. photograph by Val Brinkerhoff

Portrait of Joseph Smith (photograph of original). This oil portrait of the Prophet was painted "from life" in September of 1842, most likely by David W. Rogers of New York. It is one of the few images that compares closely with a plaster mask made of Joseph shortly after his martyrdom in 1844 and is thus considered to be an accurate reflection of his likeness. Upon the death of Joseph Smith, Apostle John Taylor reflected solemnly, "Joseph Smith, the Prophet and Seer of the Lord, has done more, save Jesus only, for the salvation of men in this world, than any other man that ever lived in it" (Doctrine and Covenants 135:3).

Ephraim Hatch, *Joseph Smith Portraits: A Search for the Prophet's Likeness* (Provo, Utah: Religious Studies Center, Brigham Young University, 1998).

∿ Joseph Smith in His Own Time

Letter from Albert Brown to James Brown (November 1, 1835). After traveling from Missouri to Kirtland, Ohio, Mormon convert Albert Brown wrote this letter to his parents. He had found relatives "all in good health and the church in great prosperity, her members increasing and the blessings of heaven pourd out apon them," while calamities awaited those who "obey not the fullness of the Gospel of our Lord Jesus Christ." Albert also mentions the purchase by the Church in Kirtland of four Egyptian mummies for $2,400 in order to obtain an ancient record "containing some of the history of Josef while in egypt and also of Jacob and many prophesise Delivered by them. . . . Many of the learned have been to kirtland to examine the characters but none of them have been able to tell but very little about them and yet Joseph without any of the wisdom of this world can read them and know what they are."

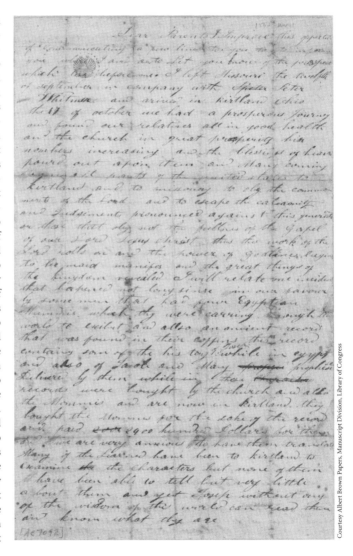

The full text of this letter was published by Christopher C. Lund in "A Letter Regarding the Acquisition of the Book of Abraham," *BYU Studies* 20, no. 4 (1980): 402–3.

Petition from Lyman Wight to President Martin Van Buren, 1839. This elegantly scripted and passionate affidavit details the injuries suffered by Lyman Wight as he was expelled by mobs from Missouri, where he had a home at Adam-ondi-Ahman in Daviess County. He protested to President Martin Van Buren: "Such was not the liberty" that his father had fought for as a Revolutionary War soldier or that he personally had stood for in the Battle of Sackets Harbour in the War of 1812. Hundreds of affidavits of plunder, rape, and murder were collected by the Latter-day Saints after their expulsion from Missouri under the governor's order of extermination. Their protests were of no avail.

For a thorough presentation of these protests, see Clark V. Johnson, ed., *Mormon Redress Petitions: Documents of the 1833–1838 Missouri Conflict* (Provo, Utah: Religious Studies Center, Brigham Young University, 1992).

Courtesy Martin Van Buren Papers, Manuscript Division, Library of Congress

Letter of Recommendation from James Adams to President Martin Van Buren, November 9, 1839. When Joseph Smith traveled to Washington, D.C., to seek help from federal officials in redressing damages suffered in the 1838 Mormon conflict in Missouri, he carried with him several letters of introduction. This letter was signed by General James Adams (1783–1843), an Indian war veteran, lawyer, and justice of the peace in Springfield, Illinois. He states that the Missouri "outrages are unparalleled in the annals of civilized communities" and encouraged President Van Buren "to sustain the rights of all the citizens of our great Republic."

See generally Robert V. Remini, *Joseph Smith* (New York: Viking, 2002).

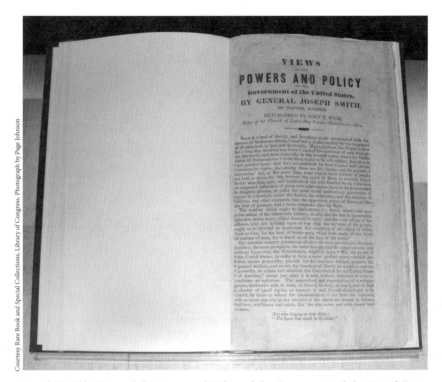

Joseph Smith's *Views of the Power and Policy of the Government of the United States* (**Nauvoo, 1844**). In April 1844 a call went out for volunteers to "electioneer for Joseph to be the next President" (*History of the Church,* 6:325). Some 340 signed up and were actively canvassing the country when Joseph Smith was murdered in Carthage, Illinois, in June 1844. They disseminated Smith's views on law and politics via this pamphlet. Joseph Smith advocated the elimination of prisons except for murderers, punishing offenders by having them work on public roads so they can be "taught more wisdom and more virtue," and the abolition of slavery by 1850, compensating slave owners with revenue from the sale of western lands. He extolled the civic virtues of honor, honesty, generosity, equality, and friendship toward all, "from any country, of whatever color, clime or tongue."

The full text of this pamphlet is published in Joseph Smith Jr., *History of The Church of Jesus Christ of Latter-day Saints,* ed. B. H. Roberts, 2d ed., rev., 7 vols. (Salt Lake City: Deseret Book, 1971), 6:197–209. On Joseph Smith's presidential campaign, see Margaret C. Robertson, "The Campaign and the Kingdom: The Activities of the Electioneers in Joseph Smith's Presidential Campaign," *BYU Studies* 39, no. 3 (2000): 147–80.

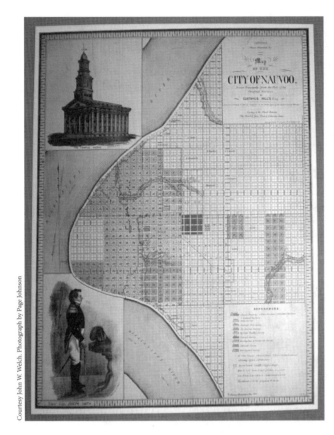

Map of Nauvoo, "The City of Joseph" (1971 reprint). This composite by Gustavus Hills, lithographed by J. Chalds, New York, is based on the plats of the original surveys of Nauvoo, Illinois, founded 1839 on the east bank of a large bend in the Mississippi River. Colors on the map indicate the different surveys. Temple Square (block 20) is in the center of town, on Wells Street between Knight and Mulholland Streets. Joseph Smith's residence is on the south waterfront. In the upper left is a preliminary drawing of the Nauvoo Temple by William Weeks, temple architect; in the lower left is Joseph Smith in his Nauvoo Legion uniform, drawn by Sutcliffe Maudsley.

Historian Richard Bushman describes how "the temple, the city, and the gathering formed a pattern of movement and preparation in a distinctive Mormon geography." With the temple at its center, Nauvoo typified Mormon city building. "The whole scheme divided space in two," Bushman explains, "with Zion and the temple at the center emanating spiritual power, and a Babylon-like world outside, where people were to be converted and brought to Zion, the missionaries going out and the converts coming in." Joseph Smith planned temples for the geographical center, and, in Nauvoo's case, the most elevated spot of the city. Chicago and Nauvoo grew apace with each other, but, as Bushman notes, "In Chicago the market drew people rather than the temple." Chicago's civic leaders were business magnates. Nauvoo's were prophets and apostles. Nauvoo's geography and sacred architecture are keys to understanding both Joseph Smith and his followers. Joseph rose to power because, in the minds of converts, he opened the heavens and accessed divine power. "He could," writes Bushman, "come to power only in a society where divine intelligence and spiritual power outranked wealth and business acumen on the scale of values."

Richard L. Bushman, "Making Space for the Mormons," Leonard J. Arrington Mormon History Lecture Series, number 2, delivered October 22, 1996, at Utah State University, Logan, Utah. The commemorative double issue of *BYU Studies* 32, nos. 1–2 (1992), contains articles devoted to Nauvoo, including maps and other images of the Mormon city.

Courtesy Family and Church History Department, The Church of Jesus Christ of Latter-day Saints. Photograph by Val Brinkerhoff

Plaster Cast of Death Mask of Joseph Smith. Joseph Smith was deeply loved by many but despised by others. For an extensive cultural biography, see Richard L. Bushman, *Joseph Smith: Rough Stone Rolling* (New York: Alfred A. Knopf, 2005).

Nauvoo resident George Cannon (father of later Church leader George Q. Cannon) cast plaster masks of both Joseph and Hyrum Smith as their bodies lay in state after their murders in June 1844. On the martyrdom of Joseph and Hyrum Smith, see Davis Bitton, *The Martyrdom Remembered: A One-Hundred-Fifty-Year Perspective on the Assassination of Joseph Smith* (Salt Lake City, Utah: Aspen Books, 1994), and Ronald D. Dennis, "The Martyrdom of Joseph Smith and His Brother Hyrum, by Dan Jones," *BYU Studies* 24, no. 1 (1984): 78–109.

Letter from Albert Brown to Albert Underwood, November 11, 1844. When Joseph Smith was murdered in June 1844, David Kilbourne of Fort Madison, Iowa Territory, hastened to write "of the wonderful events which have taken place," recounting the events of Smith's death from the perspective of an antagonist. This contrasting four-page letter by Albert Brown, written less than four months after the tragic shooting, recounts at length the widely discussed details of that event. Brown justifies the destruction of the *Nauvoo Expositor* as a public "neusance" according to the "constitution and laws of Illinois." He tells of the unlawful detention of Joseph and Hyrum, and of their murder by troops irresponsibly left in Carthage by Illinois Governor Thomas Ford. He also recounted the rumor that had spread quickly about "a flash of light" that preventing the assassins from beheading the lifeless corpse of Joseph Smith. Brown doubted that any of the murderers would be brought to justice, since "no murderer has ever bin punished I believe sinse the world began for murdering a Prophit of the Lord."

David Kilbourne's correspondence regarding Joseph Smith's martyrdom is housed in the State Historical Society of Iowa, Des Moines, and published in Warren A. Jennings, "The Lynching of an American Prophet," *BYU Studies* 40, no. 1 (2001): 205–16, quote on 207. See also Dallin H. Oaks, "The Suppression of the Nauvoo Expositor," *Utah Law Review* 9 (Winter 1965): 862–902, and Dallin H. Oaks and Marvin S. Hill, *Carthage Conspiracy: The Trial of the Accused Assassins of Joseph Smith* (Urbana and Chicago: University of Illinois Press, 1979).

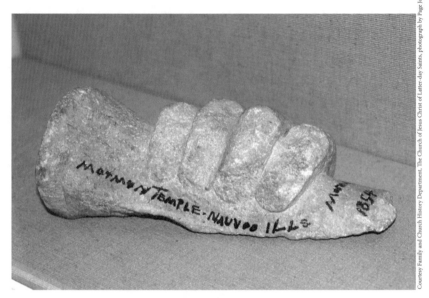

Courtesy Family and Church History Department, The Church of Jesus Christ of Latter-day Saints, photograph by Page Johnson

A Stone Remnant from the Nauvoo Temple. Built at a cost in excess of one million dollars, the Nauvoo Temple was constructed from 1841 to 1846. In the temple, thousands of Latter-day Saints received blessings and endowments of spiritual power. The temple was destroyed by arson in 1848, after which its walls were demolished by a tornado. The Nauvoo Temple has recently been reconstructed for use as originally intended. This fragment is part of a hand holding a trumpet above a sunstone. A complete sunstone is on permanent display in the National Museum of American History, Washington, D.C.

See Glen M. Leonard, *Nauvoo: A Place of Peace, a People of Promise* (Salt Lake City: Deseret Book; Provo, Utah: Brigham Young University Press, 2002).

ᢙ Joseph Smith
and the Recovery of Past Worlds

Courtesy Family and Church History Department, The Church of Jesus Christ of Latter-day Saints.

Angel Moroni Delivers the Gold Plates to Joseph Smith on Hill Cumorah, by Lewis Ramsey (1875–1941). Oil, 65" x 41", 1923. This painting depicts the delivery of the Book of Mormon plates to Joseph Smith on the Hill Cumorah in 1827. Ramsey painted it in 1923 for the centennial of the first appearance of the Angel Moroni to Joseph Smith on September 21–22, 1823. Joseph Smith described Moroni as "standing in the air, for his feet did not touch the floor. He had on a loose robe of the most exquisite whiteness. . . . His hands were naked, and his arms also, a little above the wrist; so, also, were his feet naked, as were his legs, a little above the ankles. His head and neck were also bare. . . . [H]is whole person was glorious beyond description, and his countenance truly like lightning" (Joseph Smith–History 1:30–32). Oliver Cowdery, David Whitmer, and Martin Harris testified that the angel appeared to them in 1829 and showed them the plates from which Joseph Smith translated the Book of Mormon, a testament of Jesus Christ from a past world.

See H. Donl Peterson, *Moroni: Ancient Prophet, Modern Messenger* (Bountiful, Utah: Horizon, 1983); Donald W. Parry, Daniel C. Peterson, and John W. Welch, *Echoes and Evidences of the Book of Mormon* (Provo, Utah: FARMS, 2002); and Margaret Barker, *An Extraordinary Gathering of Angels* (London: MQ Publications, 2004).

Page of the Original (Dictation) Manuscript of the Book of Mormon, 1829. The Book of Mormon was dictated by Joseph Smith to scribes, who made a verbatim word-for-word transcription, as seen here, with no punctuation. This page contains the text of 1 Nephi 2:23–3:18. Oliver Cowdery was the scribe for the first 13 lines of this page, but an unidentified scribe began writing mid-sentence on line 14, "I will go and do the things which the Lord hath commanded." This corroborates the testimony of scribes. Joseph's wife, Emma Hale, sometimes his scribe, said that when returning "after meals, or after interruptions, he would at once begin where he had left off, without either seeing the manuscript or having any portion of it read to him. This was a usual thing for him to do. It would have been improbable that a learned man could do this; and, for one so ignorant and unlearned as he was, it was simply impossible." It is noteworthy that no cross-outs or modifications were made on this manuscript as the dictation flowed, phrase after phrase.

"Last Testimony of Sister Emma," *Saints Herald* 26 (October 1, 1879): 289–90; John W. Welch, "The Miraculous Translation of the Book of Mormon," in John W. Welch, ed., *Opening the Heavens: Accounts of Divine Manifestations, 1820–1844* (Provo: Brigham Young University Press, 2005), 76–213, quote on 131.

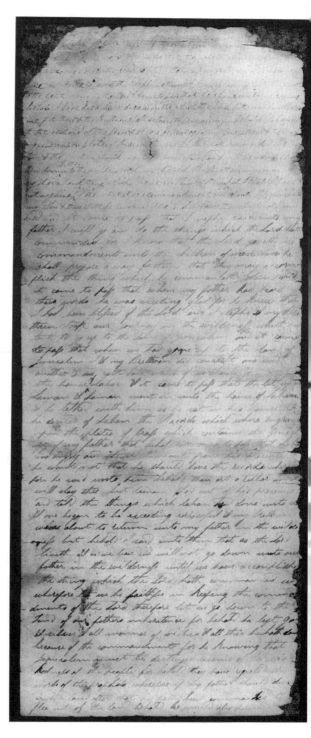

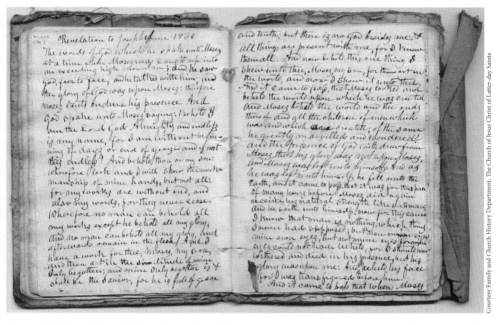

Diary of William Wines Phelps, Containing a Transcription of Moses 1, 1835. In December 1830, Joseph Smith commenced his revision of the King James Version of the Bible. He worked on this project until July 1833. While reading and pondering the Bible, Joseph received and recorded several additional scriptures. This manuscript, written by W. W. Phelps (1792–1872) in 1835 in Kirtland, Ohio, contains Joseph's dictation of Moses 1:1–6. It tells how Moses was taken up into the presence of God, was shown the endless worlds created by God, and was called to a work in the similitude of God's Only Begotten. The Book of Moses is now published in the Pearl of Great Price, considered by Latter-day Saints to be a standard work of canonized scripture along with the Bible, the Book of Mormon, and the Doctrine and Covenants.

For the documents of the Joseph Smith Translation, see Scott H. Faulring, Kent P. Jackson, and Robert J. Matthews, *Joseph Smith's New Translation of the Bible: Original Manuscripts* (Provo, Utah: Religious Studies Center, Brigham Young University, 2004).

A Page from John Lloyd Stephens, *Incidents of Travel in Central America, Chiapas, and Yucatan* **(New York, 1841).** John Bernhisel sent Joseph Smith a copy of this book. In his thank you letter, Joseph commented, "It unfolds & develops many things that are of great importance to this generation & corresponds with & supports the testimony of the Book of Mormon; I have read the volumes with the greatest interest." This impressive two-volume work was rich with etchings of buildings and monuments, such as this stela at Quirigua, Guatemala. Stephens' detailed observations led many early LDS leaders, including Parley P. Pratt, John Taylor, John E. Page, Orson Pratt, and George Q. Cannon, personally to consider Mesoamerica as the central area in the geography of the Book of Mormon.

Dean C. Jessee, ed. and comp., *Personal Writings of Joseph Smith* (1984; reprint, Salt Lake City: Deseret Book; Provo, Utah: Brigham Young University Press, 2002), 533. See also John L. Sorenson, *An Ancient American Setting for the Book of Mormon* (Salt Lake City: Deseret Book and Foundation for Ancient Research and Mormon Studies, 1985).

TIMES AND SEASONS.

"Truth will prevail."

Vol. III. No. 23.]   CITY OF NAUVOO, ILL. OCT. 1, 1842.   [Whole No. 59

ZARAHEMLA.

Since our 'Extract' was published from Mr. Stephens' 'Incidents of Travel,' &c., we have found another important fact relating to the truth of the Book of Mormon. Central America, or Guatimala, is situated north of the Isthmus of Darien and once embraced several hundred miles of territory from north to south.—The city of Zarahemla, burnt at the crucifixion of the Savior, and rebuilt afterwards, stood upon this land as will be seen from the following words in the book of Alma:—'And now it was only the distance of a day and a half's journey for a Nephite, on the line Bountiful, and the land Desolation, from the east to the west sea; and thus the land of Nephi, and the land of Zarahemla was nearly surrounded by water: there being a small neck of land between the land northward and the land southward.' [See Book of Mormon 3d edition, page 280-81.]

It is certainly a good thing for the excellency and veracity, of the divine authenticity of the Book of Mormon, that the ruins of Zarahemla have been found where the Nephites left them; and that a large stone with engravings upon it, as Mosiah said; and a 'large round stone, with the sides sculptured in hieroglyphics,' as Mr. Stephens has published, is also among the left remembrances of the, (to him,) lost and unknown. We are not agoing to declare positively that the ruins of Quirigua are those of Zarahemla, but when the land and the stones, and the books tell the story so plain, we are of opinion, that it would require more proof than the Jews could bring to prove the disciples stole the body of Jesus from the tomb, to prove that the ruins of the city in question, are not one of those referred to in the Book of Mormon.

It may seem hard for unbelievers in the mighty works of God, to give credit to such a miraculous preservation of the remains, ruins, records and reminiscences of a branch of the house of Israel; but the elements are eternal, and intelligence is eternal, and God is eternal, so that the very hairs of our heads are all numbered. It may be said of man he was and is, and is not; and of his works the same, but the Lord was and is, and is to come and his works never end; and he will bring every thing into judgment whether it be good, or whether it be evil; yea, every secret thing, and they shall be revealed upon the house tops. It will not be a bad plan to compare Mr. Stephens' ruined cities with those in the Book of Mormon: light cleaves to light, and facts are supported by facts. The truth injures no one, and so we make another

EXTRACT

From Stephens' "Incidents of Travel in Central America."

"On a fine morning, after a heavy rain, they set off for the ruins. After a ride of about half an hour, over an execrable road, they again reached the Amates. The village was pleasantly situated on the bank of the river, and elevated about thirty feet. The river was here about two hundred feet wide, and fordable in every part except a few deep holes. Generally it did not exceed three feet in depth, and in many places was not so deep; but below it was said to be navigable to the sea for boats not drawing more than three feet water. They embarked in two canoes dug out of cedar-trees, and proceeded down the river for a couple of miles, where they took on board a negro man named Juan Lima, and his two wives. This black scoundrel, as Mr. C. marks him down in his notebook, was to be their guide. They then proceeded two or three miles farther, and stopped at a rancho on the left side of the river, and passing through two cornfields, entered a forest of large cedar and mahogany trees. The path was exceedingly soft and wet, and covered with decayed leaves, and the heat very great. Continuing through the forest toward the northeast, in three quarters of an hour they reached the foot of a pyramidal structure like those at Copan, with the steps in some places perfect. They ascended to the top, about twenty-five feet, and descending by steps on the other side, at a short distance beyond came to a colossal head two yards in diameter, almost buried by an enormous tree, and covered with moss. Near it was a large altar, so covered with moss that it was impossible to make anything out of it. The two were within an enclosure.

Retracing their steps across the pyramidal structure, and proceeding to the north about three or four hundred yards, they reached a collection of monuments of the same general character with those

"Zarahemla," *Times and Seasons* (October 1, 1842, p. 927). Joseph Smith was interested in American antiquities. When John Lloyd Stephens' book was published in 1841, it attracted immediate attention among the Latter-day Saints. This article contains Stephens' descriptions of "a large round stone, with the sides sculptured in hieroglyphics," that once stood in the midst of a "large city" on the banks of a wide, fordable river but whose "name is lost, its history unknown," evoking strongly asserted connections with the Book of Mormon city of Zarahemla: "We are not agoing to declare positively that the ruins of Quirigua are those of Zarahemla, but [it would take much] to prove that the ruins of the city in question, are not one of those referred to in the Book of Mormon." Although the Church has never taken an official stand on the location of Book of Mormon geography, this 1842 editorial shows that in Joseph Smith's day Central America was considered as the plausible heartland of ancient Nephite civilization.

For general discussions of Book of Mormon geographies, see John E. Clark, "Searching for Book of Mormon Lands in Middle America," *FARMS Review* 16, no. 2 (2004): 1–54; and Noel B. Reynolds, ed., *Book of Mormon Authorship Revisited: The Evidence for Ancient Origins* (Provo: FARMS, 1997).

∾ Joseph Smith Challenges the Theological World

Joseph Smith, by Sutcliffe Maudsley, ink on paper. Probably drawn by the English portraitist Sutcliffe Maudsley in Nauvoo around 1843, this painting hung in the Nauvoo Mansion House for several years. By his own description, Joseph had a "native cheery temperament." His people had a great love for him. The Nauvoo Temple can be seen in the lower left.

On Joseph Smith's personality, see Richard L. Bushman, "The Character of Joseph Smith," *BYU Studies* 42, no. 2 (2003): 23–34.

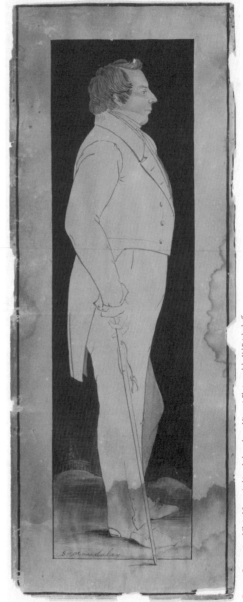

Courtesy Family and Church History Department, The Church of Jesus Christ of Latter-day Saints, photograph by Val Brinkerhoff

Joseph Smith, by Danquart Weggeland, oil on canvas. This image is attributed to Norwegian artist Danquart Anton Weggeland. It offers a strong profile of the Prophet. Beginning with his First Vision, Joseph Smith boldly challenged the theological world. As he recounted: "When the light rested upon me I saw two Personages, whose brightness and glory defy all description, standing above me in the air. One of them spake unto me, calling me by name and said, pointing to the other—This is My Beloved Son. Hear Him!" In the face of much opposition, he testified to the end of his life: "I had seen a vision; I knew it, and I knew that God knew it, and I could not deny it, neither dared I do it" (Joseph Smith–History 1:17, 25).

Documented accounts of Joseph Smith's First Vision are presented and discussed in John W. Welch, ed., *Opening the Heavens: Accounts of Divine Manifestations, 1820–1844* (Provo, Utah: Brigham Young University Press, 2005), 1–75.

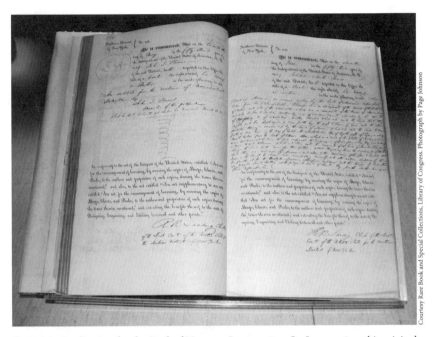

Copyright Application for the *Book of Mormon,* June 11, 1829. On June 11, 1829, this original application was filed in the Northern District of the District Court of the United States, received by clerk of the court, R. R. Lansing. The handwritten description of this form uses the words that now appear on the title page of the Book of Mormon. Joseph Smith said that these words were found on the last of the plates of Mormon. The printed text on this form shows that Joseph Smith's application was filed pursuant to federal law, which allowed "authors and proprietors" to secure a copyright on maps, charts, and books. The Book of Mormon would in fact need this protection, especially as it challenged the sensitivities and beliefs of many Americans. Joseph successfully asserted this copyright when, during publication of the Book of Mormon in Palmyra, New York, Abner Cole pilfered several pages for publication in his own newspaper.

For an expansive survey of Book of Mormon scholarship, see Terryl L. Givens, *By the Hand of Mormon: The American Scripture That Launched a New World Religion* (Oxford: Oxford University Press, 2002).

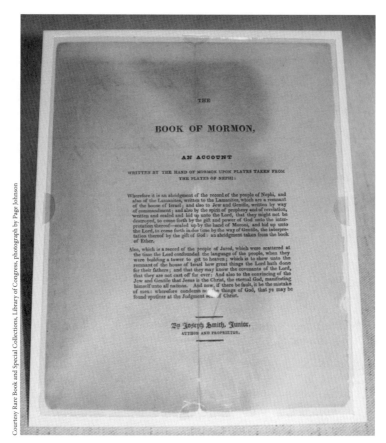

Proof Sheet of the Title Page of the *Book of Mormon*, June 11, 1829. Attached to the Book of Mormon copyright application filed on June 11, 1829, was this single printed sheet. It had been typeset as a proof of the title page of the Book of Mormon. Similar to the title page eventually used in the first edition of the Book of Mormon in 1830, this proof sheet is the earliest printed Mormon page. This page speaks of the spirit of prophesy and revelation, the coming forth of sealed scriptures, the Lord's covenants with the house of Israel, and convincing the Jew and the Gentile that Jesus is the Christ, the eternal God, who manifests himself unto all nations. These words epitomize several of Joseph Smith's challenges to the theological world.

On Mormon teachings in general, see Douglas J. Davies, *An Introduction to Mormonism* (Cambridge: Cambridge University Press, 2003).

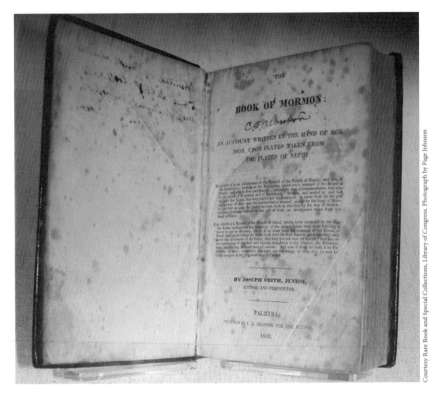

Courtesy Rare Book and Special Collections, Library of Congress. Photograph by Page Johnson

Book of Mormon (**First edition, Palmyra, New York, 1830**). Published in March 1830, the Book of Mormon testified of a premortal Jesus who had appeared as an anthropomorphic spirit to an early prophet, of messianic foreknowledge held by Israelite and Nephite prophets, of the infinite and eternal atonement of Jesus Christ, and of the physical appearance of the resurrected Jesus to the people at the temple in Bountiful in the New World. The Book of Mormon rejected the practice of infant baptism, required repentance and baptism by immersion, articulated a strong covenant theology, eschewed the use of a paid clergy, established two levels of priesthood ordination, and gave instructions for administering and partaking of the sacrament in remembrance of Jesus Christ's body and blood. On Latter-day Saint doctrines about Christ, see Robert L. Millet, *A Different Jesus? The Christ of the Latter-day Saints* (Grand Rapids: Eerdmans, 2005).

Facsimile 2 from the Book of Abraham, as published in *Times and Seasons* **(March 4, 1842).** Joseph Smith was fascinated with the world view and the priesthood powers he saw represented in ancient manuscripts. For example, Figure 1 (in the center) represents the primal point of creation. Figure 3 represents God "clothed with power and authority." Figure 7 represents God on his throne. Round disks such as this were placed under the heads of mummies to help orient their souls to the eternal cosmos. The explanations Joseph Smith gave for the figures on this hypocephalus are incomplete. Figures 9–21 were to be interpreted at some future time. The original from which this engraving was made has long been lost. Very few fragments of Joseph Smith's several papyri have survived, leaving the relationship between the lost papyri and the Book of Abraham uncertain.

Courtesy L. Tom Perry Special Collections, Harold B. Lee Library, Brigham Young University, photograph by Page Johnson

See generally, John Gee, *A Guide to the Joseph Smith Papyri* (Provo: Foundation for Ancient Research and Mormon Studies, 2000).

Book of Commandments (**Independence, Missouri, 1833**). In November 1831, Joseph Smith and a council of newly ordained high priests collected about 65 of the Prophet's early revelations for publication as "The Book of Commandments." The original plan was to print 10,000 copies. A mob destroyed the printing establishment on July 20, 1833, in the midst of the print run. Perhaps 100 copies of the incomplete book were salvaged from the fire. About 24 copies are known to survive today. These revelations, most of which are now included in the Doctrine and Covenants, issued bold warnings to the world regarding impending judgments of God, commanded people to repent, directed the organization of the Church, instructed missionaries, proclaimed the law of the Lord, described the gifts of the Spirit, and promised God's blessings for faithful obedience to Jesus Christ.

On the millenarian context of these early revelations, see Grant Underwood, *The Millenarian World of Early Mormonism* (Urbana: University of Illinois Press, 1993).

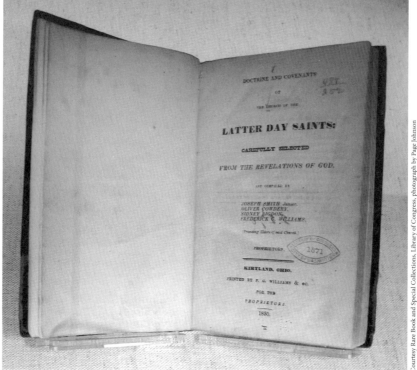

Doctrine and Covenants (**First edition, Kirtland, Ohio, 1835**). In 1835, Joseph Smith, his counselors, and the Kirtland High Council compiled and published this 284-page book entitled *Doctrine and Covenants of the Church of the Latter Day Saints: Carefully Selected from the Revelations of God.* Part 1 presented seven theological lectures on faith, including "ideas of the character, perfections and attributes of God" and the knowledge and sacrifice a person must manifest in order to exercise faith unto eternal life and salvation. Part 2 contained 99 revelations, 3 appendices, a testimony of the Twelve Apostles, and an index. Among its challenging and innovative contents are the vision of the three kingdoms of glory in the afterlife (D&C 76), several revelations on priesthood (D&C 20, 84, 86, 107), the school of the prophets (D&C 88), health and diet ("a word of wisdom," D&C 89), and the order of the Church for the benefit of the poor (D&C 104).

See Grant Underwood, "More Than an Index: The First Reference Guide to the Doctrine and Covenants as a Window into Early Mormonism," *BYU Studies* 41, no. 2 (2002), 116–47.

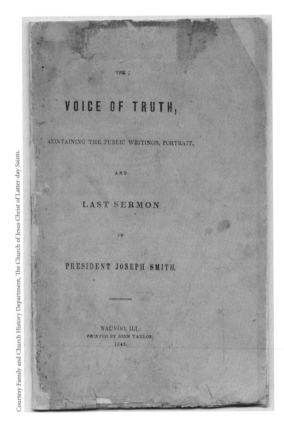

The Voice of Truth, Containing the Public Writings, Portrait, and Last Sermon of President Joseph Smith (Nauvoo, 1844). This 64-page booklet, published by John Taylor, contained Joseph Smith's famous King Follett discourse, a funeral tribute delivered at a general conference in April 1844. Notes from that speech briefly indicate that Joseph Smith declared, "It is necessary for us to have an understanding of God himself in the beginning. If we start right, it is easy to go right all the time, but . . . there are a very few beings in the world who understand rightly the character of God. . . . God himself was once as we are now, and is an exalted man." Other topics addressed by Joseph Smith on that occasion include the power of the Father and the Son; the premortal council of the Gods; creation as organization of eternally existing matter; mankind's eternal intelligence; conversing with God; death and advancing in knowledge; salvation for all mankind, living and dead; repentance; and baptism by water and the Holy Ghost by those holding priesthood keys and authority.

See generally, David L. Paulsen, "The Doctrine of Divine Embodiment: Restoration, Judeo-Christian, and Philosophical Perspectives," *BYU Studies* 35, no. 4 (1995–96): 6–94; and Douglas J. Davies, *The Mormon Culture of Salvation* (Aldershot, UK: Ashgate, 2000).

✎ Joseph Smith
and the Making of a Global Religion

First edition of *The Millennial Star* (Liverpool, May 1840). *The Latter-day Saints' Millennial Star* (1840–1970) was the official publication of the Church in the British Isles. Its inaugural editor, Elder Parley P. Pratt, boldly set the tone and purpose of this first international magazine of the Church: "The *Millennial Star* will stand aloof from the common political and commercial news of the day.—Its columns will be devoted to the spread of the fulness of the gospel—the restoration of the ancient principles of Christianity—the gathering of Israel—the rolling forth of the kingdom of God among the nations." This first issue contained extracts from Joseph Smith's revelations, responses to criticisms from other churches, articles about other religions, reports of local conferences, letters from missionaries, poetry, and two hymns.

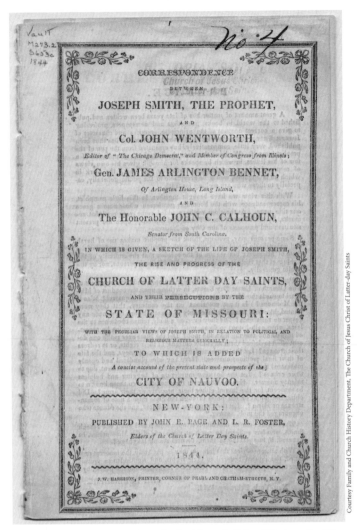

Correspondence between Joseph Smith and John Wentworth (New York, 1844). From the outset, Joseph Smith published abroad numerous revelations, newspapers, pamphlets, and proclamations. In 1831, The Church of Jesus Christ of Latter-day Saints purchased a printing press, its first major asset. As found in this 1844 pamphlet, Joseph Smith penned the thirteen Articles of Faith in an open letter to John Wentworth, editor of the *Chicago Democrat* and member of Congress. Also included is Joseph Smith's correspondence with James Arlington Bennet, of Arlington House, Long Island, and with John C. Calhoun, Senator from South Carolina, along with various political and religious statements of Joseph Smith. Missionaries made use of pamphleteering to spread their message in many lands. This pamphlet was published by Elders John E. Page and L. R. Foster in New York City.

Joseph Smith's 1842 letter to John Wentworth is published in Dean C. Jessee, ed., *The Papers of Joseph Smith,* 2 vols. (Salt Lake City: Deseret Book, 1989–92), 1:427–37.

Excerpt from the Wentworth Letter. In March 1842 Joseph Smith briefly outlined the "rise, progress, persecution, and faith of the Latter-Day Saints" as a courtesy to Chicago editor John Wentworth. The last page of the Wentworth Letter includes thirteen Articles of Faith, stating to the world the basic beliefs of The Church of Jesus Christ of Latter-day Saints, organized in 1830. From its beginning the Church assumed Christ's great commission. The command to teach and baptize all nations can hardly be overstated as a motivational force for getting missionaries to faraway places to persuade people of diverse cultures to believe in the gospel restored by Joseph Smith. An 1831 revelation, for example, urged Smith to send missionaries "unto the ends of the world" and "to lay the foundation of this church, and to bring it forth out of obscurity" (Doctrine and Covenants 1:23, 30). Missions were local in the beginning, but by 1837 stretched across the Atlantic to the British Isles. By 1842 elders of the church had "planted the gospel in almost every state in the Union," as well as in England, Ireland, Scotland and Wales. Joseph Smith articulated his global perspective to Wentworth: "Our missionaries are going forth to different nations, and in Germany, Palestine, New Holland, the East Indies, and other places, the standard of truth has been erected: no unhallowed hand can stop the work from progressing: persecutions may rage, mobs may combine, armies may assemble, calumny may defame, but the truth of God will go forth boldly, nobly, and independently till it has penetrated every continent, visited every clime, swept every country, and sounded in every ear; till the purposes of God shall be accomplished and the great Jehovah shall say the work is done."

On the rise of Mormonism in general, see Jan Shipps, *Mormonism: The Story of a New Religious Tradition* (Urbana: University of Illinois Press, 1985); Rodney Stark, *The Rise of Christianity* (Princeton, New Jersey: Princeton University Press, 1996), and his anthology *The Rise of Mormonism*, ed. Reid L. Neilson (New York: Columbia University Press, 2005).

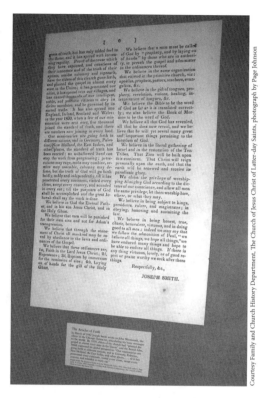

Orson Hyde, *Eine Stimme aus dem Schoose der Erde* (Frankfurt, 1842). In April 1840, Joseph Smith dispatched apostle Orson Hyde to dedicate the Holy Land for the return of the Jews. On his return in 1842, Hyde stopped in Germany, where one of his students translated into German this 115-page treatise he had written. Its title page reads: *A Call from the Wilderness, A Voice from the Depths of the Earth: A Brief Overview of the Origins and Doctrine of the Church of Jesus Christ of Latter Day Saints in America, Known by Many under the Label of "The Mormons," by Orson Hyde, a Priest of this Church, Frankfurt 1842, a self-publication of the author.* In it was published, for the first time in a foreign language, an account of Joseph Smith's First Vision.

On the publishing activities of the early Church, see David J. Whittaker, *Early Mormon Pamphleteering* (Provo, Utah: Joseph Fielding Smith Institute for Latter-day Saint History, 2003).

An Epistle of the Twelve (March 20, 1842). The great commission to spread the gospel throughout the world has been one of the main missions of The Church of Jesus Christ of Latter-day Saints since its inception. Samuel Smith became a missionary in April 1830. Heber C. Kimball was called in 1837 to open the work in the British Isles. By the 1850s, missions had been opened in Chile, France, Germany, Gibraltar, Hawaii, India, Italy, Malta, Denmark, South Africa, the South Pacific, and Switzerland. This epistle from the Quorum of the Twelve Apostles was sent to the branches and conferences of the Church in Europe. It addresses several social and economic pressures already felt by this burgeoning religion. The letter gives instructions to "facilitate the gathering of the Saints" to Nauvoo, Illinois, and teaches of unity "to ameliorate the condition of those who are struggling with poverty, and distress."

Proclamation of the Twelve Apostles of the Church to the Rulers and People of All Nations, April 6, 1845. On the fifteenth anniversary of the organization of the Church and less than a year after the martyrdom of Joseph and Hyrum Smith, the Twelve Apostles wrote this proclamation to all the kings, presidents, governors, rulers, and people of all nations on the earth. It declares that "the kingdom of God has come, as has been predicted by ancient prophets, and prayed for in all ages." The opening pages declare that God has again communed with those on earth by visions and holy messengers, by whom "the great and eternal High Priesthood" has been restored, holding the keys "to administer in all things pertaining to the ordinances, organization, government and direction of the kingdom of God." This publication, printed in Liverpool, England, was probably drafted by Parley P. Pratt.

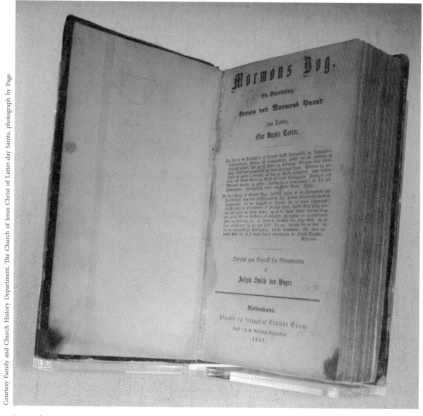

Danish Translation of Book of Mormon (1851). The first foreign language edition of the Book of Mormon was this Danish translation, printed in Copenhagen in 1851. Latter-day Saint missionaries arrived in Denmark in 1850, shortly after that country had adopted a new constitution, modeled in certain ways after the Constitution of the United States. Aided by the freedom of religion thus afforded in Denmark, Mormon missionaries met with considerable success. Thousands of Danish converts soon immigrated to Utah. As of 2005, the Book of Mormon has been translated into 104 languages.

For the full story of the early growth of the Church in Denmark, see William Mulder, *Homeward to Zion: The Mormon Migration from Scandinavia* (Minneapolis: University of Minnesota Press, 1957; reprint, Provo, Utah: BYU Press, 2000).

Courtesy Family and Church History Department. The Church of Jesus Christ of Latter-day Saints. Photograph by Page Johnson.

Joseph Smith, by Lucius Gahagan (ca. 1773–1855). Cold-cast marble, 1852 (replica). After Joseph Smith's death, he was memorialized in many ways in many lands. George Cannon made the casket in which Joseph was buried, and he also cast plaster masks of both Joseph and Hyrum Smith as their bodies lay in state. Apostle John Taylor, who witnessed the assassination of Joseph Smith and was himself critically wounded, took Cannon's mask to Lucius Gahagan, a prominent British artist in London, along with several sketches of the prophet. A committee of men who had known Joseph intimately worked directly with the artist as he produced this bust. Taylor commented that the artist had "obtained as correct a likeness as [was] possible . . . at such a period from [Joseph Smith's] death."

On recent international expansion, see Emmanuel Abu Kissi, *Walking in the Sand: A History of The Church of Jesus Christ of Latter-day Saints in Ghana* (Provo, Utah: Brigham Young University Press, 2004); Steven C. Harper, "'Nothing Less Than Miraculous': The First Decade of Mormonism in Mongolia," *BYU Studies* 42:1 (2003): 19–49.

Part 3

Joseph Smith in a Personal World

J oseph Smith cared intensely about the personal world. He related to
individuals. He championed the exercise of individual conscience.
He promoted personal revelation. For this part, the presenter was
asked to provide insights into Joseph Smith the man, who became
devoutly revered by his followers as the Prophet Joseph Smith. What
can be known of his background, his personality, his challenges, his
opposition, and his charisma? What has drawn people to him? This
presentation opens several windows into the mind and heart of a
complex human being who responded to a call from God to undertake a divine work.

Joseph Smith in a Personal World

Dallin H. Oaks

My subject is Joseph Smith in a personal world. My lens is primarily a personal one—his impact on me and believers I have known during my lifetime. I will also discuss Joseph Smith's own personal world and his impact on his acquaintances and friends. A major focus will be Joseph Smith's role as a prophet and his teachings on the reality of revelation. By *prophet* I mean one who speaks for God in revealing divine truth to others. By *revelation* I mean God's communication to man—to prophets and to every one of us, if we seek.

As several contributors to this volume discuss, revelation is the key to the uniqueness of Joseph Smith's message. That message began with his personal testimony that as a fourteen-year-old boy, without schooling, property, or family prominence, he saw the Father and the Son in person. He and his associates testified to later personal visits from other heavenly beings. Joseph taught that he was directed by a continuing flow of revelation throughout his life and that everyone could enjoy personal revelation or inspiration to guide them in their individual lives. "The Church of Jesus Christ of Latter-day Saints was founded upon direct revelation," he declared, "as the true Church of God has ever been."[1] "Take away the Book of Mormon and the revelations, and where is our religion?" he asked. "We have none," he answered.[2]

Joseph Smith's teaching about the significance of modern-day revelation is clearly the most distinctive characteristic of the Latter-day Saint religion. "Whatever we may think of revelation," Joseph taught, "without it we can neither know nor understand anything of God . . . and . . . must remain in ignorance."[3] He also taught that "salvation cannot come without revelation; it is vain for anyone to minister without it."[4] Revelation is the foundation of our church doctrine and governance, and it is also fundamental to personal conversion, personal decision making, and the ways we understand and apply the inspired texts we call scriptures.

Personal and Prophetic Revelation

When we ask in faith, Joseph Smith taught, God will give us knowledge in our mind and in our heart, by feelings (see Doctrine and Covenants 8:1–3). The New Testament describes such personal revelation. For instance, when Peter affirmed his conviction that Jesus was the divine Son of God, Jesus declared: "Flesh and blood hath not revealed it unto thee, but my Father which is in heaven" (Matthew 16:17). This biblical pattern is the one Joseph Smith followed as he acted upon James 1:5 and asked God for answers to his spiritual questions. Personal revelation also occurs when an inventor or artist or great leader receives flashes of enlightenment from a loving God for the benefit of his children.

To demonstrate the operation of revelation upon decision making, I will give two contrasting personal experiences—the familiar and the revelatory.

First, to illustrate the kind of decision making with which we are all familiar, I have chosen a personal experience that happened when I was serving as a law clerk to Chief Justice Earl Warren of the United States Supreme Court. In my personal journal for May 5, 1958, I wrote:

> Saturday afternoon Jon, Don and I [the Chief Justice's law clerks] took up our objections to [an opinion being joined by the Chief in a particular case before the Court]. After about 3 hours of tussling, in which the Chief held his own in an admirable way, it became

clear that he was fire-hardened with the majority position but might go for some slight alterations in the opinion.

That description of three law clerks' interaction with the Chief Justice of the Supreme Court is typical of the process of dialogue and decision making in the legal profession.

Second, and in contrast, just over three years later, while I was employed by a large law firm in Chicago, I engaged in a different kind of dialogue and decision making. Edward H. Levi, who was later to serve as Attorney General of the United States, approached me with a proposal that I leave the law firm and become a professor at the University of Chicago Law School, where he was dean. He said, "I know you will want to pray about this." He was right. He knew this because he knew me as his student, and we had had frequent association when I was the editor-in-chief of his school's law review.

I discussed this unexpected new career path with my wife. My personal history for that August 1961 records: "We prayed about it all through the weekend and shortly felt that this was what we should do." I wrote to our parents: "None of us knows where this will lead, but we feel perfectly peaceful in our hearts that this is another valuable preparation for us." This second experience illustrates what Latter-day Saints mean by *personal revelation*, namely an inspiration or manifestation that comes in response to earnest prayer for guidance in an important personal decision.

Joseph Smith affirmed by countless teachings and personal experiences that revelation did not cease with the early apostles, but that it continued in his day and continues in ours. He also taught that revelation was a reality for everyone. "It is the privilege of the Children of God to come to God and get Revelation," he said. "God is not a respecter of persons, we all have the same privilege."[5] Moses declared, "Would God that all the Lord's people were prophets, and that the Lord would put his spirit upon them!" (Numbers 11:29). Any sincere truth seeker can receive a personal manifestation from God by the power of the Holy Ghost.

Another example of revelation, which I will call *prophetic revelation*, occurs in the role of Joseph Smith and his successors as presidents of The Church of Jesus Christ of Latter-day Saints. Here God reveals

truths or commandments to His prophet-leader for the enlightenment of His people. This is the kind of revelation described in the
Old Testament teaching that "the Lord God will do nothing, but he
revealeth his secret unto his servants the prophets" (Amos 3:7).

It is on this subject of revelation that Joseph Smith shared something important with George Washington. In *His Excellency*, Joseph J.
Ellis's recent bestseller on Washington, Ellis gives the following analysis of the man who was the founder of the American nation:

> He was that rarest of men: a supremely realistic visionary, a pru-
> dent prophet whose final position on slavery served as the cap-
> stone to a career devoted to getting the big things right. His genius
> was his judgment. . . . But where did that come from? Clearly, it
> did not emanate from books or formal education, places where
> it is customary and often correct to look for the wellspring that
> filled the minds of such eminent colleagues as Adams, Jefferson,
> and Madison with their guiding ideas. Though it might seem sac-
> rilegious to suggest, Washington's powers of judgment derived in
> part from the fact that this mind was uncluttered with sophisti-
> cated intellectual preconceptions.[6]

When I read those words, I was struck with the parallel to Joseph
Smith. It is surely true that Joseph's mind "was uncluttered with
sophisticated intellectual preconceptions." It is also true—if one
judges him by the criteria of the quality of his followers or the fruits
of his teachings—that he got the big things right.

Joseph Smith's almost total lack of formal education or access to
the learning of his day has been a standard basis for criticizing him.
"Ignorant" is the label so familiar in the popular criticisms. Perhaps it
is time for educated nonbelievers to take the unlearned Joseph Smith
seriously and to ask the question Ellis asked about Washington:
where did his genius come from? I see revelation from God as the
best answer to that question.

My Personal View of Joseph Smith

I am a product of the teachings of Joseph Smith. What he taught
about the Fatherhood of God and the brotherhood of man has given
me my understanding of my relationship with God, my relationship

to mankind, and the worth of men and women everywhere. He also taught that "friendship is the grand fundamental principle of Mormonism, to revolutionize [and] civilize the world."[7] I believe the principles he taught have that potential.

The stated purpose of the Book of Mormon is to witness that Jesus is the Christ. That book and Joseph Smith's other teachings about the mission of Jesus Christ have grounded me in the Christian faith. "The fundamental principles of our religion," he proclaimed, "are the testimony of the Apostles and Prophets, concerning Jesus Christ."[8]

Joseph Smith taught that each individual had identity in the world of spirits before this life. "Man was also in the beginning with God," he revealed (Doctrine and Covenants 93:29). He also taught that we will each have identity and purpose in the life to come (Doctrine and Covenants 76:50–106; 137:5–10). These teachings have expanded my concept of my personal potential and the potential of every living person. His teachings have also disciplined and given significance and joy to my marriage relationships and to my relationships with my children, grandchildren, and great-grandchildren.

Joseph Smith revealed that "the glory of God is intelligence" (Doctrine and Covenants 93:36) and that a man cannot be saved in ignorance (see Doctrine and Covenants 131:6). These inspired declarations about the eternal significance of learning—sacred and secular—have powerfully motivated my efforts to learn. The Word of Wisdom (Doctrine and Covenants 89), which he gave by revelation long before it became socially or scientifically fashionable, has kept me away from any use of tobacco or alcohol or drugs throughout my life. The health benefits of that abstinence are now evident in scientific terms. Even without such evidence, I am convinced that all of the teachings of Joseph Smith would make the world a better place for everyone.

That is my personal view of the man we call a prophet. And, of course, those teachings are the foundation of The Church of Jesus Christ of Latter-day Saints. "Everything we have is a lengthened shadow of Joseph Smith," said Gordon B. Hinckley, our church president. "Our foundation of doctrine and practice and procedure all come down from him."[9] Accordingly, I welcome the opportunity to contribute to scholarship on Joseph Smith under the title "Joseph Smith in a Personal World." He would have liked that, for his relationships with those around him were always personal—never institutional.[10]

Joseph Smith was a personal leader. His teachings always encouraged men and women to have their own personal relationship with God. For this reason, missionary work that is based on Joseph's teachings always focuses on individuals, not groups. Thus, when Latter-day Saint missionaries encounter tribal or other leaders who are attracted to their message and offer to bring all of their followers into membership, we refuse. I recall directing that response in one example in the southern Philippines. For Joseph and for us, each individual must decide for himself or herself, without pressure from peers or higher authorities.

Since religious faith and affiliation must always be a personal decision, Joseph Smith's followers vigorously defend the freedom to choose for all people. That is an article of our faith (Article of Faith 11). Joseph Smith taught it in these words: "If it has been demonstrated that I have been willing to die for a Mormon, I am bold to declare before heaven that I am just as ready to die for a presbyterian, a baptist, or any other denomination."[11] He obviously recognized that the same tyranny that would trample on the rights of believers who were unpopular and too weak to defend themselves would trample on the rights of Latter-day Saints.

The Personal World of Joseph Smith's Character and Personality[12]

I am a fifty-year student of the life of Joseph Smith. I was born in 1932, when the church was just over one hundred years old, so my lifetime corresponds closely to the second century of the church Joseph Smith founded. In my studies and my conclusions, I believe I am typical of the Latter-day Saints of this second century. We did not meet Joseph Smith, but we feel we know him, and we love him personally through what he taught. We are witnesses of the truth of the poetic prediction by one of his adult associates that "millions shall know 'Brother Joseph.'"[13]

The Joseph Smith I met in my personal research was a man of the frontier—young, emotional, dynamic, and so loved and approachable by his people that they often called him "Brother Joseph." His comparative youth overarched his prophetic ministry. He was fourteen at the time of the First Vision, twenty-one when he received the golden plates, and just twenty-three when he finished translating the Book of Mormon (in less than sixty working days). Over half of the revelations in our Doctrine and Covenants were given through this prophet when he was twenty-five or younger. He was twenty-six when the First Presidency was organized, and just over thirty-three when he escaped from imprisonment in Missouri and resumed leadership of the Saints gathering in Nauvoo. He was only thirty-eight and a half when he was murdered.

During his thirty-eight and a half years of life, Joseph Smith had more than his share of mortal afflictions. When he was about seven, he suffered an excruciatingly painful leg surgery. Because of the poverty of his family, he had little formal education and as a youth was compelled to work long hours to help put food on the family table. He was attacked physically on many occasions. In the midst of trying to fulfill the staggering responsibilities of his sacred calling, he had to labor as a farmer or merchant to provide a living for his family. He did this without the remarkable spiritual gifts that sustained him in his prophetic calling. The Lord had told him that "in temporal labors thou shalt not have strength, for this is not thy calling" (Doctrine and Covenants 24:9).

In spiritual matters, Joseph Smith had no role models from whom he could learn how to be a prophet and a leader. He had to rely on inexperienced associates. They struggled and learned together, and Joseph was extremely rapid in his acquisition of knowledge and maturity. He unquestionably had unique gifts. As we would say today, he was "a quick study." He said he was taught by heavenly messengers and by other revelations from God, and I believe him.

One of his personal gifts is evidenced by the love and loyalty of the remarkable people who followed him. When Joseph challenged his followers to overcome their mortal imperfections, he did not raise himself above them and they loved him for it. In a sermon preached a little over a month before he was murdered, he declared, "I never told you I was perfect—but there is no error in the revelations which I have taught."[14] Joseph Smith had a "native cheery temperament" that endeared him to almost everyone who knew him (Joseph Smith–History 1:28). We have record of many adoring tributes like that of an acquaintance who said, "The love the saints had for him was inexpressible."[15]

The companionship of his friends was a delight to Joseph Smith, who saw society- and community-building as major purposes of the gospel. According to a careful notetaker, one of Joseph Smith's sermons used these words, which go on to reveal his attitude toward the members of his Latter-day Saint community: "I see no faults in the church—let me be resurrected with the saints, whether to heaven or hell or any other good place—good society. What do we care [where we are] if the society is good?"[16] The Book of Mormon teaches, "Men are, that they might have joy" (2 Nephi 2:25).[17] I believe a subsequent compiler had it right when he represented Joseph as saying that "if we go to hell, we will turn the devils out of doors and make a heaven of it."[18]

All of his life, Joseph Smith lived on the frontier, where men had to pit their brute strength against nature and sometimes against one another. He did not shrink from physical confrontation, and he had the courage of a lion. Once he was kidnapped by two men who punched cocked pistols into his ribs and repeatedly threatened to shoot him if he moved a muscle. Joseph endured these threats for a time and then snapped back, "Shoot away; I have endured so much persecution and oppression that I am sick of life; why then don't you shoot, and have done with it instead of talking so much about it?"[19] His persecutors did not shoot on that occasion, but few men have been the targets of more assaults on their mission or their memory than Joseph Smith. I investigated some of these charges by personal research in original records in Illinois, where Joseph lived the last five years of his life.

One such charge arose when Joseph Smith, then mayor, and the Nauvoo City Council suppressed an opposition newspaper. This event focused anti-Mormon hostilities and led directly to Joseph's murder. Early Latter-day Saint historians, including B. H. Roberts, conceded that this action was illegal. However, as I researched this subject as a young law professor, I was surprised to find a legal basis for this action in the Illinois law of 1844. My law review article noted that the guarantee of freedom of the press in the United States Constitution was not declared applicable to the actions of city and state governments until 1931, and then only by a five-to-four Court's reliance on a constitutional amendment adopted in 1868.[20] There were many suppressions of newspapers on the frontier in the period before the Civil War. One should judge the actions of Joseph Smith on the basis of the laws and circumstances of his day, not ours.

As students at the University of Chicago, historian Marvin S. Hill and I were intrigued with the little-known fact that five men went to trial in Illinois for the murder of Joseph Smith. For over ten years we scoured libraries and archives across the nation to find every scrap of information about this trial and those involved in it. Our book reviewed the actions and words of Illinois citizens who knew Joseph Smith personally—some who hated him and plotted to kill him and others who loved him and risked their lives for him. Nothing in our discoveries in the original court records or in the testimony at the lengthy trial disclosed anything that reflected dishonor on the murdered man.[21]

The accessibility of Illinois court records led to another previously untouched area of research on Joseph Smith. Joseph I. Bentley, a law student at Chicago, and I discovered numerous records showing the business activities of Joseph Smith. We coauthored a law review article on this subject.[22] The 1840s followed a period of nationwide financial panic and depression. Economic conditions in frontier states like Illinois were ruinous. The biographers of an Illinois contemporary, Abraham Lincoln, have described his financial embarrassments during this decade, when business was precarious, many obligations were in default, and lawsuits were common.[23]

Joseph Smith was not spared. His enemies charged him with fraud in various property conveyances, most conducted in behalf of the church. A succession of court proceedings that extended for nearly a decade examined these claims in meticulous detail. Finally, in 1852, long after the Saints' exodus from Illinois (so there was no conceivable political or other cause for anyone to favor the Saints or their leader), a federal judge concluded this litigation with a decree that found no fraud or other moral impropriety by Joseph.[24]

Poor legal advice seriously disadvantaged Joseph and his fellow church leaders and members. As one familiar with early Illinois property law and as a lawyer enjoying the benefit of over one hundred years of hindsight, I can readily see where this was the case in some of Joseph's legal controversies. This poor advice may account for Brigham Young's 1846 declaration that he "would rather have a six-shooter than all the lawyers in Illinois."[25]

Joseph Smith's character was perhaps best apprehended by men who knew him best and stood closest to him in church leadership. They adored him. Brigham Young declared, "I do not think that a man lives on the earth that knew [Joseph Smith] any better than I did; and I am bold to say that, Jesus Christ excepted, no better man ever lived or does live upon this earth."[26]

Joseph's Impact on Personal Worlds in the Philippines

Latter-day Saints frequently mention the fulfillment of the remarkable prophecy that the name of this obscure youth on the American frontier "should be had for good and evil among all nations" (Joseph Smith–History 1:33). Today, with Latter-day Saint missionaries in over one hundred twenty nations and with more than half of the twelve million church members living outside the United States, that statement is much easier to understand than when it was first uttered to a seventeen-year-old boy in 1823. With that background in mind, I will now describe how Joseph Smith has changed lives—personal worlds—in one such nation, the Philippines.

My wife and I recently returned from two years in the Philippines. There we lived among a people who endured over four hundred years of colonial rule. After the Spanish yoke was lifted, they had a forty-year administration by the United States and a brief, harsh occupation by Japan. Today they have been independent for almost sixty years, but it seemed to us that their colonial heritage still haunts them. Economically, their culture is one of dependency. A landed and wealthy aristocracy of their own people has replaced the foreign masters, but the wonderful Filipino people still lack many of the political freedoms and economic opportunities they desire. They are like an eagle shown the joy of flight but still kept on a tether.

In the Philippines, my wife and I experienced the impact of the teachings of Joseph Smith and the practices of our faith in what we call the developing world. It is now just a little over forty years since the first Latter-day Saint missionaries commenced their work in that nation. When they began, they had just one local church member. Today, there are over 500,000 in that country, and we must modulate our missionary activities in order to ensure that our growth does not exceed our capacity to train local leaders.

I am often asked why our church has grown so rapidly in the Philippines and in other parts of the developing world. The label "rice Christians" memorializes the reality that some of the converts of Christian preaching in underdeveloped lands were persons in search of economic rather than religious gain. Our growth includes some of this. Some of our new members in the Philippines undoubtedly expected personal advantages from their friendship with American missionaries or their membership in a financially strong American church. But this cannot be a major factor, since for many years the greater part of Latter-day Saint missionaries in the Philippines have been native Filipinos or other Pacific islanders.

The most important ingredient at work in the remarkable growth and staying power of the Latter-day Saint church in the Philippines is the investigators' personal conversion to the doctrines of the church. To cite one objective test of that staying power, attendance records indicate that about 100,000 Filipino members attend the three-hour Sunday meetings at least once each month in 1,100 congregations presided over and taught entirely by local Filipinos. Tens of thousands regularly serve in voluntary leadership and teaching positions. In a nation with the cultural traditions, transportation difficulties, and economic challenges of the Philippines, this level of attendance and leadership activity is impressive by any measure.

Why do the teachings and example of the prophet Joseph Smith have such power in the Philippines and in other nations in the developing world?

The first reason, which applies in every nation, is revelation. The Book of Mormon tells of a people who "had many revelations" (Jacob 1:6). When those investigating our church hear what we call the message of the Restoration, including the account of Joseph Smith's first vision and the key doctrines he taught, they are invited to pray to God in the name of Christ and ask if these things are true. They are promised that if they ask with real intent, having faith in Christ, he will manifest the truth to them by the power of the Holy Ghost (see Moroni 10:4). They are told that they should not be baptized until they know by personal revelation that the message is true and that this church is still led by a prophet.

"The best way to obtain truth and wisdom," Joseph Smith taught, "is not to ask it from books, but to go to God in prayer, and obtain divine teaching."[27] This teaching and challenge is especially meaningful in a culture where many feel insignificant and isolated, politically and economically. Persons in that circumstance can identify with a prophet who was unschooled and poor. They welcome the message that even the poor and downtrodden are children of a Heavenly Father who loves them and has a plan for them. And they feel ennobled as well as challenged by the teaching that persons can know the truth for themselves by personal revelation from God rather than by depending on others of greater education or standing.

Sometimes that revelation comes after baptism, as it did with Arsenio Pagaduan. He was baptized in the Philippines in 1973, but continued to wonder about the truth of the Book of Mormon. Two years later, when he was sent to England to do post-graduate work in Agricultural Engineering, he determined to study the Book of Mormon carefully along with his graduate studies. While doing so he received clear, strong impressions of its truthfulness. According to his written account, as he read the promise in Moroni 10:4:

> My eyes were [so] saturated with tears that I had to stop reading. The impressions of the Holy Ghost in my being [were] so strong that I knelt down in prayer of gratitude to our Heavenly Father. . . .

This personal knowledge borne by the Holy Ghost of the truthful-
ness of the Book of Mormon led me to other important truths: that
Joseph Smith was indeed a prophet of God and that The Church of
Jesus Christ of Latter-day Saints is really true.[28]

Whenever this knowledge comes with surety—whether before or
after baptism—it ties the convert closely to Joseph Smith. A convert
serving as a missionary recorded this experience with someone who
attacked Joseph Smith:

> I allowed him to finish his tirade and calmly testified about the
> prophet Joseph. As I was sharing my testimony, a warm feeling
> started to fill my whole being until it completely enveloped me.
> It was a special kind of warm, sweet, tender glowing feeling that
> tells me what I was saying is true. I know it was the Holy Ghost
> telling me that Joseph Smith is truly a prophet of God.[29]

A similar expression came from an isolated island where an
elderly rice farmer was taught by the missionaries and baptized. One
of my associates heard him speak. Trembling with emotion, with
big tears running down his cheeks, he said: "I am so grateful to the
Prophet Joseph Smith. I am thankful at last to know about the Lord's
true church—His church is now restored to the earth. I am thankful
to understand His plan of salvation. Oh, how happy I am to finally
have the truth."[30] This old rice farmer was also grateful to be taught
about a God he can understand as "an exalted man."[31] Joseph Smith
revealed God to be a personal being with "a body of flesh and bones
as tangible as man's" (Doctrine and Covenants 130:22).

The teachings of Joseph Smith require individual responsibility,
and they promise rewards for efforts at self-improvement.[32] That
assurance and promise is very meaningful to those who are poor
and desirous to improve. It is especially powerful when combined
with continuing revelation, which promises that we are not locked
into or limited by the conditions or rules of the past. "We are differently situated from any other people that ever existed upon this
earth," Joseph Smith taught, "consequently those former revelations
cannot be suited to our conditions; they were given to other people,
who were before us."[33]

Another attraction to the theology Joseph Smith taught is that it presents mortal life in a context preceded by a premortal existence and followed by assurances of continued progress in the world to come. In this view of life all stand equal before God, without regard to the conditions of their mortal birth or citizenship or their current attainments of property or prominence. That message attracts the poor and the disadvantaged in every land, just as it did my ancestors in England and Scandinavia in the earliest days of Latter-day Saint missionary work there.

The Book of Mormon, brought forth by Joseph Smith, contains many of these teachings that I have cited as reasons for the rapid growth of our church in the developing world and among the poor and oppressed in all nations. Its first chapter states that God's "power, and goodness and mercy are over all the inhabitants of the earth" (1 Nephi 1:14). It later declares that God has not only spoken to the Jews who wrote his teachings in the Bible and to the people who wrote them in the Book of Mormon, but that he "shall also speak unto all nations of the earth and they shall write it" (2 Nephi 29:12). The book also affirms that the Savior appeared to people in more lands than just in Judea (3 Nephi 16:1–3; 17:4). It also teaches that the gospel of Jesus Christ, for which it is a second witness, will "be declared to every nation, kindred, tongue, and people" (Mosiah 15:28). "Ye shall not esteem one flesh above another," a Book of Mormon prophet declared, "or one man shall not think himself above another" (Mosiah 23:7). In sum, the Book of Mormon contains a universal message and it affirms the value of all people everywhere. In a circumstance where the rich and the proud persecuted the poor, a Book of Mormon prophet declared this to be "abominable unto him who created all flesh," for "the one being is as precious in his sight as the other" (Jacob 2:21; see also verses 12–20). Persons who had "set their hearts upon riches" were told that they were "cursed because of your riches, and also are your riches cursed because ye have set your hearts upon them" (Helaman 13:20–21).

The faithful in the Philippines look to a prophet for guidance in their personal lives, just as the people of Kirtland and Nauvoo looked to Joseph Smith. A prophet has taught them to shun the culture of dependency and take the responsibility for their personal support and that of their families. He has taught them to be honest. He has taught them to be good law-abiding citizens, and to help one another in their towns and villages and in their communities of faith. And he has promised them that if they are faithful in paying their tithes and offerings, as increasing numbers are, the Lord will bless them and their entire nation.[34] All these teachings are twenty-first-century applications of principles taught in the nineteenth century by Joseph Smith.

Joseph Smith on Revelation and Scripture[35]

The principle of independent verification by revelation introduces my last subject, which is Joseph Smith's teachings on the relationship of revelation to the interpretation of the Bible or any other inspired text. The Latter-day Saint approach to scriptural interpretation follows from our belief in continuing revelation. We encourage everyone to study the scriptures and to prayerfully seek personal revelation to know their meanings for themselves.

Most Christians believe that the scriptural canon—the authoritative collection of sacred books used as scriptures by true believers in Christ—is closed because God closed it some centuries following the death of Christ and he has not given any comparable revelations since that time. Joseph Smith taught that the scriptural canon is open.[36] In fact, the canon of scripture is open in several ways, and the idea of continuing revelation is crucial to all of these.

First, Joseph taught that God will guide his children by giving new additions to the body of scriptures. The Book of Mormon is such an addition. So are the revelations in the Doctrine and Covenants. Often, those new revelations explain the meaning of scriptures previously canonized—meanings that may not have been evident in earlier times. As Joseph taught, "We never can comprehend the things of God and of heaven, but by revelation."[37] Sometimes these new meanings are the ones most valuable and useful to us as we seek to obtain answers to our personal questions and to understand what the Lord would have us do in our own time and circumstances.

These new revelations on the meaning of existing scriptures are of two types. They may be *public* revelations, such as the numerous additions and clarifications in the Joseph Smith translation of the Bible and the revelations published in the Doctrine and Covenants on the meaning of Bible passages. They may also be *private* revelations on the meaning of existing scriptures, to help us with our personal studies and decisions.

Joseph Smith and an associate, Oliver Cowdery, set the example. After their baptism, they were filled with the Holy Ghost. Then, as Joseph Smith explained in his personal history, "Our minds being now enlightened, we began to have the scriptures laid open to our understandings, and the true meaning and intention of their more mysterious passages revealed unto us in a manner which we never could attain to previously, nor ever before had thought of" (Joseph Smith–History 1:74). Joseph Smith applied that principle to the Apocrypha. He was reported to have taught that much of the Apocrypha was true, but one had to be guided by the Spirit of God to select the truth out of those writings.[38]

The ordinary person obviously needs help in understanding the meaning of obscure ancient texts with diverse meanings. The traditional approach has been to rely on scholarship and historical methods, such as authoritative commentaries. Latter-day Saints, of course, know that learned commentaries can help with interpretation, but we maintain that they must be used with caution. Commentaries are not a substitute for the scriptures any more than a good cookbook is a substitute for food. The apostle Paul wrote that "all scripture is given by inspiration of God" (2 Timothy 3:16; also see 2 Peter 1:21) and that "the things of God knoweth no man, except he has the Spirit of God" (1 Corinthians 2:11, Joseph Smith Translation). Consequently, while Latter-day Saints rely on scholars and scholarship, that reliance is preliminary in method and secondary in authority.

Similarly, Latter-day Saints believe that as a source of sacred knowledge, the scriptures are not the ultimate but the penultimate. The ultimate knowledge comes by personal revelation through the Holy Ghost. We read the scriptures not only for knowledge, but also for direction. We seek inspiration in interpretation, but we also seek revelation in applying God's commandments to the circumstances of our day.

Because of our reliance on revelation, Joseph Smith's lack of formal education in languages and scholarship is seen in a different light by Latter-day Saints than by our scholarly colleagues of other faiths. Joseph Smith declared, "Could you gaze into heaven five minutes, you would know more than you would by reading all that ever was written on the subject."[39] Joseph Smith's teaching on this subject is clearly stated in this passage from the Book of Mormon: "For he that diligently seeketh shall find; and the mysteries of God shall be unfolded unto them, by the power of the Holy Ghost, as well in these times as in times of old, and as well in times of old as in times to come; wherefore, the course of the Lord is one eternal round" (1 Nephi 10:19). So it is that the Lord said to a Book of Mormon leader named Nephi: "For unto him that receiveth I will give more; and from them that shall say, We have enough, from them shall be taken away even that which they have" (2 Nephi 28:30; see also Matthew 13:12).

Personal Conclusion

Some may wonder how members of The Church of Jesus Christ of Latter-day Saints, both in Joseph Smith's time as well as today, accept the direction of a prophet in their personal lives, something that is unusual in most religious traditions. The answer is revelation—and in this case it is personal revelation.

The principle of personal revelation—difficult to describe in analytic terms—is explainable by an analogy from the law. As a former lawyer and judge, I am familiar with the use of certified copies of official documents, like a death certificate or an honorable discharge from military duty. Such copies are accepted as if they were originals, because of their official certificate. This acceptance is based on the fact that anyone who doubts the authenticity of the content can verify its accuracy by going to the original. So it is with the prophetic revelation of a prophet of God. He is the certifying authority that his teaching or direction is from God. Anyone who doubts this—and none are discouraged from personal doubts—can verify the authenticity and content of the message by checking it with the official source, by personal revelation.

The principle also applies to the message in sacred music. For Joseph Smith, the experience of divine disclosure was beautifully distilled in the words of one of his favorite hymns, "A Poor Wayfaring Man of Grief."[40] When he and his associates were confined in the Carthage Jail on that hot afternoon of June 27, 1844, he requested that it be sung for him. Less than an hour later he was dead. The words of the first and the last two verses are these:

> A poor wayfaring Man of grief
> Hath often crossed me on my way,
> Who sued so humbly for relief
> That I could never answer nay.
> I had not power to ask his name,
> Whereto he went, or whence he came;
> Yet there was something in his eye
> That won my love; I knew not why.
>
> In pris'n I saw him next, condemned
> To meet a traitor's doom at morn.
> The tide of lying tongues I stemmed,
> And honored him 'mid shame and scorn.
> My friendship's utmost zeal to try,
> He asked if I for him would die.
> The flesh was weak; my blood ran chill,
> But my free spirit cried, "I will!"
>
> Then in a moment to my view
> The stranger started from disguise.
> The tokens in His hands I knew;
> The Savior stood before mine eyes.
> He spake, and my poor name He named,
> "Of Me thou hast not been ashamed.
> These deeds shall thy memorial be;
> Fear not, thou didst them unto Me."

Notes

1. Joseph Smith Jr., *History of the Church of Jesus Christ of Latter-day Saints*, ed. B. H. Roberts, 2d ed., rev., 7 vols. (Salt Lake City: Deseret Book, 1971), 6:9 (hereafter cited as *History of the Church*).

2. *History of the Church*, 2:52.

3. *History of the Church*, 4:574.

4. *History of the Church*, 3:389.

5. Andrew F. Ehat and Lyndon W. Cook, *The Words of Joseph Smith: The Contemporary Accounts of the Nauvoo Discourses of the Prophet Joseph*, Religious Studies Monograph Series, no. 6 (Provo, Utah: Religious Studies Center, Brigham Young University, 1980), 13, 15.

6. Joseph J. Ellis, *His Excellency* (New York: Knopf, 2004), 271.

7. Ehat and Cook, *The Words of Joseph Smith*, 234.

8. Joseph Fielding Smith, comp., *Teachings of the Prophet Joseph Smith* (Salt Lake City: Deseret News Press, 1949), 121.

9. Quoted in Gerry Avant, "Moving Church Forward with Faith," *LDS Church News*, published by *Deseret Morning News*, March 19, 2005, 3.

10. See Mark L. McConkie, *Remembering Joseph: Personal Recollections of Those Who Knew the Prophet Joseph Smith* (Salt Lake City: Deseret Book, 2003).

11. Ehat and Cook, *The Words of Joseph Smith*, 229.

12. This section is an edited version of a talk given in 1996, with some omissions and other slight editing. See Dallin H. Oaks, "Joseph, the Man and the Prophet," *Ensign* 26 (May 1996): 71–72.

13. "Praise to the Man," in *Hymns of The Church of Jesus Christ of Latter-day Saints* (Salt Lake City: The Church of Jesus Christ of Latter-day Saints, 1985), no. 27, verse 4.

14. Ehat and Cook, *The Words of Joseph Smith*, 369.

15. Mary Alice Cannon Lambert, *Young Women's Journal*, 16 (December 1905): 554.

16. Ehat and Cook, *The Words of Joseph Smith*, 234.

17. In this paper, when I refer to Joseph Smith's teachings and personal views, I include statements from his sermons and letters, as well as revelations and translations brought forth by Joseph Smith.

18. *History of the Church*, 5:517.

19. Joseph Smith, in *Journal of Discourses*, 26 vols. (Liverpool: F. D. Richards, 1855–86), 2:167, June 30, 1843; see also *History of the Church* 5:440.

20. Dallin H. Oaks, "The Suppression of the *Nauvoo Expositor*," *Utah Law Review* 9 (1965): 862–903.

21. Dallin H. Oaks and Marvin S. Hill, *Carthage Conspiracy: The Trial of the Accused Assassins of Joseph Smith* (Urbana: University of Illinois, 1975).

22. See Dallin H. Oaks and Joseph I. Bentley, "Joseph Smith and Legal Process: In the Wake of the Steamboat *Nauvoo*," *BYU Law Review* (1976): 735–82.

23. David Herbert Donald, *Lincoln* (New York: Simon and Schuster, 1995), 94–118.

24. Oaks and Bentley, "Legal Process," 767–82.

25. *History of the Church*, 7:386.

26. Brigham Young, in *Journal of Discourses*, 9:332, August 3, 1862.

27. *History of the Church*, 4:425.

28. Arsenio Pagaduan, "The Power of the Book of Mormon," manuscript in author's possession.

29. M. J. Balledos Perez, "I Didn't Know I Know," manuscript in author's possession.

30. Words of Berlie M. Patricio, quoted in memorandum of D. Rex Gerratt, in author's possession.

31. *History of the Church*, 6:305.

32. He taught, for instance, "God has created man with a mind capable of instruction, and a faculty which may be enlarged in proportion to the heed and diligence given to the light communicated from heaven to the intellect." Smith, *Teachings of the Prophet Joseph Smith*, 51, see also 12–13.

33. *History of the Church*, 2:52.

34. Gordon B. Hinckley, "Manila Philippines Temple Dedicatory Prayer," in *Selected Manifestations,* comp. David M. Reay and Vonda S. Reay (Oakland: n.p., 1985), 340–42.

35. This section uses some material from a talk given to the BYU Studies Academy in 1993; see Dallin H. Oaks, "Scripture Reading and Revelation," *Ensign* 25 (January 1995): 7–9.

36. See Dean C. Jessee, ed. and comp., *Personal Writings of Joseph Smith* (1984; repr., Salt Lake City: Deseret Book; Provo, Utah: Brigham Young University Press, 2002), 321–24.

37. *History of the Church*, 5:344.

38. Recollection of Edward Stevenson, quoted in *They Knew the Prophet,* comp. Hyrum L. Andrus and Helen Mae Andrus (Salt Lake City: Deseret Book, 1999), 96.

39. *History of the Church*, 6:50.

40. "A Poor Wayfaring Man of Grief," in *Hymns*, no. 29.

Part 4

Joseph Smith and the Theological World

While Joseph Smith lived in what could be called early nineteenth-century Protestant America, many of his teachings, though bearing a close resemblance to biblical Christianity, stood in stark contrast with the theologies of other religions. Distinctively, he insisted on the need for modern and continuing revelation. While Joseph Smith never thought of himself as a theologian, his experiences and declarations have theological implications. What theological answers did Joseph Smith offer the world? What problems do those answers solve? What problems do they raise? Authors in this part also address the issue of divine discourse beyond the Bible and the odyssey involved in being not only a "true" but also a "living" church over time.

Joseph Smith Challenges the Theological World

David Paulsen

In his illuminating book *The Story of Christian Theology,* Roger Olson states:

> Christian theology does not begin at the beginning. That is, Christian theology began well after Jesus Christ walked the earth with his disciples and even after the last disciple and apostle died. . . . The apostles [had] tremendous prestige and authority. . . . While they were alive, there was no need for theology in the same sense as afterward. Theology was born as the heirs of the apostles began to reflect on Jesus' and the apostles' teachings to . . . settle controversies about Christian belief and conduct.[1]

These words invite consideration of a fundamental question: Why was theology unnecessary before the death of the apostles? Pertinent to this inquiry is John 15:16, where Jesus declares to his apostles, "Ye have not chosen me, but I have chosen you, and *ordained* you, that ye should go and bring forth fruit" (emphasis added). Clearly, this apostolic authority is not something that can be chosen—it was a divine calling issued by the Lord himself, the fruits of which are evidence of the call's divine origin.[2]

Perhaps the most important fruit of that divine call and ordination was revelation, which enabled the apostles to direct the church's affairs under God's direction. It was by revelation that

Peter received the commandment to take the gospel to the Gentiles, and it was by revelation that the apostles decided that gentile converts to the faith would not be bound by the law of circumcision.[3] It should come as no surprise, then, that the loss of apostolic authority and its attendant revelation was seen as problematic by early Christians, and Olson explains, "The last disciple . . . to die was John 'the Beloved' . . . who . . . is a pivotal figure in the story of Christian theology because his death marked an important turning point. . . . No longer would it be possible to settle doctrinal or other disputes by turning to an apostle."[4]

Lacking apostolic authority and revelation, Christian theologians have been unable to settle controversies about Christian belief, as Olson's section titles disclose:

> "The Opening Act: Conflicting Christian Visions in the Second Century"
>
> "The Plot Thickens: Third-Century Tensions and Transformations"
>
> "A Great Crisis Rocks the Church: The Controversy about the Trinity"
>
> "Another Crisis Shakes the Church: The Conflict over the Person of Christ"
>
> "A Tale of Two Churches: The Great Tradition Divides between East and West"
>
> "A New Twist in the Narrative: The Western Church Reforms and Divides"
>
> "The Center of the Story Falls Apart: Protestants Follow Diverse Paths"
>
> "The Overall Plot Divides: Liberals and Conservatives Respond to Modernity."

As we enter the new millennium, Olson says, unsettled conflicts in Christendom have not subsided; they have increased, with no end in sight.[5]

To this diverse and ambivalent world that we call Christian theology, doctrines taught by Joseph Smith pose several challenges. To be

sure, he poses *different* challenges to the varieties of generally orthodox Christian thought (which will be my focus here) than he does
to the many variants of liberal Christian theologies. Unfortunately,
there is not room to compare Joseph with each individual theologian.
Instead, I will discuss, usually in his own words, several of Joseph
Smith's revelations and invite everyone to examine his or her own
theological world in light of these. It is not my intent to argue for
their truth but rather to make clear their content and their challenging implications for Christian theology.

Six of Joseph's most fundamental challenges are his teachings
(1) of God's resumption of direct revelation in our day; (2) of God's
restoration of divine authority to man to speak and act in his name,
and as a corollary, of a greatly enlarged (and still open) canon. Within
this enlarged canon is found the basis for many more challenges,
including (3) a clear and very high Christology that affirms that Jesus
is both God and the Savior; (4) a reaffirmation of the living God of
Abraham, Isaac, and Jacob as opposed to the God of the philosophers
and theologians; (5) an ennobling, theomorphic understanding of
human potential; and (6) a comprehensive and consistent soteriology that, among other things, solves the puzzle of the fate of the
unevangelized. I will explain and illustrate each of these challenges.

1. Revelation and Canon

Of all Joseph's challenges to the theological world, none is more
fundamental than his claim to direct revelation from God. This claim
challenges every variety of Christian thought and, at the same time,
grounds all of Joseph's additional claims. However biblically consistent, rationally plausible, or existentially appealing Joseph's theological insights may be, the force of their challenge hinges most critically
on his claim they were directly revealed by God.[6] The authoritative-
ness of the Bible for Christians hinges on a similar claim to its being
God's revealed word. As Richard Bushman explains:

> The reason for embracing the Bible was that its words had come
> from heaven. Christianity had smothered this self-evident fact by
> relegating revelation to a bygone age, making the Bible an archive

rather than a living reality. . . .[Hence,] Joseph aimed a question at the heart of the culture: Did Christians truly believe in revelation? If believers in the Bible dismissed revelation in the present, could they defend revelation in the past? . . . [And] if revelation in the present was so far out of the question that Joseph's claims could be discounted without serious consideration, *why believe revelation in the past?*[7] (emphasis added)

Joseph's claim of new revelation is, as Bushman suggests, a challenge based on the Bible itself, a fact of which the Prophet was fully aware. In response to a minister inquiring "wherein we [the Mormons] differ from other christian denominations," the Prophet replied, "We believe the Bible, and they do not."[8]

Extrabiblical Revelation: Representative Christian Views. Is prophetic and apostolic revelation an archive rather than a living reality? In his book *The Formation of the Christian Biblical Canon*, Evangelical Bible scholar Lee M. McDonald points out that the passing of the apostles and the formation of the canon led to a significant change in attitude regarding the possibility of continuing revelation: the biblical canon came to be viewed as containing all the truths necessary for human life and salvation.[9] The Westminster Confession gives creedal status to this view:

> The whole counsel of God concerning all things necessary for his own glory, man's salvation, faith and life, is either expressly set down in Scripture, or by good and necessary consequence may be deduced from Scripture: unto which nothing at any time is to be added, whether by new revelations of the Spirit or traditions of men.[10]

And in a slightly expanded version of the same view, the *Catholic Encyclopedia* explains:

> While the Church recognizes that God has spoken to His servants in every age, and still continues thus to favour chosen souls, she is careful to distinguish these revelations from the Revelation which has been committed to her charge . . . *That Revelation was given in its entirety to Our Lord and His Apostles.* After the death of the last of the twelve it could receive no increment. It was, as the Church calls it, a deposit—"the faith once delivered to the saints" (Jude, 2)—*for which the Church was to "contend" but to which she could*

add nothing. . . . The gift of Divine assistance, . . . sometimes con-
founded with Revelation by the less instructed of anti-Catholic
writers, merely preserves the supreme pontiff from error in defining the faith; it does not enable him to add jot or tittle to it.[11]
(emphasis added)

Not all Christian thinkers hold as dogma the finality of God's
revelation in biblical times. Indeed, the status of the biblical canon,
whether open or closed, has become a hotly debated issue among
current biblical scholars. In the "Final Reflections" of his book on
the formation of the canon, McDonald raises several very thoughtful questions challenging Christian belief in a closed canon; I list the
most relevant ones:

> The first question, and the most important one, is whether the
> church was right in perceiving the need for a closed canon of
> scriptures.[12] If the term "Christian" is defined by the examples and
> beliefs passed on by earliest followers of Jesus, then we must at
> least ponder the question whether the notion of a biblical canon
> is necessarily "Christian." They did not have such canons as the
> church possesses today, nor did they indicate that their successors
> should draw them up. . . .[13]
>
> . . . Did such a move toward a closed canon . . . ultimately (and
> unconsciously) limit the presence and power of the Holy Spirit in
> the Church? . . . Does God act in the Church today and by the same
> Spirit? On what biblical or historical grounds has the inspiration of
> God been limited to the written documents that the Church now
> calls its Bible?
>
> . . . If apostolicity is still a legitimate criterion for the canonic-
> ity of the NT literature . . . should the church today continue to
> recognize the authority of . . . nonapostolic literature of the NT?
> If the Spirit's activity was not considered to be limited to apostolic
> documents, . . . can we and should we make arguments for the
> inclusion of other literature in the biblical canon? . . .[14]
>
> . . . One must surely ask about the appropriateness of tying the
> church of the twentieth century to a canon that emerged out of
> the historical circumstances in the second to the fifth centuries CE.
> How are we supposed to make the experience of that church abso-
> lute for all time? . . .[15]

If the Spirit inspired specific, authoritative instruction on the issues contemporary to the biblical writers, is there no voice today to give such needed guidance in our increasingly complex world?

God's Word and Joseph Smith. Almost two centuries ago, Joseph challenged the theological world with answers to McDonald's questions, always with a witness of revelatory events. For example, consider Joseph's response to the question: On what biblical ground has the inspiration of God been limited to the written documents that the church now calls its Bible? None! reasoned Joseph: "If [the canon is closed] there is a great defect in the book, or else it would have said so."[16] Elsewhere, he argued:

> To say that God never said anything more to man than is recorded [in the Bible], *would be saying at once that we have at last received a revelation*: for it must require one to advance thus far, because it is nowhere said in that volume by the mouth of God, that He would not, after giving what is there contained, speak again; and if any man has found out for a fact that the Bible contains all that God ever revealed to man he has ascertained it by an immediate revelation, other than has been previously written by the prophets and apostles.[17] (emphasis added)

Joseph's argument seems persuasive. Given the silence of the Bible as a whole on this issue, the only way one could know for certain that there can be no extrabiblical revelation would be by means of an extrabiblical revelation. But this is obviously incoherent.

Joseph's most fundamental challenge, however, to those who deny the possibility of extrabiblical revelation is not based on argument; it is grounded in his testimony of receiving direct revelations from God. Joseph's experience with these matters began in his fifteenth year as he struggled to decide which Christian church to join:

> It was impossible for a person young as I was, . . . to come to any certain conclusion [as to] who was right and who was wrong . . . for the teachers of religion . . . understood the same passages of scripture so differently as to destroy all confidence in settling the question by an appeal to the Bible. (Joseph Smith–History 1:8–12)

In 1820, he prayed for divine guidance in choosing a church. In his canonized account of the experience, Joseph reports, "I saw two

Personages, whose brightness and glory defy all description, standing above me in the air. One of them spake unto me, calling me by name and said, pointing to the other—*This is My Beloved Son. Hear Him!*" (Joseph Smith–History 1:17).

In this revelation, Joseph conversed with God and Jesus Christ face to face as one man converses with another.[18] In this transcendent, tradition-shattering experience, Joseph received personal assurance of forgiveness of his sins, he was instructed to join none of the existing churches, and he was advised that God had a work for him to do. He later learned that this work was to usher in a new gospel dispensation—"the dispensation of the fullness of times," when all things would be gathered together in one to prepare the human family for the Second Coming of the Lord (Ephesians 1:10).[19]

God also brought heaven to earth by divine visitations and angelic messengers. Through these instructions, Joseph revealed much about God's kingdom and his purposes for humankind, apostolic authority, ancient scriptures, the divine church, the temple, temple ordinances, and theology. As a result the Latter-day Saints have greatly enlarged the Christian canon, adding "plain and precious" gospel truths not found in the Bible (1 Nephi 13:40). Thus Joseph could pen as the ninth Article of Faith for the Saints, "We believe all that God has revealed, all that He does now reveal, and we believe that He will yet reveal many great and important things pertaining to the Kingdom of God."

With Joseph Smith's revelations in mind, let us return to some of McDonald's questions. Joseph's answers to these questions are tacit in his report of his revelations but are also often explicit in their specific content. Thus, being Christian, he asserted, does not "necessarily" mean having a closed canon; it means having an open one, as Moroni in the Book of Mormon explicitly and prophetically wrote:

> And again I speak unto you who deny the revelations of God, and say that they are done away, that there are no revelations. . . . Behold I say unto you, he that denieth these things knoweth not the gospel of Christ; . . . For do we not read that God is the same yesterday, today, and forever, and in him there is no variableness neither shadow of changing? (Mormon 9:7–9)

Does the same Spirit that produced the written documents of the first century still speak today? In most of the revelations Joseph received directly, he recorded the Lord speaking in first person; the phrase "thus saith the Lord" appears ninety-nine times in uniquely Latter-day Saint scripture. In a dramatic fashion, Joseph burst open the canon that had been regarded as closed for hundreds of years.

2. Divine Authority

Joseph's claims to revelation shake the theological world at its very foundation. But at the same time, he proclaimed that the revelations offer the "more sure word of prophecy" (2 Peter 1:19) and a firmer foundation: a foundation of living prophets and apostles who have the authority to say, "Thus saith the Lord."

Christendom and Divine Authority. Jesus Christ is the only source from which claims to divine authority can be credibly based in Christendom. The first to claim such divine authority, as we have seen, were Jesus's apostles, whom he personally called and ordained. The apostles claimed, and were recognized by fellow Christians, to possess teaching, sacramental, and governing authority. With their passing, the question of authority became critical. The practical precedent that was established presumed authority in those who were tutored by the apostles. Olson explains:

> Men like Polycarp [who had been tutored by John or other apostles] were considered the best and most authoritative sources of information about what the apostles taught and how they led the churches. Polycarp's aura of special authority [subsequently] fell upon his own disciples—men like Irenaeus who were trained in the Christian faith by him. . . . [U]ntil the New Testament was identified and agreed upon by Christians in the fourth century, this oral tradition and the authority of apostolic succession proved invaluable in the Christian struggle against heresies and schisms within the church.[20]

After the adoption of Christianity by the Roman Empire and attempts to establish orthodoxy by way of creedal decree, the Western churches adopted the Bishop of Rome as the "single supreme head" to which all other officers in the church became subordinate.[21] Thus, the Catholic Church claims that (1) "apostolic succession is found in the Catholic Church," (2) "none of the separate Churches have any valid claim to it," and (3) the Roman Bishop possesses the supreme power to govern the church.[22] The Orthodox Church claims exactly the same apostolic succession while maintaining that all bishops are equal in authority. For them, "no particular bishop per se or document . . . has say over the churches."[23]

In time, Protestantism emerged with a new answer to the question of authority: Olson writes, "Three major Protestant principles are usually identified as setting them apart from the church of Rome and its official theology: *sola gratia et fides* (salvation by grace through faith alone), *sola scriptura* (scripture above all other authorities for Christian faith and practice) and the priesthood of all believers."[24] Thus, for the Reformers doctrinal authority is founded solely in the Bible. Furthermore, sacramental authority is found in the virtuous lives of believers, rather than by authoritative call and hand-to-head ordination. The *Catholic Encyclopedia* diplomatically outlines the central argument:

> Now in this respect there are several points of controversy between Catholics and every body of Protestants. Is all revealed truth consigned to Holy Scripture? or can it, must it, be admitted that Christ gave to His Apostles to be transmitted to His Church, that the Apostles received either from the very lips of Jesus or from inspiration or Revelation, Divine instructions which they transmitted to the Church and which were not committed to the inspired writings? Must it be admitted that Christ instituted His Church as the official and authentic organ to transmit and explain in virtue of Divine authority the Revelation made to men?[25]

Joseph Smith and Divine Authority. Into the confusing whirlwind of answers to these complex questions stepped a theologically untrained young man of twenty-four years of age. Armed with claims of direct conferrals of divine authority by angelic ministrants, Joseph Smith challenged the foundations of Christendom with his claim of authority from God to both speak and act in his name. Here, I will briefly set out Joseph's witness that angelic visitants conferred upon him divine authority, which, they said, had long been absent from the church.

In 1829 as Joseph Smith and Oliver Cowdery were engaged in translating the Book of Mormon, they came across certain passages that made it clear to them that, in Oliver's words, "none had authority from God to administer the ordinances of the gospel."[26] Subsequently, on May 15, 1829, Joseph and Oliver went to a wooded area in Pennsylvania to pray to the Lord concerning the matter. In answer to their prayers, John the Baptist "descended in a cloud of light" and, acting under the direction of Peter, James, and John, laid his hands upon them and ordained them, conferring the Aaronic Priesthood, "which holds the keys of the ministering of angels, and of the gospel of repentance, and of baptism by immersion for the remission of sins" (Joseph Smith–History 1:68–69).[27] Not long after John the Baptist's appearance, Peter, James, and John visited Joseph and Oliver and conferred on them the Melchizedek Priesthood, which empowered them to confer the gift of the Holy Ghost and to officiate in the higher ordinances of the gospel.[28] They also ordained Joseph and Oliver to be apostles of Jesus Christ, thus restoring the office that they themselves had held while on the earth.[29]

These ordinations by angelic ministrants grounded Joseph Smith's claims to divine authority. Whereas Catholics claim an unbroken line of authority from the days of Peter, Joseph proclaimed that through apostasy the chain had been broken and the authority lost. Whereas Protestants claim that all believers hold priesthood authority, Joseph claimed that God restored divine authority by literal hand-to-head transfer by the very prophets and apostles whose lives and words are recounted in the Bible.[30] On the basis of these revelatory events, Joseph taught that there is no salvation between the two ends of the Bible without divine authority.[31] He elaborated:

> We believe that no man can administer salvation through the gospel, to the souls of men, in the name of Jesus Christ, except he is authorized from God, by revelation or by being ordained by some one whom God hath sent by revelation, as it is written by Paul, Romans 10:14, "and how shall they believe in him, of whom they have not heard? and how shall they hear without a preacher? and

how shall they preach, except they be sent?" and I will ask, how can they be sent without a revelation, or some other visible display of the manifestation of God. And again, Hebrews 5:4, "And no man taketh this honor unto himself, but he that is called of God as was Aaron."—And I would ask, how was Aaron called, but by revelation?[32]

3. Jesus Christ[33]

As one claiming to have apostolic authority and to be a "special witness" of Christ, Joseph had much to teach about the identity and mission of Jesus of Nazareth that would challenge Christendom's Christologies.

Christendom's Christologies. Christology attempts to answer the question Jesus asked of his first disciples: "Whom say ye that I am?" (Matthew 16:15). As "the keystone of theology for serious Christians," Christology has been pursued using two fundamentally different methodologies: "Christology from above" and "Christology from below."[34] Christology from above takes at face value the confessions of faith in the deity of Christ as expressed in the New Testament, affirming that Christ is both God and Savior. Conversely, Christology from below begins with an inquiry into the historical Jesus. It goes behind the theological interpretations of the New Testament writers and attempts to ascertain the historical and factual foundation of Christological claims. Currently, there is a constant flux of both from-above and from-below scholarship.

Although Christologies vary considerably, one noteworthy attempt at a unifying declaration has been made by the World Council of Churches, which requires that all applicants believe in "the Lord Jesus Christ as God and Savior."[35] Yet even this declaration has found its Christian critics. Some assert that Jesus was not a special revelation of God but only an extraordinary person. While some deny the God-nature of Jesus, other Christologies deny the actuality of his resurrection and atonement and even deny that Christ was morally perfect. In some Christologies, even the sayings of Jesus are turned into the "theological interpretations of his followers."[36] The most famous work in this regard has been done by the Jesus Seminar in California.

The Seminar scholars assert that Jesus was not born of a virgin, not born of David's lineage, and not born in Bethlehem.[37] The divide in contemporary Christologies is astonishingly wide.

Joseph's Christology. Joseph Smith's "method" of arriving at Christological insights differs from both the traditional from-above and from-below approaches. In fact, it most closely parallels the method of Paul. Pauline Christology begins with his conversion experience, in which the resurrected Christ appeared and spoke with him.[38] Joseph, like Paul, also reported that he saw and conversed with the risen Lord on several occasions.[39] The source of Joseph's knowledge is thoroughly reflected in his deliverance of his Christology. Instead of lengthy prose articulating reasoned historical research or sustained exegeses of biblical texts, one finds in Joseph's statements short, clear descriptions.[40]

In the resulting unique and expansive portrait of Christ, Joseph Smith agreed with, added to, and sometimes repudiated contemporary Christologies. He did so not only through direct personal encounters with the risen Lord, but also from revealed biblical and extrabiblical recorded encounters of others. Many of the latter are recorded in the Book of Mormon. Throughout the century preceding Christ's birth, Book of Mormon prophets foretold his incarnation, atonement, and resurrection. For instance, King Benjamin prophesied (ca. 124 BC):

> The Lord Omnipotent who reigneth, who was, and is from all eternity to all eternity, shall come down from heaven among the children of men, and shall dwell in a tabernacle of clay, and shall go forth amongst men, working mighty miracles.... And lo, he shall suffer temptations, and pain of body, hunger, thirst, and fatigue, even more than man can suffer, except it be unto death; for behold, blood cometh from every pore, so great shall be his anguish for the wickedness and the abominations of his people. And he shall be called Jesus Christ, the Son of God ... the Creator of all things.... And lo, he cometh ... that salvation might come unto the children of men even through faith on his name; and even after all this they ... shall crucify him. And he shall rise the third day from the dead. (Mosiah 3:5–10)[41]

According to the Book of Mormon, these transcendent events were established most clearly and powerfully by the risen Lord himself when, following his ascension in Jerusalem, he visited an expectant community of believers in the Western Hemisphere. He was introduced by God, the Father:

> Behold my Beloved Son, in whom I am well pleased, in whom I have glorified my name—hear ye him. . . . As [the multitude] understood they cast their eyes . . . towards heaven; and behold, they saw a Man descending out of heaven; and he was clothed in a white robe; and he came down and stood in the midst of them . . . [And he] spake unto the people saying: Behold, I am Jesus Christ, whom the prophets testified shall come into the world. . . . Arise and come forth unto me, that ye may thrust your hands into my side, and . . . feel the prints of the nails in my hands and in my feet, that ye may know that I am the God of Israel, and the God of the whole earth, and have been slain for the sins of the world. (3 Nephi 11:7–14)

But this is not all. Consider two further disclosures. According to a canonized account, the risen Lord appeared to Joseph Smith and Sidney Rigdon in Hiram, Ohio, on February 16, 1832. Of this experience, they wrote:

> And now, after the many testimonies which have been given of him, this is the testimony, last of all, which we give of him: That he lives! For we saw him, even on the right hand of God; and we heard the voice bearing record that he is the Only Begotten of the Father—That by him, and through him, and of him, the worlds are and were created. (Doctrine and Covenants 76:22–24)

Four years later in the newly dedicated temple in Kirtland, Ohio, Christ again appeared and spoke, this time to Joseph Smith and Oliver Cowdery. They described their experience:

> We saw the Lord standing upon the breastwork of the pulpit, before us . . . His eyes were as a flame of fire; the hair of his head was white like the pure snow; his countenance shone above the brightness of the sun; and his voice was as the sound of the rushing of great waters . . . saying: I am the first and the last; I am he who liveth, I am he who was slain; I am your advocate with the Father. (Doctrine and Covenants 110:2–4)

When accepted as true, these self-disclosures of the risen Lord repudiate the humanistic conclusions of the Jesus Seminar and of liberal Christologies, and they powerfully confirm the faith of Christians who affirm with Joseph that Jesus Christ is the Eternal God, the Creator, the God of Israel, God incarnate, merciful Savior, risen Lord, and advocate with the Father.

4. God and the Godhead

Reflection on his first vision in due time yielded Joseph more insights: Jesus Christ is truly God's beloved Son; God the Father and Jesus Christ are two distinct persons, gloriously embodied and humanlike in form; and men and women were literally created in their image. These experiential insights stand in dramatic contrast with the typical propositions found in conventional theologies.

The Nature of God: Conventional Theism. The God of Abraham, Isaac, and Jacob has sometimes been distinguished from the god of the philosophers and theologians.[42] The latter is a human construction—a product of rational theologizing, with no explicit basis in revelation. While the philosophers' god is variously conceived, it is commonly portrayed as absolutely sovereign, all-controlling and all-determining, wholly other, absolutely simple, immaterial, nonspatial, nontemporal, immutable and impassible, the creator of all things out of nothing.[43] Although there is, as already seen, much diversity within Christian understandings of God, I will refer to this composite portrait of God as "the god of the philosophers."[44]

The God of Joseph Smith. The God who revealed himself to Joseph Smith is radically unlike the god of the philosophers. He did not create all things out of nothing; to the contrary, he created the physical universe out of chaotic matter. That God is not all-controlling and all-determining; to the contrary, we on earth have morally significant freedom. Even God's gracious gift of forgiveness of sins awaits our free acceptance. Joseph's God is neither timeless, immutable, impassible, nor eternally static. To the contrary, he is "the living God" who is profoundly "touched with the feeling of our infirmities," and responsive to our needs and petitionary prayers

(Hebrews 3:12; 4:15).[45] God is not absolutely simple, immaterial, non-spatial, nor wholly other. To the contrary, he formed our bodies in the very image and likeness (Genesis 1:26) of his own, and he speaks with people "face to face, as a man speaketh unto his friend" (Exodus 33:11). In sum, the God who revealed himself to Joseph is the God of Abraham, Isaac, and Jacob and not the god of the philosophers and theologians. Of the many differences between Joseph's living God and the god of human constructions, I will focus on three: divine embodiment, the Godhead, and God's loving passibility.

Divine Embodiment. In language again reflecting direct experience over reasoned discourse, Joseph declared, "The Father has a body of flesh and bones as tangible as man's; the Son also; but the Holy Ghost has not a body of flesh and bones, but is a personage of Spirit" (Doctrine and Covenants 130:22). In similar simple declarations of revealed fact, Joseph made it clear that the Father and the Son created our bodies in the very image and likeness of their own. Thus, he taught that humans are theomorphic. "When the Savior shall appear we shall see him as he is. We shall see that he *is a man like ourselves*" (Doctrine and Covenants 130:1; emphasis added).

> God himself was once as we are now, and is an exalted man, and sits enthroned in yonder heavens! That is the great secret. If the veil were rent today, and the great God who holds this world in its orbit, and who upholds all worlds and things by His power, was to make himself visible,—I say, if you were to see him today, you would see him like a man in form—like yourselves in all the person, image, and very form as a man.[46]

Indeed, "it is the first principle of the gospel to know for a certainty the character of God, and to know that we may converse with Him as one man converses with another."[47] From these self-disclosures, it became evident to Joseph Smith that the Father's and the Son's risen bodies, while like human bodies in form are, in some respects, substantially unlike our corruptible bodies. In Joseph's account of his First Vision, he reports that the "brightness and glory [of the Father and the Son] defy all description" (Joseph Smith–History 1:17). And a newly revealed report of Moses' face-to-face encounter with God reads:

The presence of God withdrew from Moses, that his glory was not upon Moses; and Moses was left unto himself. And as he was left unto himself, he fell unto the earth. And it came to pass that it was for the space of many hours before Moses did again receive his natural strength like unto man; and he said unto himself: Now, for this cause I know that man is nothing, which thing I never had supposed. But now mine own eyes have beheld God; but not my natural, but my spiritual eyes, for my natural eyes could not have beheld; for I should have withered and died in his presence; but his glory was upon me; and I beheld his face, for I was transfigured before him. (Moses 1:9–11)

So glorious is God's personage that Moses had to undergo a temporary transfiguration of his own body simply to withstand God's presence.

The Godhead. Joseph penned this simple first Article of Faith: "We believe in God, the Eternal Father, and in His son, Jesus Christ, and in the Holy Ghost." On the basis of his revelations, Joseph taught that the Godhead consists of three distinct persons, each separately embodied. Thus, Joseph rejected (and explicitly so) the traditional but extrabiblical idea that they constitute one metaphysical substance. Rather, they constitute one mutually indwelling divine community, perfectly united in mind, will, purpose, work, and love. The recorded revelations given to and through Joseph repeatedly declare, "Father, Son, and Holy Ghost are one God"; in these revelations, the word "God" is used to designate the individual members of the Godhead, as well as the divine community (cf. Doctrine and Covenants 20:28; 2 Nephi 31:21; Alma 11:44; 3 Nephi 11:36). Taken in their totality, Joseph's revelations disclose a social trinity, rather than a "one substance," tritheistic or modalistic model of the Godhead.[48]

Passibility. Conventional theism, influenced by Greek metaphysics, reasons that God must be timeless and unchanging and, hence, impassible—that is, unchangeable by another. In contrast, the revelations that came to and through Joseph Smith disclose God's tender and profound passibility. Consider two such passages from these revelations, the first from the Pearl of Great Price record of Enoch, an antediluvian prophet:

And it came to pass that the God of heaven looked upon the residue of the people, and he wept. . . . And Enoch said unto the Lord: How is it that thou canst weep, seeing thou art holy, and from all eternity to all eternity? . . . The Lord said unto Enoch: Behold these thy brethren; they are the workmanship of mine own hands, and I gave unto them their knowledge, in the day I created them; and in the Garden of Eden, gave I unto man his agency; And unto thy brethren have I said, and also given commandment, that they should love one another, . . . but behold they are without affection, and they hate their own blood. (Moses 7:28–29, 32–33)

The second comes from the Book of Mormon account of the visit of the resurrected Lord to a gathering of ancient Americans. As his visit was drawing to a close, the Lord advised the gathering that he was leaving. But he "cast his eyes round about again on the multitude, and beheld they were in tears, and did look steadfastly upon him as if they would ask him to tarry a little longer with them." Discerning their desires, the Lord lingered, responding, "Behold, my bowels are filled with compassion towards you." He inquired if there were any sick among them and told them, "Bring them hither and I will heal them, for I . . . see that your faith is sufficient that I should heal you." Next, Jesus invited them to bring their little children to him, and he prayed for them. The record continues: "No one can conceive of the joy which filled [their] souls." Seeing that *their* joy was full, Jesus said, "Blessed are ye because of your faith. And *now* behold, *my* joy is full. And when he had said these words, he wept." Then he "took their little children, *one by one*, and blessed them, and prayed unto the Father for them. And when he had done this he wept again" (3 Nephi 17:3–8, 17–25; emphasis added). The resurrected Lord had planned to leave his people earlier, but he lingered because he discerned that the people wanted him to stay. And when their joy was full, *then* was his joy full.

Dallas Willard once caricatured the god of the philosophers as "a great unblinking cosmic stare."[49] In Joseph's theology, there is no ground for such a caricature. His revelations powerfully and reassuringly disclose the tender passibility of God, who profoundly loves each of us.

5. A Theomorphic Understanding of Men and Women

But what or who are we? Where did we come from? Why are we here? Let's begin at the beginning.

Beginningless Beginning. In his book *Eternal Man*, Latter-day Saint philosopher Truman G. Madsen succinctly summarizes Joseph's answers to the above questions:

> Regarding the ultimate identity of man, the Prophet Joseph Smith taught that man as a primal intelligence is eternal. Likewise the spirit-elements that compose his Divinely-sired spirit and the matter-elements that compose his physically-sired body are eternal. Except in procreation, these elements of the total self never become an *essential* part of any other self. Once united, their destiny is to be glorified and "inseparably connected" throughout all eternity.[50]

While acknowledging that Joseph's affirmations about intelligences leave much that remains indeterminate, Madsen suggests that a careful reading yields these four points:

> *Individuality.* A person as a self had a beginningless beginning. He or she has never been identified wholly with any other being. Nor is he or she a product of nothing. "Intelligence is eternal and exists upon a self-existent principle. . . . There is no creation about it."[51]
>
> *Autonomy.* The self is free. All intelligence "is independent in that sphere in which God has placed it, to act for itself . . . otherwise there is no existence."
>
> *Consciousness.* There is no inanimate intelligence or unconscious mind. These are contradictions in terms. Selfhood and individual consciousness are unending. "The intelligence of spirits had no beginning; neither will it have an end."
>
> *Capacity for Development.* "All the minds and spirits that God ever sent into the world are susceptible of enlargement."[52]

Spirits Begotten, Not Made. A revelation pronounced by Joseph states that the inhabitants of the world are the "begotten sons and daughters unto God" (Doctrine and Covenants 76:24). Thus the entire human family are God's children, not creatures merely. Joseph's successors in the prophetic office have spelled out this concept more fully:

The Father of Jesus is our Father also. Jesus Himself taught this truth, when He instructed His disciples how to pray: "Our Father which art in heaven," etc. Jesus, however, is the firstborn among all the sons of God—the first begotten in the spirit, and the only begotten in the flesh. . . . All men and women are in the similitude of the universal Father and Mother, and are literally the sons and daughters of Deity.[53]

Bodies Created in God's Image. In an early account in the Book of Mormon, a prophet was permitted to see the preincarnate Lord and his premortal spirit body (ca. 2200 BC). The Lord explained to the brother of Jared, "Seest thou that ye are created after mine own image? Yea, even all men were created in the beginning after mine own image. Behold, this body, which ye now behold, is the body of my spirit; . . . and even as I appear unto thee to be in the spirit will I appear unto my people in the flesh" (Ether 3:15–16). This passage corroborates Genesis 1:27, which appears in slightly altered form in another revelation given through Joseph: "And I, God, created man in mine own image, in the image of mine Only Begotten created I him; male and female created I them" (Moses 2:27).

Morally Significant Freedom. As eternal intelligences begotten as sons and daughters of God, humans have morally significant freedom. This is clearly taught in the revelations that came through Joseph. "All truth is independent in that sphere in which God has placed it, to act for itself, as all intelligence also; otherwise there is no existence" (Doctrine and Covenants 93:30). Thus, humans "are free to choose liberty and eternal life, through the great Mediator of all men, or to choose captivity and death, according to the captivity and power of the devil" (2 Nephi 2:27). Joseph told the Saints that "Satan was generally blamed for the evils which we did, but if he was the cause of all our wickedness, men could not be condemned. The devil could not compel mankind to do evil; all was voluntary," and later in the same address he affirmed that "God would not exert any compulsory means, and the devil could not; and such ideas as were entertained [on these subjects] by many were absurd."[54]

The Purpose of Mortal Existence and Our Eschatological Potential. Joseph taught, "The relationship we have with God places us in a situation to advance in knowledge. He has power to institute laws to instruct the weaker intelligences." He further argued that, as noted earlier, our minds "are susceptible of enlargement."[55]

And just how much enlargement did Joseph have in mind? He took as his paradigm the relationship between God the Father and God the Son, Jesus Christ. In much the same way that Christ "received not of the fulness at first, but continued from grace to grace, until he received a fulness" (Doctrine and Covenants 93:13), and so are we expected to advance from grace to grace until we, too, receive a fullness from the Father. Consider these words from Joseph Smith:

> You have got to learn how to be Gods yourselves, and to be kings and priests to God, the same as all Gods have done before you, namely, by going from one small degree to another, and from a small capacity to a great one; from grace to grace, from exaltation to exaltation, until you attain to the resurrection of the dead, and are able to dwell in everlasting burnings, and to sit in glory, as do those who sit enthroned in everlasting power. . . .
>
> What did Jesus do? Why; I [Jesus] do the things I saw my Father do when worlds came rolling into existence. My Father worked out his kingdom with fear and trembling, and I must do the same; and when I get my kingdom, I shall present it to my Father, so that he may obtain kingdom upon kingdom, and it will exalt him in glory. He will then take a higher exaltation, and I will take his place, and thereby become exalted myself. So that Jesus treads in the tracks of his Father, and inherits what God did before; and God is thus glorified and exalted in the salvation and exaltation of all his children.[56]

Joseph viewed this process as one that would take a very substantial amount of time to complete: "It will be a great while after you have passed through the veil before you will have learned them [the principles of exaltation]. It is not all to be comprehended in this world; it will be a great work to learn our salvation and exaltation even beyond the grave."[57] Mortals are, indeed, in many ways extremely lacking in Godly attributes, yet so profound was Joseph's doctrine of their potential that he taught that with time, growth, and grace men and women could eventually arrive at a Godlike station:

"Then shall they be gods, because they have no end; . . . then shall they be above all, because all things are subject unto them. Then shall they be gods, because they have all power." The blessings of this exaltation are placed under strict principles and guidelines, which only those who endure on the gospel path in faithful obedience shall find: "Verily, verily, I say unto you, except ye abide my law ye cannot attain to this glory" (Doctrine and Covenants 132:20–21).

The Fall. Joseph's views of the fall and its effects presented (and still present) a major challenge to the varying theologies of Christendom. Contrary to the negative view of the fall prevalent in traditional Christianity, Joseph affirmed that the fall was a "fortunate fall" wherein mankind fell "downward, yet forward."[58] As usual, Joseph's thought was shaped by the revelations that he received and the records he translated.

Nowhere is Joseph's theology of a fortunate fall more explicit than in the book of Moses. Here one reads of Adam and Eve's reaction to the consequences brought about by their transgression, fall, and subsequent removal from the Garden of Eden. Surprisingly, they both rejoice in, rather than lament, their new condition. Adam says:

> Blessed be the name of God, for because of my transgression my eyes are opened, and in this life I shall have joy, and again in the flesh I shall see God. And Eve, his wife heard all these things and was glad, saying: Were it not for our transgression we never should have had seed, and never should have known good and evil, and the joy of our redemption, and the eternal life which God giveth unto all the obedient. And Adam and Eve blessed the name of God, and they made all things known unto their sons and their daughters (Moses 5:10–12).

Similarly, Lehi (ca. 600 BC), a prophet-leader in the Book of Mormon, explained the benefits of the fall. He taught that Adam and Eve's fall placed them in a world wherein moral opposites are allowed to coexist. "For it must needs be, that there is an opposition in all things. If not so, . . . righteousness could not be brought to pass, neither wickedness, neither holiness nor misery, neither good nor bad" (2 Nephi 2:11). The fall, then, far from being an unanticipated aberration from God's will, is to be embraced as a crucial component of

God's salvific designs for the whole of his creation. As Lehi's text goes on to note, "All things have been done in the wisdom of him who knoweth all things. Adam fell that men might be; and men are, that they might have joy" (2 Nephi 2:24–25).

Joseph's own words affirm the wisdom of the fall: "Adam did not commit sin in eating the fruits, for God had decreed that he should eat and fall . . . [That] he should die was the saying of the Lord; therefore, the Lord appointed us to fall and also redeemed us—for where sin abounded grace did much more abound."[59] When coupled with the atonement of Christ, the fall becomes an indispensable blessing by affording us meaningful moral freedom to choose righteousness from among the evils of a fallen world.

In affirming such an unorthodox, positive view of the fall, Joseph did not overlook the untoward consequences of the fall that plague our mortal condition. Joseph's revelations concur with traditional Christianity teachings that because of the fall humanity was universally lost and became estranged from God's presence.[60] Yet Joseph did not teach that all humans inherit a totally depraved nature (original sin). Rather, he understood that all humans inevitably sin (universal sinfulness) because of opposition and moral imperfection. Even with the inevitability of our failures, Joseph taught that however existentially estranged we may become by our sinful choices, by Christ's justifying and sanctifying grace, we can be reconciled. Joseph advocated an extremely ennobling image of humans in which *every* person possesses the capacity, with divine assistance and grace, to refine his or her own fallen nature toward righteousness. Joseph stated, "I believe that a man is a moral, responsible, free agent; that although it was foreordained he should fall, and be redeemed, yet after the redemption it was not foreordained that he should again sin."[61]

In summary, Joseph's teachings present a unique portrait of humanity. A person is a child, not a creature, of God; thus, we are of the same species as God. This relationship, Joseph taught, has profound implications for our ultimate potential: we contain within ourselves the capacity to grow unto the likeness of God. We possess morally significant freedom, which we may use for our ultimate exaltation or condemnation. The fall, coupled with the atonement, is a necessary part of God's plan for our moral development.

Indeed, Joseph's ennobling view of humans and their eschatological potential stands in striking contrast and challenge to more negative views of men and women within conventional Christian theologies. Carl Mosser, Evangelical theologian and coeditor and author of *The New Mormon Challenge,* astutely views the contrast from another angle: "Smith's teachings about the eschatological potential of men and women challenges Christian theology to think more deliberately about what the redeemed are redeemed *for*. Too often, in my view, Christian theologians are content to reflect on *how* we are redeemed (the mechanics) and on what we are redeemed *from*."[62]

6. Salvation for the Unevangelized

By resolving long-standing theological perplexities, the risen Lord's self-disclosures reported by Joseph Smith can greatly increase one's understanding of the Lord's salvific gifts. The fate of the unevangelized is one such difficulty. Thomas Morris explains the perplexity (which he calls a "scandal") this way:

> The scandal . . . arises with a simple set of questions asked of the Christian theologian who claims that it is only through the life and death of God incarnated in Jesus Christ that all can be saved and reconciled to God: How can the many humans who lived and died before the time of Christ be saved through him? They surely cannot be held accountable for responding appropriately to something of which they could have no knowledge. Furthermore, what about all the people who have lived since the time of Christ in cultures with different religious traditions, untouched by the Christian gospel? . . . How could a just God set up a particular condition of salvation, the highest end of human life possible, which was and is inaccessible to most people?[63]

Stephen Davis expresses a similar perplexity in an article in *Modern Theology*: "Is it right for God to condemn [a woman "who lived from 370–320 B.C. in the interior of Borneo"] to eternal hell just because she was never able to come to God through Christ? Of course not . . . God is just and loving."[64]

The perplexity that Morris and Davis express appears to be more than a paradox; we seem to stare contradiction right in the face. It can be expressed in the form of an inconsistent triad, a set of three premises, the conjunction of any two of which logically entails the falsity of the third:

(1) God is almighty, perfectly loving and just, and desires that all of his children be saved.

(2) Salvation comes only in and through one's knowledge and personal acceptance of Christ and his atonement.

(3) Vast numbers of God's children have lived and died never having heard of Christ, let alone having had a fair chance to accept his salvific gift.

The third premise appears indisputable, forcing us to give up either the first or the second, both of which seem warranted on biblical authority. So how is this inconsistent triad to be resolved?

Christian Solutions. Christian theologians are not without answers, most of which have been grouped into three broad categories: restrictivism, universalism, and "wider-hope" theories. Restrictivists hold that all who, prior to death, do not know of and accept Christ's salvific gift will be damned.[65] Universalists argue that eventually all mankind will be saved, although there are several variations on this theme.[66]

Between the two extremes—restrictivism and universalism—wider-hope theories affirm that while salvation may not be universally achieved, it is nonetheless universally *accessible*. There are basically three wider-hope views: inclusivism, universal evangelization before death, and eschatological evangelization. Inclusivists believe that while Christ's atonement is ontologically necessary for salvation, it is not epistemically necessary. "Those who never hear the gospel of Christ may nevertheless attain salvation before they die if they respond in faith to the revelation they do have."[67] Those who believe in universal evangelization *before death* advance three main stances: (1) all who seek God will find him in this life; (2) all people who have not heard the gospel will have that opportunity at the moment of dying; and (3) God will judge the unevangelized by how they would have responded had they heard the gospel message (middle knowledge). Proponents of eschatological evangelization affirm that the unevangelized will hear and have the chance to receive the gospel after this life; whether it occurs immediately after death or in a purgatory-like state is in dispute, but both affirm that persons must freely accept Christ.

Proponents all claim biblical warrant for their respective positions. But this is precisely the problem. For instance, in 1 Corinthians 15:29, Paul alludes to a contemporaneous Christian practice of living persons being baptized on behalf of the dead. *Die Taufe für die Toten*, a study by German scholar Mathis Rissi, reveals that this verse has been interpreted in over a hundred different ways.[68] Many of these interpretations are mutually exclusive, and, meanwhile, people with salvation at stake live and die with no way to definitively resolve the issue by appealing to the Bible.

Joseph Smith and Salvation for the Unevangelized. Joseph received a number of revelations that offer to settle the question definitively. Interestingly, the answer can be seen as a comprehensive synthesis of all the major Christian responses, allowing one to make sense of all the biblical data. It affirms important strands of universalism, inclusivism, and restrictivism, all of which coherently coalesce in a doctrine of postmortem evangelization. What makes this synthesis of otherwise inconsistent ideas possible is God's revelations to Joseph, which affirm that in the eschaton, there are multiple degrees of salvation within three broad kingdoms of glory.[69] Salvation, Joseph clearly taught, is not an all-or-nothing affair.

What Joseph's revelations articulated is *very* good news, indeed, evidencing our Savior's love, grace, and mercy, while confirming universalism in four ways. First, resurrection is universal; Christ has saved the entire human family from permanent bodily death.[70] Second, "all children who die before they arrive at the years of accountability [will be] saved in the celestial kingdom of heaven [the highest kingdom of glory]" (Doctrine and Covenants 137:10). Third, all persons except the "sons of perdition" will ultimately be saved from the second death ("an everlasting death as to things pertaining unto righteousness," for "the plan of redemption could have no power" [Alma 12:32]), and, most significantly, fourth, the saved will all dwell in a heavenly kingdom, the glory of the least of which exceeds all human comprehension.[71]

The inclusivist insights in these revelations give good news, including (1) God desires the salvation of all of his children and invites everyone to come unto him;[72] (2) God endows all of his children with "the Light of Christ," which enables them to distinguish between good and evil and which, without overriding agency, inclines them toward God;[73] (3) God reveals saving light in addition to the Light of Christ to every people;[74] and (4) God will base his judgment on how faithfully human persons adhere to whatever light they have.[75] The Book of Mormon makes clear that God does not confine his revelations to Christians.[76]

Joseph's revelations also confirm the partial truth of restrictivism. The exclusivist conditions for salvation in the celestial kingdom are clearly set out.[77] Thus, the risen Lord affirms his earlier teaching that "strait is the gate, and narrow is the way, which leadeth unto . . . exaltation" (Doctrine and Covenants 132:22; cf. Matthew 7:14). The good news is that, in God's graciousness and love, he will ensure that every person, either on this side or the other side of veil, will have a full chance to satisfy these conditions.

The crown of Joseph's contribution to this issue is found in the revelations he received from Christ affirming postmortal evangelization and proxy sacraments for the dead performed by the living. Modern-day revelation affirms that Christ himself initiated the work of redemption of the dead when he descended into spirit prison in the period between his death on the cross and his resurrection (Doctrine and Covenants 138). This knowledge and the sealing authority to perform these sacred ordinances came to Joseph through a series of revelations, the most pertinent of which was Elijah's restoration of the sealing powers of the priesthood (Doctrine and Covenants 110). Holders of these sealing powers are authorized to perform vicarious ordinances for the dead, all of which, if the partakers thereof are faithful to the covenants related to the ordinances, are efficacious for eternity. In a powerful funeral sermon delivered in Nauvoo, Illinois, on August 15, 1840, the Prophet disclosed that the Lord would permit the Saints to be baptized on behalf of their friends and relatives who had departed this life. He told the Saints, "The plan of salvation was calculated to save all who were willing to obey the requirements of the law of God."[78]

On the basis of subsequent revelations, Joseph taught that the living and the dead are dependent upon each other for salvation: "They [the dead] without us cannot be made perfect—neither can we without our dead be made perfect" (Doctrine and Covenants 128:15). The vicarious ordinances to help accomplish this mutual perfection, he later explained, include not only baptisms for the dead but also the endowment of the holy priesthood and sealings of family members to each other for eternity.

I began this section by outlining the soteriological problem of evil, which I expressed in the form of an inconsistent triad. Joseph Smith affirmed that Jesus Christ, himself, is the resolution to this inconsistent triad. Christ, Joseph declared, has revealed himself to be not only Lord but also Savior of both the living and the dead. His arms are extended to all people of all times and places.[79]

Conclusions

In bringing his story of Christian theology to a close, Olson explores the possibility of Christian unity in the future. He suggests that "diverse voices, when brought together in harmony, can make a chorus out of cacophony and a choir out of confusion."[80] Such harmony might be accomplished, Olson believes, with the arrival of a new Christian theologian—perhaps one from a third-world country who has fresh ideas.[81]

After pondering Olson's story of Christian theology, I find his hoped-for solution puzzling indeed. If the gifted theologians who have graced the Christian scene for the past two thousand years have failed to unite the diverse voices, why hold out hope that one will yet do so? Can a person by reason alone find out God? (cf. Job 11:7). The history of Christian theology demonstrates the dubiety of such a method. The need for revelation seems to be unavoidable.

So what about God? Where is he? Can he speak? Will he speak? Did he speak to Joseph Smith? Joseph Smith challenged Christianity with answers he claimed were revealed, not reasoned. Some may conclude the truth of his claims from the mere fact of his witness, but Joseph never advocated this sort of logical or circular justification. Rather, because he knew from experience that God will speak now, Joseph taught that if a person wants to know the truth, he or she should "search the revelations which we publish, and ask your Heavenly Father, in the name of His Son Jesus Christ, to manifest the truth unto you, and if you do it with an eye single to His glory nothing doubting, He will answer you by the power of His Holy Spirit. You will then know for yourselves."[82]

Notes

David Paulsen gratefully acknowledges the substantial assistance of Craig Atkinson, Adam Bentley, Robb Duffin, Brett McDonald, Abraham Skousen, and Tyler Stoehr in the research and writing of this paper.

1. Roger E. Olson, *The Story of Christian Theology: Twenty Centuries of Tradition and Reform* (Downers Grove, Ill.: InterVarsity, 1999), 25.

2. Especially pertinent to this point is the declaration in Hebrews 5:4 that "no man taketh this honour unto himself, but he that is called of God, as was Aaron." Divine authority cannot be acquired at will. Thus, *a fortiori*, as Peter explained to Simon Magus, who wanted the power to bestow the Holy Ghost, it cannot be acquired by purchase: "Thy money perish with thee, because thou hast thought that the gift of God may be purchased with money. Thou hast neither part nor lot in this matter: for thy heart is not right in the sight of God. Repent therefore of this thy wickedness, and pray God, if perhaps the thought of thine heart may be forgiven thee" (Acts 8:20–22).

3. Acts 10:9–17, 34–48; 15:1–11, 23–29. The apostles claim divine guidance for this decision in Acts 15:28: "For it seemed good to the Holy Ghost, and to us, to lay upon you no greater burden than these necessary things."

4. Olson, *Story of Christian Theology*, 25.

5. Olson, *Story of Christian Theology*, 610–13.

6. Elsewhere I have argued at length that no natural or cultural explanations can adequately account for the range, depth, and unique synthesis of Joseph Smith's vision. Even the most determined cultural reductionist must still, in the end, deal with Joseph's claims to divine revelation. See my article

"The Search for Cultural Origins of Mormon Doctrines," in *Excavating Mormon Pasts: The New Historiography of the Last Half Century* (Salt Lake City: Greg Kofford Books, 2004), 27–52.

7. Richard Lyman Bushman, *Believing History: Latter-day Saint Essays* (New York: Columbia University Press, 2004), 272–73.

8. Dean C. Jesse, ed., *The Papers of Joseph Smith*, 2 vols. (Salt Lake City: Deseret Book, 1992), 2:155.

9. Lee M. McDonald, *The Formation of the Christian Biblical Canon*, rev. ed. (Peabody, Mass.: Hendrickson Publishers, 1995). This issue is discussed by Carl Mosser and Paul Owen, "How Wide the Divide? A Mormon and an Evangelical in Conversation," *FARMS Review* 11, no. 2 (1999): 5–6. They assert that the Bible *does not say* that it is insufficient in providing information on how one is to be saved and go on to state what they believe is the real issue: "(1) What body of information is necessary for salvation? and (2) Does the Bible contain this information? If the Bible contains a sufficient body of information for the establishment and continuing proclamation of the Christian gospel, then no more scripture is *necessary*." They cite the third and fourth Articles of Faith to support the view that even Latter-day Saints would have to agree that faith, repentance, water baptism, and the laying on of hands for the gift of the Holy Ghost is sufficient for salvation; and all of this is taught in the Bible.

Additionally, Mosser and Owen quote Grudem's "concise and helpful definition" of the "sufficiency of Scripture": "The *sufficiency of Scripture* means that Scripture contains all the words of God which he intends his people to have at each stage of redemptive history, and that it contains everything we need God to tell us for salvation, for trusting him perfectly and for obeying him perfectly." According to the "Advent Argument," the next *stage of redemptive history* has not yet arrived (the Second Coming); therefore, at this time, the canon is closed in practice, but can reasonably be said to be open in theory. Mosser and Owen, "How Wide the Divide?" 5, 8, emphasis in original.

10. The Westminster Assembly of Divines, convened by the English Parliament in 1643, completed the *Confession of Faith, Shorter Catechism and Larger Catechism* in 1647. These documents have served as the doctrinal standards, subordinate to the word of God, for Presbyterian and other churches around the world. The text of the *Confession* is that adopted by the Orthodox Presbyterian Church in 1936. It is derived from a 1646 manuscript edited by S. W. Carruthers and incorporates revisions adopted by American Presbyterian churches as early as 1788. Database online. Available from http://www.opc.org/documents/standards.html.

11. G. H. Joyce, "Revelation," *Catholic Encyclopedia*, Database online, available from http://www.newadvent.org/.

12. Here, McDonald's historical study demonstrates that the scripture available and used by the earliest Christians was much more expansive than

the present closed canon. According to McDonald, "even in regard to the OT canon, it has been shown that the early church's collections of scriptures were considerably broader in scope than those presently found in either the Catholic or Protestant canons and that they demonstrated much more flexibility than our present collections allow" (254). McDonald recognizes a disturbing inconsistency between the content and understanding of scripture in the days of Christ and the earliest Christians and the content and understood "closed-ness" of today's scriptures.

13. McDonald identifies several ancient writings that purport to tell us about Christ but were left out of the current canon of the Church. He mentions specifically the Apocryphal writings and Pseudepigrapha as well as the *agrapha* (literally, unwritten—isolated sayings of Jesus that were preserved in first instance by oral tradition and eventually found their way into the early church fathers, in ancient manuscripts, and in some apocryphal sources). He suggests that inasmuch as these sources can be proven authentic and useful, they ought to inform our modern understanding of Christ. But he also firmly states that "I for one am not in favor of rejecting the present biblical canon in order to create *a new closed canon of scriptures*" (257). And concerning the currently *known* collection of noncanonical literature, he concludes "that there are no other ancient documents which are on the whole *more* reliable in informing the church's faith than our present biblical canon, even though we have suggested that some noncanonical sources are *as* reliable in their portrayal of the teaching and preaching of early Christianity" (257). It would seem then, that he would leave the canon open for early documents, which would add to our understanding of Christ.

14. McDonald uses as an example the epistle to the Hebrews: "Although there was considerable doubt about [its] authorship . . . among the church fathers, the book nevertheless was included in the biblical canon because its message was both relevant and important to the Christian communities that adopted and preserved it as scripture." Perhaps McDonald reveals his own opinion in his concluding question on the issue: "Is it not the intrinsic worth of the writing to the church in establishing its identity and facilitating its ministry that is the ultimate criterion for canonicity?" (255).

15. As McDonald shows, the Bible as closed canon is not accepted on the authority of the biblical writings themselves, but on the decisions of a collection of church leaders hundreds of years removed from the time of Christ. Thus, the legitimacy of a closed canon rests heavily on one's answer to his question: "Was the church in the Nicene and post-Nicene eras infallible in its decisions or not?" (256).

16. Larry E. Dahl and Donald Q. Cannon, eds., *Encyclopedia of Joseph Smith's Teachings* (Salt Lake City: Bookcraft, 1997), 73.

17. Dahl and Cannon, *Encyclopedia*, 73.

18. All extent accounts of the vision (1832, 1835, 1838, 1842, 1840, 1869, 1871, 1874, 1842, 1843, and 1844) corroborate Joseph's claim of both seeing and hearing Jesus Christ. While unified on this issue, the accounts vary in other ways. See Milton V. Backman, Jr., "Joseph Smith's Recitals of the First Vision," *Ensign* 15 (January 1985): 8–17; Dean C. Jessee, "The Earliest Documented Accounts of Joseph Smith's First Vision," in *Opening the Heavens: Accounts of Divine Manifestations,* ed. John W. Welch (Salt Lake City: Deseret Book; Provo, Utah: Brigham Young University Press, 2005), 1–33; James B. Allen and John W. Welch, "The Appearance of the Father and the Son to Joseph Smith in 1820," in *Opening the Heavens,* 35–75.

19. In the 1832 and 1835 accounts, Joseph receives a forgiveness of sins, taken from Scott H. Faulring, ed., *An American Prophet's Record: The Diaries and Journals of Joseph Smith* (Salt Lake City: Signature Books, 1989), 3, 4–6, 50–51, 59; the command to "go not after" the existing churches is recounted in the 1838 (canonized) version, the 1842 "Wentworth Letter" account, as well as Pratt's later accounts (1840, 1869, 1871, 1874); the promise of a later restoration is taken from the 1842 account in Joseph Smith, *History of The Church of Jesus Christ of Latter-day Saints,* 6 vols. (Salt Lake City: Deseret Book 1980), 4:536, where the exact language reads: "I was expressly commanded 'to go not after them,' at the same time receiving a promise that the fullness of the Gospel should at some future time be made known unto me."

20. "At times, however, this special aura of authority could present problems for Christianity as some of the apostles' successors introduced their own ideas into the stream of early theology. As we will see, occasionally these fathers of the generation after the apostles gave the gospel their own unique interpretations" (Olson, 40–41). The introduction of personal ideas by persons who could not definitively and authoritatively say "thus saith the Lord," Olson says, was the most problematic aspect of giving precedent to those who could trace chronologically through relationships back to the Savior.

21. G. H. Joyce, "The Pope," *Catholic Encyclopedia.*

22. J. Wilhelm, "Apostolic Succession," *Catholic Encyclopedia.*

23. In practice, the Church of Constantinople has functioned for centuries as the church responsible for guiding and preserving the worldwide unity of the family of self-governing Orthodox Churches. But it must be noticed that this responsibility is merely a practical and pastoral one. It carries no sacramental or juridical power with it and it is possible that in the future this function may pass to some other church.

24. Olson, *Story of Christian Theology,* 370–71.

25. Jean Bainvel, "Tradition and Living Magisterium," *Catholic Encyclopedia.*

26. Oliver Cowdery in *Messenger and Advocate* 1 (October 1834): 15.

27. See also Brian Q. Cannon and *BYU Studies* Staff, "Seventy Contemporaneous Priesthood Restoration Documents," in *Opening the Heavens*, 215–63. Presupposed here is authority existing in varying degrees within a framework of various offices, just as the New Testament church attests. As the sixth Article of Faith states, "We believe in the same organization that existed in the Primitive Church, namely, apostles, prophets, pastors, teachers, evangelists, and so forth."

28. While the exact date is not known, scholars place the event sometime between May 15, and the end of June 1829. For a fuller treatment of this issue, see "The Restoration of the Priesthood (Doctrine and Covenants 13 and 27)" by Charles R. Harrell in *Studies in Scripture, Vol. 1: The Doctrine and Covenants*, ed. Kent P. Jackson and Robert L. Millet (Salt Lake City: Deseret Book, 1984), 86–99.

29. In Doctrine and Covenants 27:12, the Lord confirms this bestowal of divine authority: "I have sent unto you [Peter, James, and John], by whom I have ordained you and confirmed you to be apostles, and especial witnesses of my name, and bear the keys of your ministry and of the same things which I revealed unto them."

30. G. R. Evans, *Problems of Authority in the Reformation Debates* (New York: Cambridge University Press, 1992), 219, 223, 218. "Both sides in the sixteenth century could broadly agree that 'every power which was in the college of the apostles is now in the Church.' The difference of opinion was about the distribution of that power (with its connotation of 'dominion') in the Church. . . . They said that the ordained ministry had, not a special or higher power, but a license to 'use' a power which belongs to all Christians equally. This *usus* is what is bestowed by popular assent (*plebes assensu*) and taken away by the same means" (219). "The Trent Fathers found the same contentions in Calvin's writings as in Luther's that if bishops alone (*soli episcopi*) confer 'priesthood' (*sacerdotium*), they do it *illegitime*, for the true agent (*agens*) and conferring authority (*conferens*) is the people. It is the people who have *auctoritas et potestas* from God to ordain" (223). The Protestant reformers described all Christians as 'equally priests' . . . with an 'equal power.' . . . Luther's case in *Concerning the Ministry* (the treatise he wrote for Bohemia in 1523) is set out like this: Christ is our High Priest, and through union with him we are all priests, without rite of ordination, and without having a special character impressed on us. The primary office of ministry, the ministry of the Word, is, he says, common to all Christians. There is no other baptism than the one which any Christian can bestow; no other remembrance of the Lord's Supper than that which any Christian can observe; there is no other kind of sin than that which any Christian can bind or loose; any Christian can pray; any Christian may judge of doctrine. These make up the royal and priestly office. The emphasis

here was upon the equality of individuals, not upon the collective character of the 'Priesthood of all believers', that is, their shared participation in the single Priesthood which is unique to Christ" (218–19).

31. Dahl and Cannon, *Encyclopedia,* 59.

32. Dahl and Cannon, *Encyclopedia,* 56–57.

33. In the year 2000, the First Presidency and the Quorum of the Twelve of The Church of Jesus Christ of Latter-day Saints issued a declaration to the world entitled "The Living Christ: The Testimony of the Apostles, The Church of Jesus Christ of Latter-day Saints." This is an official statement of Latter-day Saint Christology. I will reference Joseph's revelations to corresponding passages in the Declaration.

34. Veli-Matti Kärkkäinen, *Christology: A Global Introduction* (Grand Rapids, Mich.: Baker Academic, 2003), 10, 12. As a general rule, the "from above" method was dominant in the early centuries, up until the enlightenment. During the enlightenment, the main orientation of Christology was "from below."

35. "Basis," Constitution of the World Council of Churches, http://www.wcc-coe.org/wcc/who/con-e.html. The World Council of Churches is an umbrella organization for cooperation between over a hundred churches worldwide.

36. Kärkkäinen, *Christology,* 120.

37. These include Roman Catholic John Dominic Crossan and seventy-three other scholars.

38. Kärkkäinen, *Christology,* 45.

39. Acts 26:14; 1 Corinthians 9:1; Joseph Smith–History 1:16–20; Doctrine and Covenants 110:1–10.

40. See, for example, Doctrine and Covenants 76:22–24 and 110:2–4, quoted later in the paper.

41. See also 2 Nephi 25:26; Mosiah 15:1; Alma 7:9–10; 34:9–16.

42. Among the prominent thinkers who have drawn this distinction are Blaise Pascal, Martin Buber, Jehuda Halevi, Charles Hartshorne, and Clark Pinnock. Pascal believed in a personal God. During his spiritual conversion experience, Pascal penned these words: "From about half-past ten in the evening until about half-past midnight. Fire. The God of Abraham, the God of Isaac, the God of Jacob. Not of the philosophers and intellectuals. . . . The God of Jesus Christ" (Marvin R. O'Connell, *Blaise Pascal: Reasons of the Heart* [Grand Rapids, Mich.: Eerdmans, 1997], 96). Jehuda Halevi argued that philosophy's practice of inference has led to false notions of God, which includes the belief that "God neither benefits nor injures, nor knows anything of our prayers or offerings, our obedience or disobedience" (Isaak Heinemann, ed., "Jehuda Halevi: Kuzari," *Three Jewish Philosophers* [New York: Harper and Row,

1965], 113–4). In the words of Martin Buber, "the man who says, 'I love in God the father of man,' has essentially already renounced the God of the philosophers in his innermost heart" (Martin Buber, *To Hallow This Life: An Anthology*, ed. Jacob Trapp [New York: Harper and Brothers, 1958], 10). For a rigorous defense of the claim that these two god-descriptions cannot refer to the same being see Norbert Samuelson, "That the God of the Philosophers is not the God of Abraham, Isaac, and Jacob," *Harvard Theological Review* 65, no. 1 (January 1972): 1–27. And see also Anthony Kenny, *The God of the Philosophers* (Oxford: Oxford University Press, 1979), especially chapter 10, "The God of Reason and the God of Faith," 121–29.

43. I use the definite description, "*the* god of the philosophers" to refer to god-concepts which are significantly constituted by attributes derived through rational theologizing without explicit basis in biblical revelation, including most notably those attributes enumerated in the text corresponding to this note. So understood, the description encompasses both the god of scholastic theism and the god of nineteenth-century transcendental idealism—the two god-concepts which bear the brunt of William James's pragmatic critique. There are, of course, significant differences between the various gods denominated by my description. For instance, the god of Thomas Aquinas is a person while the god of F. H. Bradley is not.

44. Of course, these summary descriptions of God are a gloss over the richly diverse portraits of deity found in the different Christian theological traditions. There is no time to identify their most fundamental differences, let alone delineate their subtle nuances. Instead, I will focus on Joseph's vision of God. Partisans of particular Christian theologies will have to make more specific comparisons, discerning which aspects of their own views are confirmed and which are challenged by those of Joseph.

45. The "living God" reference is in several places in the book of Hebrews: 9:14, 10:31, and 12:22.

46. Dahl and Cannon, *Encyclopedia*, 295. More particularly, God revealed that that he had a body of flesh and bones. Joseph continues: "That which is without body or parts is nothing. There is no other God in heaven but that God who has flesh and bones" (293).

47. "And that he was once a man like us; yea, that God himself, the Father of us all, dwelt on an earth, *the same as Jesus Christ himself did*; and I will show it from the Bible. . . . The Scriptures inform us that Jesus said, As the Father hath power in Himself, even so hath the Son power—to do what? Why, what the Father did. The answer is obvious—in a manner to lay down His body and take it up again. As the Father hath power in Himself, so hath the Son power in Himself, to lay down His life and take it again, so He has a body of His own. The Son doeth what he hath seen the Father do: then the Father hath some day laid

down His life and taken it again; so He has a body of His own; each one will be in His body; and yet the sectarian world believe the body of the Son is identical with the Father's." Dahl and Cannon, *Encyclopedia*, 295.

48. Many Christian thinkers are showing a renewed interest in this kind of trinitarian thought. One of the preeminent theological ideas that is circling in the midst of this intellectual revival is that of social trinitarianism. Social trinitarianism, or the social analogy of the Trinity, reasserts the religious teaching that the Godhead is composed of three separate and distinct persons who are perfectly one in thought, word, intention, and action. Those who affirm this doctrinal notion of deity largely base their perspective on primitive Christian views of the Godhead and the economic vision of the Trinity.

49. Dallas Willard, *The Divine Conspiracy: Rediscovering Our Hidden Life in God* (San Francisco: Harper, 1998), 244–45.

50. Truman G. Madsen, *Eternal Man* (Salt Lake City: Deseret Book, 1970), 23–24.

51. Dahl and Cannon, *Encyclopedia*, 341. Speaking of our conscious identity, our spirit, Joseph taught:

> Where did it come from? All learned men and doctors of divinity say that God created it in the beginning; but it is not so: the very idea lessens man in my estimation. I do not believe the doctrine; I know better. Hear it, all ye ends of the world; for God has told me so; and if you don't believe me, it will not make the truth without effect. . . . We say that God himself is a self-existent being. Who told you so? It is correct enough; but how did it get into your heads? Who told you that man did not exist in like manner upon the same principles? Man does exist upon the same principles. . . . The mind or the intelligence which man possesses is co-equal [co-eternal] with God himself. (Dahl and Cannon, *Encyclopedia*, 340–41).

52. Madsen, *Eternal Man*, 24–25.

53. "The Origin of Man" (1909), quoted in *Messages of the First Presidency of the Church of Jesus Christ of Latter-day Saints*, comp. James R. Clark, 6 vols. (Salt Lake City: Bookcraft, 1965–1975), 4:205.

54. Dahl and Cannon, *Encyclopedia*, 134.

55. Dahl and Cannon, *Encyclopedia*, 519. The preceding remarks were part of the King Follett Discourse, Nauvoo, April 7, 1844.

56. Joseph Fielding Smith, ed., *Teachings of the Prophet Joseph Smith* (Salt Lake City: Deseret Book, 1976), 347–48.

57. *Teachings of the Prophet Joseph Smith*, 348.

58. Robert L. Millet, *Alive in Christ: The Miracle of Spiritual Rebirth* (Salt Lake City: Deseret Book Company, 1997), 75; Elder Orson F. Whitney observed

that "The fall had a twofold direction—downward, yet forward. It brought man into the world and set his feet upon progression's highway." Forace Green, comp., *Cowley & Whitney on Doctrine* (Salt Lake City: Bookcraft, 1963), 287.

59. Dahl and Cannon, *Encyclopedia*, 238.

60. See 2 Nephi 2:21, 26; Mosiah 3:19; Mosiah 16:3–5; Alma 12:22; Alma 42:7–9; Doctrine and Covenants 20:18–20.

61. Andrew F. Ehat and Lyndon W. Cook, *The Words of Joseph Smith: The Contemporary Accounts of the Nauvoo Discourses of the Prophet Joseph*, Religious Studies Monograph Series, no. 6 (Provo, Utah: Religious Studies Center, Brigham Young University, 1980), 33.

62. Carl Mosser, email message to author, January 2, 2005.

63. Thomas V. Morris, *The Logic of God Incarnate* (Ithaca, N.Y.: Cornell University Press, 1986), 174–75. Morris is not sure how to resolve the "scandal," although he offers several solutions, including universalism (176) and inclusivism (177). "I think the most that can reasonably be said," he concludes, "is that a measure of pious agnosticism is appropriate here" (180). Reflection on the soteriological problem of evil is hardly new in the history of Christianity as evidenced by Dr. Jeffrey A. Trumbower's recent book, *Rescue for the Dead: the Posthumous Salvation of Non-Christians in Early Christianity* (New York: Oxford University Press, 2001).

64. Stephen T. Davis, "Universalism, Hell and the Fate of the Ignorant," *Modern Theology* 6, no. 2 (January 1990): 176.

65. For the biblical proof-texts for which the restrictivists base their position see John Sanders, *No Other Name: An Investigation into the Destiny of the Unevangelized* (Eugene, Ore.: Wipf and Stock, 2001).

66. Some universalists hold that God sovereignly overrides human freedom unilaterally, fulfilling his desire to save all mankind. Others contend that all persons, given eons of time, will eventually *freely* choose salvation in Christ. Another division separates universalists into restorationists and ultra-universalists. Restorationists believe that the hell is something that can be escaped, a purgatory that one may leave through accepting Christ; ultra-universalists reject any notion of hell, believing that all will be saved immediately at or following death.

67. Sanders, *No Other Name*, 215.

68. Mathis Rissi, *Die Taufe für die Toten* (Zürich: Zwingli, 1962).

69. See Doctrine and Covenants 76:50–113.

70. Book of Mormon prophet Amulek is explicit: "The day cometh that *all* shall rise from the dead and stand before God, and be judged according to their works. . . . Now, this restoration shall come to *all*, both old and young, both bond and free, both male and female, both the wicked and the righteous" (Alma 11:41, 44; emphasis added). See also 2 Nephi 9:22; Jacob 6:9; Alma 40:4–10; 3 Nephi 26:4–5; Doctrine and Covenants 29:26; 76:15–85; 88:14–32.

71. "And this is the gospel, the glad tidings, . . . that he came into the world, even Jesus, to be crucified for the world, and to bear the sins of the world, and to sanctify the world, and to cleanse it from all unrighteousness; *That through him all might be saved* . . . except those sons of perdition who deny the Son after the Father has revealed him" (Doctrine and Covenants 76:40–43; emphasis added).

> And thus we saw, in the heavenly vision, *the glory of the telestial, which surpasses all understanding;* And no man knows it except him to whom God has revealed it. And thus we saw the glory of the terrestrial which excels in all things the glory of the telestial, even in glory, and in power, and in might, and in dominion. And thus we saw the glory of the celestial, which excels in all things—where God, even the Father, reigns upon his throne forever and ever. (Doctrine and Covenants 76:89–92; emphasis added)

72. (1) 2 Nephi 26:33; Alma 5:33.

73. (2) The religious teaching that all people, regardless of the time of their birth in relation to the birth, life, death, and resurrection of the Savior Jesus Christ, are able to access the inspiration of Heaven, can be found throughout Christian history. One such example is found in Trumbower's statement that even, "according to Justin Martyr (ca. 150 CE) Abraham, Socrates, Heraclitus, and others had had a share of the Logos, which was later fully embodied in Christ." See *Rescue for the Dead*, 49.

74. (3) Alma 29:8, see also 2 Nephi 29:12.

75. (4) Joseph taught: "He [God] will judge them, 'not according to what they have not, but according to what they have,' those who have lived without law, will be judged without law, and those who have a law, will be judged by that law" (Dahl and Cannon, *Encyclopedia*, 389). See also Doctrine and Covenants 82:3; Alma 39:6.

76. Alma 29:8; Compare with the following pronouncements by the First Presidency in 1978:

> The great religious leaders of the world such as Mohammed, Confucius, and the Reformers, as well as philosophers including Socrates, Plato, and others, received a portion of God's light. Moral truths were given to them by God to enlighten whole nations and to bring a higher level of understanding to individuals. The Hebrew prophets prepared the way for the coming of Jesus Christ, the promised Messiah, who should provide salvation for all mankind who believe in the gospel. Consistent with these truths, we believe that God has given and will give to all peoples sufficient knowledge to help them on their way to eternal salvation, either in this life or in the life to come . . . Our

message therefore is one of special love and concern for the eternal welfare of all men and women, regardless of religious belief, race, or nationality, knowing that we are truly brothers and sisters because we are sons and daughters of the same Eternal Father. Robert L. Millet, *The Mormon Faith: A New Look at Christianity* (Salt Lake City: Deseret Book, 1998), 203–4.

77. See Doctrine and Covenants 76:51–69. For instance, the restrictivist conditions for entrance into the celestial kingdom include faith in Christ, repentance, baptism by immersion for the remission of sins, receipt of the Gift of the Holy Ghost by the laying on of hands, and enduring faithfully unto the end.

78. Ehat and Cook, *Words of Joseph Smith*, 49.

79. Of the prophet to whom Christ revealed this good news and on whom he restored the sealing powers to redeem the dead, the apostle John Taylor wrote these canonized words: "Joseph Smith, the Prophet and Seer of the Lord, has done more, save Jesus only, for the salvation of men in this world, than any other man that ever lived in it" (Doctrine and Covenants 135:3).

80. Olson, *Story of Christian Theology*, 591, 609.

81. Olson, *Story of Christian Theology*, 612.

82. *Teachings of the Prophet Joseph Smith*, 11. Joseph continues, "You will not then be dependent on man for the knowledge of God; nor will there be any room for speculation" (11–12).

Joseph Smith's Theological Challenges: From Revelation and Authority to Metaphysics

Richard J. Mouw

In his published dialogue with the Evangelical theologian Craig Blomberg, Stephen Robinson observed that one of the factors that makes it so difficult for Mormons and Evangelicals to understand each other is the issue of terminology. The theology of the Latter-day Saints, he noted, has not been shaped by the same developments that Protestants have experienced since the days of the Reformation. This means, Robinson said, that "Latter-day Saints are generally quite naïve when it comes to the technical usage of theological language."[1]

David Paulsen is one of several Latter-day Saint scholars who have provided, in a decidedly non-naïve manner, helpful explanations of Mormon doctrines in a careful interaction with thinkers in the mainstream of historic Christianity. He has focused—and I think helpfully—on the question of authority. Certainly when we Evangelicals have critiqued Latter-day Saint thought, we have typically focused, not on the issue of authority as such, but on *Joseph Smith's* claim to authority. In doing so we have largely limited the options to the ones described by Joseph Smith himself. In his account of the reactions of his Protestant neighbors to his testimony regarding the First Vision he wrote, "I felt much like Paul, when he made his defense before King Agrippa, and related the account of the vision he had when he saw a light, and heard a voice; . . . there were but few who believed him; some said he was dishonest, others said he was mad" (Joseph Smith–History 1:24). And so has it continued to be in the Protestant world; we have responded to Joseph's claim that the ancient prophetic office had been restored in his own person by insisting that he was either a clever huckster or a possessed agent of Satan.

David Paulsen challenges us to look more directly at the theological issues proper. To do this, we must temporarily bracket the questions about the truth of Joseph Smith's actual claims to have directly encountered the members of the Godhead, and to think instead about the very possibility of authoritative new revelations. As Paulsen lists the questions that he asks us to consider, he rightly prefaces the question of whether God has actually spoken through the prophet Joseph Smith with the more fundamental questions: "So what about God? Where is he? Can he speak? Will he speak?"[2]

I do think it is good for those representing traditional Christian thought to engage in the theological exercise of bracketing the specific concerns about Joseph Smith's personality in order to explore the more basic questions posed by Paulsen. Whatever one makes of the account, say, of the First Vision, there is no doubt that it has provided the foundation for developing a highly influential religious perspective and that it is important for us to examine critically the basic features of that perspective. I once came across a comment by Karl Barth, in response to someone who had criticized him for making positive use of something that Søren Kierkegaard had written, with the critic insisting that Kierkegaard was not reliable because he had been mentally unstable. Barth replied that while Kierkegaard may have been mentally unstable, it is important to attend to the fact that many mentally stable people agreed with Kierkegaard's views. Similarly, in bracketing our assessments of Joseph Smith's character, we can acknowledge that many clear-thinking Latter-day Saints have been deeply influenced by the theological perspective set forth by the founder of Mormonism. It is no small question why that perspective has taken such a firm hold in the lives of so many people. And there is no doubt that the fundamental emphasis on the very idea of a "living prophet" has resonated in many Latter-day Saint hearts and lives.

As David Paulsen rightly notes, the question of whether we can acknowledge new teachings that are in some sense to be accorded equal weight to the revelations set forth in the Old and New Testaments has long been a matter of major disagreement between Protestants and Roman Catholics.[3] The Catholic view is that there is a legitimate "development of dogma" that provides teachings that can be gathered together under the rubric of "tradition," and these teachings are to be received by the Christian community as the Spirit's continuing normative guidance to the church. Thus, for example, the doctrine of the virgin birth of Christ is to be believed because it is set forth in the New Testament, but the doctrine of the immaculate conception of Mary is to be believed because it came to be considered an authoritative extension of that biblical doctrine by the office of the *magisterium*.

The basic issue between Protestants and Catholics on this issue was addressed by the great American Jesuit theologian John Courtney Murray. He observes that since both Protestant and Catholic communities have experienced considerable theological development over the centuries, the issue is not whether to accept theological teachings that go beyond the formulations set forth in the Bible. Both Protestants and Catholics, for example, accept as authoritative those formulations about the Trinity that employ language and concepts—including the term *Trinity* itself—that go beyond the explicit language of the biblical writers. Where Protestants and Catholics differ, says Murray, is on questions of this sort: "What is legitimate development, what is organic growth in the understanding of . . . the primitive discipline of the church, and what, on the other hand, is accretion, additive increment, adulteration of the deposit, distortion of true Christian discipline . . . what are the valid dynamisms of development and what are the forces of distortion?"[4]

A key word here for understanding the Catholic perspective is "organic." When Catholic authorities exercise their teaching function, "they bring forth," in the words of the Vatican II document *Lumen Gentium*, "from the treasury of Revelation new things and old, making it bear fruit and vigilantly warding off any errors that threaten their flock."[5] This "bearing fruit" metaphor is often used to explain

how the Roman Church's magisterial deliverances are to the contents
of scripture as a piece of fruit is to the original seed. These teachings
do not, for Catholics, provide us with new information; rather, they
are considered an explanation of that which is already implicit in
biblical revelation.

As Murray's questions indicate, we Protestants worry that what
Catholics consider proper organic development is in fact an "adulteration of the deposit." Thus, we insist that various dogmas about Mary
and the teaching regarding papal infallibility are not only extrabiblical in their content but are actually incompatible with the "deposit"
of revealed truths in the scriptures. The doctrine of the Trinity, on
the other hand, is seen by Protestants as a legitimate doctrinal development because it does capture and does explicate the clear sense of
what the Bible teaches. While we believe that the original apostles
would not recognize various present-day teachings about Mary, we
believe that they could sing without any sense of puzzlement the
words of the classic Protestant hymn, "Holy, Holy, Holy! Merciful
and Mighty/God in three Persons, blessed Trinity."[6]

We can admit, then, that debates within historic Christianity
about adding to the original revelations contained in the Old and
New Testaments have a kind of rough parallel with, say, Protestant
differences with Mormonism's claims to new revelations. But we
cannot push the fact of that parallel too far. Joseph Smith did not
talk about a new magisterial teaching office; instead, he insisted on
a restored office of *prophet*. His new teachings, then, came not as
the result of reflections on the meaning of an original revelation
in the Old and New Testaments but from new information that
he claimed to receive directly from the members of the Godhead.
In this sense, it is not even so important that he brought forth the
Book of Mormon, now subtitled by The Church of Jesus Christ of
Latter-day Saints as "Another Testament of Jesus Christ." As Richard
Bushman has pointed out,

> From the outset doctrine came day by day in revelations to Joseph
> Smith. Those revelations comprised the backbone of belief, the doc-
> trine and covenants for the church. . . . [Indeed] most of the appli-
> cable Book of Mormon doctrines and principles were revealed

anew to Joseph Smith, and [they] derived their authority from the modern revelation as much as from the Book of Mormon.[7]

The real authority for Mormonism resides not in books but in deliverances from living prophets. The written word has power only as the record of prophetic utterances that have already been received.

Actually, if we are looking for parallels to the Mormon view of authority within mainstream Christianity, Pentecostalism provides us with a better example than does Roman Catholicism. Here, too, there is a strong emphasis on the present-day restoration of the supernatural gifts of the original apostolic era. Indeed, it would not be difficult to find in Pentecostal literature words similar to Joseph Smith's account, in an 1831 Kirkland deliverance, of the gifts that have been restored for the church; [8] on that occasion Joseph spoke of some being "given, by the Spirit of God, the word of wisdom," to others "the word of knowledge," to others "to have faith to be healed," to others "the working of miracles," as well as prophesying, "discerning of spirits," speaking in tongues, etc. (Doctrine and Covenants 46:17–26).

Here, too, though, the parallel is not strict. Pentecostals typically affirm a high view of biblical authority, insisting that while present-day prophecies may go beyond the content of the Bible, they may not conflict with biblical teaching. Indeed, the prophecies that are regularly delivered in Pentecostal circles are usually not doctrinal teachings at all. Rather, they have the character either of very specific pieces of counsel, as in, "Go ahead with the plans for a new church building," or warnings about judgments that will come about if people continue in their present course.[9] While Pentecostal Christians might not use the word "organic," they would insist that present-day prophecy must in an important sense "bring forth"—to use the words again of the Vatican II document quoted earlier—"from the treasury of Revelation new things and old, making it bear fruit and vigilantly warding off any errors that threaten their flock."

In contrast to "extrabiblical" themes in both Catholic and Pentecostal thought, Joseph Smith's view does not require strict continuity with the content of past revelations. The Mormon prophetic office is not strictly bound by its previous utterances. The prophet may even call for major teachings of the past to be repealed and for major practices that were once mandated to be overturned.[10] Joseph Smith's theology of the extrabiblical allows for and promotes an expectation of "newness" in the "extra" that goes beyond anything advocated in either Catholicism or Pentecostalism.

David Paulsen is right when he contends that Joseph Smith's "claim to direct revelation from God" in fact "challenges every variety of Christian thought and, at the same time, serves to ground all of Joseph's additional claims." To be sure, those claims may turn out to be, as Paulsen puts it, "biblically consistent, rationally plausible or existentially appealing"—but those features do not make them authoritative. What really counts, as Paulsen says, is that those claims "were directly revealed by God" to a living prophet.[11]

In the final analysis, then, after looking at the basic theological issues, we have no alternative but to "un-bracket" the question of the truth of Joseph Smith's claims to having received direct revelations from God. And that is obviously a key item for continuing dialogue. For now, however, I want simply to acknowledge the importance of a question that I referred to briefly earlier: Why has Joseph Smith's theology had such an appeal for so many people? Mormonism has gone from being a small and rather exotic manifestation of the restorationist-primitivist impulses that came to play in the half-century or so after the American Revolution to what is now an emerging world religion.

Joseph Smith saw that the restoration of the prophetic office brought doctrinal certainty amid what he described as "this war of words and tumult of opinions" (Joseph Smith–History 1:10) in the religious world of his own day—a factor that David Paulsen sees as commending Mormonism to our present theologically pluralistic environment. That is obviously an important attraction for many. But I see another factor also at work.

One of Joseph Smith's key doctrinal emphases was his theology of God proper. Although he and Mary Baker Eddy went in opposite directions on metaphysical issues—with Joseph arguing for a thorough-going physicalism and the founder of Christian Science insisting on a thorough-going mentalism—their respective theologies have had a similar spiritual result, namely, bringing God and human beings much closer together. Mrs. Eddy, for example, would endorse the Mormon claim that God and human beings are of the same species with her own teaching that "in divine science, man is the true image of God."[12]

This teaching is, of course, deeply offensive to both Jews and Christians, for whom the denial of a radical metaphysical distance between Creator and creature violates the biblical warnings against idolatry. But it is one thing to make that point, and another for Christians to ask ourselves whether the early- to mid-nineteenth-century movements that reduced this metaphysical distance can, in any significant way, be seen as a corrective to weaknesses in our own theology and practice.

Joseph Smith's theology, along with that of other restorationist-primitivist groups and Mrs. Eddy (and we can also mention here the transcendentalism of Joseph's contemporary Ralph Waldo Emerson) emerged in an environment shaped significantly by the high Calvinism of New England Puritanism. As a high Calvinist myself, I think I can make a case that the legitimate *metaphysical* distance between God and his human creatures as advocated by the Puritans tended to reinforce in the Puritan mind and heart an unhealthy *spiritual* distance from the Calvinist deity. Thus it should not surprise us that movements arose to shrink the spiritual distance, even if we must deeply regret that they did so by also shrinking the distance of Being.

There are correctives to this problem that New England Calvinism could have found within the resources of its own orthodox Christian theology. But whatever the efforts to draw on those resources at the time, they were not enough to stem the tide of the movements that challenged the metaphysics of Calvinism as such. When traditional Christians condemn those movements without also acknowledging the spiritual realities that the dissenting groups were addressing, we are missing an important opportunity for theological self-understanding.

David Paulsen has invited us to think long and hard about whether God is still alive and whether he can still speak new things to us.[13] I am willing to continue to debate that subject. But even more fundamental to me than the debate about whether or not God is still alive is the question of what it takes for a human being to enter into a restored positive relationship with a living God. And I find the actual words of Joseph Smith in dealing with this central concern to be a helpful place to focus. For example, on the occasion of the founding of The Church of Jesus Christ of Latter-day Saints in April 1830, Joseph proclaimed, "We know that all men must repent and believe on the name of Jesus Christ, and worship the Father in his name, and endure in faith on his name to the end, or they cannot be saved in the kingdom of God." And then he added, "And we know that justification through the grace of our Lord and Savior Jesus Christ is just and true; . . . to all those who love and serve God with all their mights, minds, and strength" (Doctrine and Covenants 20:29–31).

I have no problem saying these same words in addressing the basic issues of sin and salvation. I am pleased that Ezra Taft Benson asked that the hymn, "How Great Thou Art," be made a part of Latter-day Saint hymnody. I find it hopeful that we can sing these words together:

> And when I think that God, his Son not sparing,
> Sent him to die, I scarce can take it in,
> That on the cross my burden gladly bearing
> He bled and died to take away my sin,
> Then sings my soul, my Savior God, to thee,
> How great thou art! How great thou art![14]

My continuing question for my Latter-day Saint friends is whether we mean the same things by the words of this hymn, and, if we do, whether the metaphysics set forth by Joseph Smith attributes to God those features that grant him the power to save us. I can think of no more important subject for our ongoing conversations.

Notes

1. Craig L. Blomberg and Stephen E. Robinson, *How Wide the Divide? A Mormon and an Evangelical in Conversation* (Downers Grove, Ill.: InterVarsity Press, 1997), 13.

2. David Paulsen, "Joseph Smith Challenges the Theological World," in this volume, 202.

3. Paulsen, "Joseph Smith Challenges the Theological World," 179, 182–83.

4. John Courtney Murray, *The Problem of God: Yesterday and Today* (New Haven, Conn.: Yale University Press, 1964), 53.

5. Second Vatican Council, "Dogmatic Constitution on the Church," *Lumen Gentium* (November 21, 1964), chap. 3, sec. 25, http://www.vatican.va/archive/hist_councils/ii_vatican_council/documents/vat-ii_const_19641121_lumen-gentium_en.html.

6. Reginald Heber, "Holy, Holy, Holy" (1826), http://www.cyberhymnal.org/htm/h/o/holyholy.htm.

7. Richard L. Bushman, *Joseph Smith and the Beginnings of Mormonism* (Chicago: University of Illinois Press, 1984), 142.

8. For an account of how these various gifts were seeing as being restoried in the famous Pentecostal "Azousa Street Revival" of 1906, see Vinson Synon, *The Holiness-Pentecostal Movement in the United States* (Grand Rapids, Mich.: Eerdmans, 1971), 95–116.

9. For an account of how counsel regarding specific life-situations fits into the larger Pentecostal understanding of various modes of revelation, see Grant Wacker, *Heaven Below: Early Pentecostalism and American Culture* (Cambridge: Harvard University Press, 2001), 81–84.

10. See Doctrine and Covenants, Official Declarations 1 and 2.

11. See Paulsen, "Joseph Smith Challenges the Theological World," 177.

12. Mary Baker Eddy, *Science and Health with Key to the Scriptures* (1875; repr., Boston: The First Church of Christ, Scientist, 1991), 259.

13. See Paulsen, "Joseph Smith Challenges the Theological World," 177.

14. "How Great Thou Art," in *Hymns of The Church of Jesus Christ of Latter-day Saints* (Salt Lake City: The Church of Jesus Christ of Latter-day Saints, 1985), no. 86.

Speaking of Faith:
The Centrality of Epistemology and the Perils of Circularity

Randall Balmer

It is difficult for me to respond to David Paulsen. I am not—nor have I ever claimed to be—a theologian. I will not presume to engage many of the issues or to intrude on the conversations in his paper. I am intrigued, however, by several themes raised in his paper. I will comment, first, on the crisis of authority; second, on the centrality of epistemology and the perils of theological circularity; and third, on the quintessentially modern enterprise of apologetics.

The Crisis of Authority

Every religious tradition, sooner or later, has to deal with the issue of authority. Paulsen asserts that "apostolic authority is not something that can be chosen," and he goes on to review the story of Joseph Smith's calling as a prophet. Paulsen attributes the sorry history of conflict in the Christian church over the centuries to what he calls "the loss of apostolic authority and its attendant revelation."[1] This, of course, nicely sets up the case for the resumption of apostolic authority in the "latter days" in the person of Smith himself.

Paulsen rightly points out that the issue of authority has been vexing throughout Christian history. He cites the importance of Matthew 16:18–19 in the formulation of authority structures. "And I tell you that you are Peter," Jesus says, "and on this rock I will build my church, and the gates of Hades will not overcome it. I will give you the keys of the kingdom of heaven; whatever you bind on earth will be bound in heaven, and whatever you loose on earth will be loosed in heaven" (NIV). In the various interpretations of this passage, Protestants generally say that Peter's confession itself is the rock upon which the church will be constructed. Catholics believe that Peter, the first bishop of Rome, is the rock. Finally, Latter-day Saints believe that revelation itself is the rock.[2]

These divergent interpretations, of course, have given rise to equally divergent polities and institutional structures. The Protestant embrace of confessions coupled with Luther's insistence on the priesthood of believers has produced a kind of free-for-all, a miasma of conflicting interpretations and institutional structures. Roman Catholics, employing the doctrine of apostolic succession and tracing their authority back to Peter himself, insist on the unity of the one true church. Theirs is an institutional structure whose extent and whose rigidity is virtually unrivalled.

Except, perhaps, by the Mormons. The assertion of a living prophet as the conduit for divine revelation trumps the Catholic, Orthodox, and Anglican doctrines of apostolic succession. None of these traditions claims prophetic revelation, though they do insist on apostolic authority.

My own admittedly unorthodox gloss on Matthew 16:18–19 draws on distinctively Protestant sensibilities, but even most Protestants would probably consider my view heretical. I happen to believe that the Matthew passage, where Jesus affirms Peter as the rock (in a play on words: *petra* = rock), is a rare stab at humor in the New Testament. Peter, of course, can be seen as anything but solid. He was notoriously spineless and dithering, prone to making bold declarations, as when he assured Jesus that he would never deny him, and then caving like a cheap suit in the face of criticism. When Peter, full of bravado, sought to walk on the Sea of Galilee, he promptly disappeared beneath the waves, sinking like a rock. So when Jesus proclaimed Peter a rock, he was indulging in a rhetorical device known as irony. Peter, as protean as a windsock, was anything but solid—and yet, and here is the beauty of the passage: Jesus elects to entrust his ministry and his church to fallible human beings like Peter, with all of his faults and shortcomings. If Jesus had truly wanted solidity, he should have chosen Andrew, and if he wanted authority, he should probably have pointed to John, who was forever touting himself as the disciple closest to Jesus himself. Instead, he chose Peter, the everyman of humanity and the apotheosis of fallibility.

I concede that such an unorthodox reading runs afoul of almost every Christian tradition, but such an interpretation would vitiate some of the authoritarianism of the episcopal polity in the Roman Catholic Church. The Latter-day Saints, having recognized Smith and all successors as prophets, take the notion of authority to another level altogether. But for non-Mormons, that position begs the question: Why Smith? Was it merely, as Paulsen says, that Smith claimed to be a prophet, a source of divine revelation? Why not, say, Mother Ann Lee or William Miller or Emmanuel Swedenborg or Father Divine or the Noble Drew Ali? Mormons reply that the difference lies in the fact that Smith really *is* a prophet. Paulsen himself writes: "I will discuss . . . Joseph Smith's revelations and invite everyone to examine his or her own theological world in light of these."[3] This invitation brings us face to face with the difficult issues of epistemology.

The Centrality of Epistemology and the Perils of Circularity

In addition to authority, epistemology (how we know) is another of the perennial themes surrounding the study of religion. Christianity has traditionally spoken of God's revelation to humanity and has generally divided revelation into two categories: general revelation, or the way that God reveals himself in creation, and special revelation. This latter category has been a source of contention. Most Christians would agree that God's primary vehicle for special revelation was Jesus: God become man. The other source of special revelation, of course, is the scriptures. But what counts as scripture? Judaism recognizes the Hebrew Bible as Yahweh's special revelation to humanity; Christians add the New Testament, generally agreeing that the canon was effectively closed "by the late 4th and early 5th centuries";[4]

Muslims (ostensibly, at least) acknowledge both the Hebrew Bible and the New Testament, but they add the revelations to the prophet Muhammad contained in the Qur'an. Although Joseph Smith once referred to himself as the "second Mohamet,"[5] Smith's Mormon followers accepted the Hebrew Bible and the New Testament as divinely inspired revelation, but they rejected the Qur'an. More important, Mormons added the Book of Mormon, Doctrine and Covenants, the Pearl of Great Price, and continuing revelations to the prophet and president of the church, from Smith himself all the way down to the current president, Gordon B. Hinckley, and (presumably) to future presidents.[6]

All of this complicates the question of epistemology. How does one know what is and is not scripture, God's special revelation to humanity? The early church settled the issue of canonicity through a kind of emerging consensus, codified finally in various church councils. But Paulsen raises an important question: Does this mean, as most Christians believe, that the canon was necessarily closed?[7] The followers of Joseph Smith obviously think not.

But how do we know anything? What is the basis for our epistemology? Here we encounter the perils of circularity. "Joseph's most fundamental challenge . . . to those who deny the possibility of extra-biblical revelation is not based on argument," Paulsen writes; "it is grounded in his testimony of receiving of direct revelations from God."[8] Paulsen then proceeds to the familiar story of what he terms the "canonized account" of Smith's First Vision. He hails Smith as the person who "revealed much about God's kingdom and his purposes for humankind, apostolic authority, ancient scriptures, the divine church, the temple, temple ordinances, and theology." Because of Smith, Paulsen writes, "the Latter-day Saints have greatly enlarged the Christian canon, adding 'plain and precious' gospel truths not found in the Bible."[9]

Here, the logic behind Paulsen's paper becomes circular. It is one thing to state with clarity and zeal the doctrines taught by Joseph Smith or anyone else; it is another thing to know whether those assertions or their inferences are true or not. We know the answer to this, Paulsen in effect says, because Smith's revelations tell us so. Paulsen cites Smith's ninth Article of Faith: "We believe all that God has revealed, all that He does now reveal, and we believe that He will yet reveal many great and important things pertaining to the Kingdom of God."[10] As for breaking out of the restraints of a closed canon, Paulsen cites two justifications. First, he rightly states that the New Testament itself makes no mention of a closed canon. Fair enough, though it's not clear to me how or in what context such a statement might ever have appeared. Would we expect Paul to insert a postscript at the conclusion of his second letter to the Thessalonians and say, "This is it; I've given you the last word, and the canon is hereby closed"? By the time Paulsen adds another element to his argument against a closed canon, however, the circularity becomes dizzying. How do we know that revelation is still open and that the Book of Mormon is inspired scripture? We know, Paulsen insists, because the Book of Mormon tells us so. He cites as evidence passages from Mormon 9.[11]

In fairness, many non-Mormon Christians also engage in the same kind of circularity, the serpent devouring its own tail, when talking about the inspiration of the Bible. Many Christians, Evangelicals in particular, quote the Bible in defense of the Bible. Paul writes: "All Scripture is God-breathed and is useful for teaching, rebuking, correcting and training in righteousness, so that the man of God may be thoroughly equipped for every good work" (2 Timothy 3:16–17, NIV). If this is as far as one's argument extends, circularity leaves such assertions unsupported, which casts doubt on the enterprise of apologetics itself.

Apologetics as a Modern Enterprise

Paulsen's paper, despite its merits, ultimately fails to persuade, due to this circularity of argumentation. The difficulty lies not so much with the author's reasoning as with the enterprise itself, relying as it does on the canons of Enlightenment rationalism. At least since the Civil War, much of conservative Christian apologetics in America has sought to vindicate the claims of the faith by means of various proofs and proof texts. The arguments include the numberless cosmological and ontological arguments for the existence of God. These theologians also sought to marshal empirical evidence for the historicity of the resurrection. One of the nineteenth-century battles that extended well into the twentieth century concerned the reliability of the Bible itself. In order to counter the assaults of Darwinism and higher criticism, the nineteenth-century Princetonians constructed the ultimate Enlightenment redoubt: the inerrancy of the Bible in the original autographs, neglecting to mention that they were no longer extant. (That is not so much circular reasoning as evasive reasoning!)

All of this argumentation, informed by the canons of Enlightenment rationalism, was essentially modern, concerned as it was with linear thought and empirical evidence. The postmodern approach of the late twentieth and early twenty-first centuries, however, views faith from an entirely different angle. In short, the postmodern approach to faith resorts to faith itself. That is, it seeks to vindicate the faith by invoking experience rather than argument. Not all postmodernists have abandoned apologetics, but the list of essential doctrines has been pared down. Theologically conservative Christians, following the lead of St. Paul in 1 Corinthians 15, would insist on the Incarnation and the historicity of the resurrection—much the way, I imagine, that Paulsen and his fellow Mormons would assert their belief in the historical veracity of Smith's First Vision—but those approaching the faith in a postmodern way would view the resurrection as an article of faith rather than something to be proven by means of rational argumentation. In much the same way that New Lights in the eighteenth century prized the new birth or that pentecostals of the twentieth century sought the baptism of the Holy Spirit, so too these believers prefer experience to argument. We can celebrate or lament that development, but it points beyond the shopworn Enlightenment-inspired arguments, with all of their attendant pitfalls.

An alternative approach is illustrated by a conversation with a historian whose work I very much admire and who happens to be a Mormon. We were discussing a piece I had written about my struggles to claim for myself the Evangelical faith of my childhood. I had reflected on my own encounters with doubt and then finally finding comfort in those remarkable words of the father of a young child in the Gospel of Mark: "I believe; help my unbelief" (Mark 9:24, ESV). I have come to believe, by the way, that doubt is not the antithesis of faith; it is, in fact, an essential component of faith, and I refuse to allow the canons of Enlightenment rationalism to be the final arbiter of truth. This Mormon scholar spoke of a similar process of faith bedeviled by doubt. In the midst of his doubts, he decided simply to embrace the faith—in his case to accept on faith the veracity of Smith's First Vision.

Richard Hughes has invited us to consider Alexander Campbell as a creature of the Enlightenment and Joseph Smith as a Romantic.[12] That may be, but it seems to me that other scholars, including Paulsen in this particular paper, list decidedly in the direction of Enlightenment reasoning. That is understandable, given the announced scholarly theological purposes of Paulsen's undertaking; and few would argue that all who are people of faith should not have a reasonable defense for what they believe (1 Peter 3:15). But an unalloyed Enlightenment approach to faith carries with it certain perils. Religious beliefs and theology in general do not readily submit to empirical scrutiny, and those who invest themselves solely in the Enlightenment enterprise must at some point deal with the maxim, "Those who live by the sword die by the sword" (see Matthew 26:52), including the criticism of circular reasoning. Some circles are tighter than others, but all propositional logic eventually turns back on itself.

As Joseph Smith taught and most Latter-day Saints realize, personal experience with spiritual truths is far more significant than logical analysis.[13] Thus, I have found the testimonies of docents at Temple Square much more compelling than theological exposition. The last time I took the official Latter-day Saint tour of Temple Square in Salt Lake City, the docent frequently punctuated her narrative with personal testimony. For example, after recounting the story of the seagulls devouring the crickets and saving the crops of the early settlers in the Salt Lake Valley, she paused to say what that story meant to her as a believer. The performance occasionally came off as formulaic, even contrived, but I found that presentation of the Mormon faith much more compelling than Enlightenment-style ratiocination.

Toward the end of his life, Karl Barth, probably the greatest theologian of the twentieth century, was traveling on a plane and fell into a conversation with a seatmate, who asked the venerable theologian to summarize his thoughts. Barth, who had filled several shelves with his ruminations about the transcendence of God and the centrality of Christ, thought for a moment. I imagine him staring out the airplane window and scratching the stubble on his chin before responding with the words of a simple Sunday-school ditty: "Jesus loves me, this I know; for the Bible tells me so."

Enlightenment-style theological expositions or defenses of the faith have their place, but I confess that I find them rather less than persuasive. Call me a Romantic.

Notes

1. David Paulsen, "Joseph Smith Challenges the Theological World," in this volume, 175–76.

2. See John F. Hall, "Peter," in *Encyclopedia of Mormonism,* ed. Daniel H. Ludlow, 4 vols. (New York: Macmillan, 1992), 3:1078.

3. Paulsen, "Joseph Smith Challenges the Theological World," 177.

4. Discussed by Harry Y. Gamble, "Canon: New Testament," in *Anchor Bible Dictionary,* ed. David Noel Freedman, 6 vols. (New York: Doubleday, 1992), 1:852–56, although "no *ecumenical* council of the ancient church ever undertook to define the scope of the canon" (856, emphasis in original).

5. See the sources cited in Richard L. Bushman, *Joseph Smith: Rough Stone Rolling* (New York: Knopf, 2005), 352 n. 36.

6. On the Mormon concept of scripture, see the articles under the headings of "Canon" and "Scripture" in *Encyclopedia of Mormonism,* 1:254, 3:1277–84.

7. Paulsen, "Joseph Smith Challenges the Theological World," 177–80.

8. Paulsen, "Joseph Smith Challenges the Theological World," 180.

9. Paulsen, "Joseph Smith Challenges the Theological World," 181.

10. Paulsen, "Joseph Smith Challenges the Theological World," 181.

11. Paulsen, "Joseph Smith Challenges the Theological World," 181.

12. Richard T. Hughes, "Joseph Smith as an American Restorationist," in this volume, 34.

13. Paulsen agrees with this primacy of personal spiritual experience, the ultimate point on which his paper ends.

Joseph Smith's Christology: After Two Hundred Years

Robert L. Millet

During the last decade, a recurring question has been posed to members of The Church of Jesus Christ of Latter-day Saints: Is the church "changing?" In addition, it is asked, Is there some effort on the part of church leadership to have the church and its teachings, particularly those concerning Jesus Christ, become more acceptable to and thus more accepted by other Christians? The natural Latter-day Saint inclination is to react sharply that the church's doctrines concerning Jesus Christ are intact and even eternal, that the doctrines of Joseph Smith's day and the doctrines of our own day are one and the same, that little of consequence has been altered.

To be sure these doctrines remain intact, church leaders since the days of Joseph Smith have made significant doctrinal pronouncements about Jesus Christ, such as those in "The Origin of Man" in 1909,[1] "The Father and the Son" in 1916,[2] the two revelations (one of which was given to Joseph Smith) that were added to the canon of scripture in 1976 (now Doctrine and Covenants 137 and 138), the "Statement of the First Presidency on God's Love for All Mankind in 1978,"[3] and "The Living Christ" in 2000.[4]

Still today, the basic doctrines found in Joseph Smith's own words, in the revelations given to and through him, and in his translations of ancient records remain unaltered. Jesus's suffering and death on the cross and the grace of God have been taught consistently by church leaders and can readily be traced back to Joseph Smith. What has changed in the last few decades is the emphasis placed upon these subjects and upon the church's belief in Christ. This shift has been particularly evident as the general church membership has increased in scriptural understanding and as members and leaders have responded to their beliefs being misunderstood and misrepresented.

Joseph Smith on the Doctrine of Christ

"God is my friend," Joseph wrote to his wife Emma at a difficult time. "In him I shall find comfort. I have given my life into his hands. I am prepared to go at his call. I desire to be with Christ. I count not my life dear to me, only to do his will."[5] As much as Joseph Smith believed in, loved, and centered his life and teachings in the Savior—and he certainly did—only a few of his sermons deal principally with Jesus Christ and the atonement. Why would this be the case? For one thing, all of the scriptures given to the church through Joseph Smith are filled with passages having to do with the nature of fallen humanity, the character and power of Jesus, the doctrine of spiritual rebirth, and the myriads of blessings that flow from the infinite atonement.

As I have reflected on this for years, it appears to me that for Joseph Smith, "Jesus Christ and him crucified" (1 Corinthians 2:2) was a given, a fundamental and foundational truth, the message of messages, the doctrine of doctrines. Everything else, though supplementary, was secondary. He did not feel the need to preach endless sermons on the subject that underlay everything else he taught. Faith, repentance, baptism, the sacrament of the Lord's Supper, resurrection, judgment, and a myriad of other theological issues have meaning only because of the atonement. I suppose it would be somewhat like hearing a preacher stand before a large congregation and say, "I am a Baptist pastor. And I am also a Christian, a believer in the divinity of Jesus of Nazareth." The second sentence, though informative, is generally not necessary. Clearly if the man is a Baptist he is a Christian. Likewise, Joseph Smith was convinced that the central role of a prophet of God was to bear testimony of Jesus, since, as John the Revelator explained, the testimony of Jesus is the spirit of prophecy (Revelation 19:10).[6]

Past Emphasis upon Differences

When the Saints moved from Illinois to the Great Basin, that move was, I believe, as much ideological as it was geographical. Latter-day Saint people had been insulted, accosted, attacked, robbed, persecuted, and martyred, and their desire was to get away and find a place where they could think and act and worship without hindrance or interference. One can fully appreciate why the Latter-day Saints would develop an attitude toward all others of "us versus them"[7] and begin to erect a doctrinal fortress to protect themselves from any invading theological forces. Indeed, it seems that Mormons began to focus more and more upon their distinctions, those doctrinal matters that were either slightly or greatly different from Protestant and Catholic teachings.

This kind of doctrinal dialectic continued well into the twentieth century. Let me illustrate with a personal example. Just before leaving for a mission, I found myself reading and thinking about the gospel with a bit of trepidation. After spending several days browsing through some of the great doctrinal chapters in the Book of Mormon, I approached my father with a question. (I need to add at this point that my father had grown up in Louisiana as a member of The Church of Jesus Christ of Latter-day Saints, taught seminary to the youth for many years, and knew the principles and doctrines of the gospel well.) I asked, "Dad, what does it mean to be saved by grace?" He stared at me for a moment and then said firmly, "We don't believe in that!" I responded with, "We don't believe in it? Why not?" He promptly added, "Because the Baptists do!"

My father's statement speaks volumes. We had grown up in the Bible Belt, where we were surrounded by many noble and dedicated Christians who loved the Lord and had given their hearts to him. Over the years, we had watched scores of revivals on television and spent hours listening to radio broadcasts in which the pastor had affirmed that salvation comes "by grace alone." Knowing as he did that Latter-day Saints believed in the necessity of good works, my father had simply put the matter to rest by stating that we believed something very different.

One does not travel very far in his or her study of the New Testament or the Book of Mormon, however, without recognizing the central and saving need to trust in and rely upon the merits and mercy and grace of the Holy Messiah. That teaching is not just found in a few obscure passages; it is throughout holy writ, one of the burdens of scripture.

Same Doctrines, Greater Emphasis

Several of the doctrines concerning Christ that are found in the revelations and translations of Joseph Smith seem to have received increased emphasis in recent decades. Two that have been particularly commented on by Christian observers are the saving efficacy of the cross and the magnificent grace of God.

The Cross. One of my Christian friends asked me about what he called our "changing views on the role of the cross." He suggested that if a group of one hundred Latter-day Saints had been asked some years ago the question, "Where did the atonement of Jesus Christ take place?" probably eighty to ninety persons would have answered, "In the Garden of Gethsemane." I think his assessment is probably accurate; most Mormons were brought up on the idea that while the Protestants and Catholics taught that the atonement took place on the cross of Calvary, Latter-day Saints believe the greater suffering took place in Gethsemane. My friend suggested that if that same query were posed to a hundred Mormons today, sixty to seventy would answer that the atonement took place in Gethsemane *and* on the cross, that what began in the Garden was culminated, climaxed on Golgotha. My experience teaching hundreds of students at Brigham Young University corroborates this trend.

Nonetheless, a brief survey of statements by church leaders demonstrates that from the days of Joseph Smith the cross of Christ has held a prominent place in the faith. I will represent Joseph by passages from the Book of Mormon and the Doctrine and Covenants. Nephi, a Book of Mormon prophet, foresaw some six hundred years before the birth of the Savior that Jesus would be *"lifted up upon the cross and slain for the sins of the world"* (1 Nephi 11:33; emphasis added).

Much like Paul, Jacob in the Book of Mormon called upon the followers of the Redeemer to experience for themselves the power of the cross: "Wherefore, we would to God that we could persuade all men not to rebel against God, to provoke him to anger, but that all men would believe in Christ, and *view his death, and suffer his cross* and bear the shame of the world" (Jacob 1:8; emphasis added; compare Moroni 9:25). Notice the language of the risen Lord to the people of the Book of Mormon:

> Behold I have given unto you my gospel, and this is the gospel which I have given unto you—that I came into the world to do the will of my Father, because my Father sent me. And *my Father sent me that I might be lifted up upon the cross*; and after that I had been lifted up upon the cross, that I might draw all men unto me, that as I have been lifted up by men even so should men be lifted up by the Father, to stand before me, to be judged of their works, whether they be good or whether they be evil. (3 Nephi 27:13–14; emphasis added)

The testimony of the Doctrine and Covenants is that "Jesus was *crucified by sinful men for the sins of the world*, yea, for the remission of sins unto the contrite heart" (Doctrine and Covenants 21:9; emphasis added). "I am Jesus Christ, the Son of God," another passage begins, "who was crucified for the sins of the world, even as many as will believe on my name, that they may become the [children] of God, even one in me as I am one in the Father, as the Father is one in me, that we may be one" (Doctrine and Covenants 35:2). At the start of a brief passage on various spiritual gifts, a revelation in the Doctrine and Covenants affirms, "To some it is given by the Holy Ghost to know that Jesus Christ is the Son of God, and that *he was crucified for the sins of the world*. To others it is given to believe on their words, that they also might have eternal life if they continue faithful" (Doctrine and Covenants 46:13–14; emphasis added). Additionally, it is written, "Behold, I, the Lord, who was crucified for the sins of the world, give unto you a commandment that you shall forsake the world" (Doctrine and Covenants 53:2).

I have not even begun to list the scores of passages in the Book of Mormon and Doctrine and Covenants that speak of the vital need for Christ's suffering *and death*. For it was not just his suffering, but also his death on the cruel cross of Calvary that was an indispensable element of the atoning sacrifice. As Mormon explained in the Book of Mormon, "Now Aaron began to open the scriptures unto them concerning the coming of Christ, and also concerning the resurrection of the dead, and that there could be no redemption for mankind save it were through the death and sufferings of Christ, and the atonement of his blood" (Alma 21:9; compare Alma 22:14). In short, "he surely must die that salvation may come" (Helaman 14:15).[8]

Added to all the statements about the cross is this about Gethsemane, as dictated by Joseph Smith:

> For behold, I, God, have suffered these things for all, that they might not suffer if they would repent; but if they would not repent they must suffer even as I; which suffering caused myself, even God, the greatest of all, to tremble because of pain, and to bleed at every pore, and to suffer both body and spirit—and would that I might not drink the bitter cup, and shrink—nevertheless, glory be to the Father, and I partook and finished my preparations unto the children of men. (Doctrine and Covenants 19:16–19)

The following series of statements shows how both Gethsemane and the cross are mentioned, sometimes separately and sometimes together, by church leaders from Joseph Smith's day to the present. John Taylor, the third president of the church, stated, "The plan, the arrangement, the agreement, the covenant was made, entered into, and accepted before the foundation of the world; it was prefigured by sacrifices, and was carried out and consummated on the cross."[9]

In June 1888, Wilford Woodruff, Joseph F. Smith, and Moses Thatcher (the general superintendency of the Young Men's Mutual Improvement Association) wrote, "Alone, while treading the winepress of the wrath of devils and men, [Christ] gained *the keys of death, hell and the grave*." These keys "were forged," they added, while Christ prayed in Gethsemane, endured the acts of malice that followed, and suffered the agony of the cross.[10]

George Q. Cannon, counselor in the First Presidency of the church, stressed in 1899 that "so effectually and permanently does the Lord wish to impress the remembrance of that great sacrifice at

Calvary on our memories that He permits us all to partake of the emblems—the bread and wine."[11]

Joseph F. Smith, president of the church from 1901 to 1918, reminded us that "having been born anew, which is the putting away of the old man sin, and putting on of the man Christ Jesus, *we have become soldiers of the Cross*, having enlisted under the banner of Jehovah for time and for eternity."[12] President Smith was taught in his 1918 vision of the redemption of the dead that salvation has been "wrought through the sacrifice of the Son of God upon the cross" (Doctrine and Covenants 138:35).

George F. Richards, an apostle of the church, stated in 1914, "We read in the Book of Mormon (Mosiah 3:7), a prediction of the coming of the Lord in the meridian of time, and how he would suffer for the sins of the people: 'For behold, blood cometh from every pore, so great shall be his anguish for the wickedness and the abominations of his people.' It was in the Garden of Gethsemane that this prophecy was fulfilled."[13]

In 1921, Rudger Clawson, counselor to President Heber J. Grant, declared that "the atonement made upon Mount Calvary was the supreme sacrifice ever made in all the world."[14] In their 1921 Christmas epistle, he and the other members of the First Presidency again testified to the efficacy of Christ's suffering on the cross: "He whose mortal birth in the Manger of Bethlehem the world celebrates at this festive season, is indeed the Son of God and the Savior of mankind through the atonement wrought out on the Cross of Calvary."[15]

Church leader B. H. Roberts explained: "If it be true, and it is, that men value things in proportion to what they cost, then how dear to them must be the Atonement, since it cost the Christ so much in suffering that he may be said to have been baptized by blood-sweat in Gethsemane, before he reached the climax of his passion, on Calvary."[16]

In a 1952 general conference talk, Joseph L. Wirthlin, presiding bishop of the church, discussed what it means "to take upon one the name of Jesus Christ." One requirement was that a person must "remember the great sacrifice that [Christ] made upon Calvary's hill."[17]

Bruce R. McConkie, an apostle of the church, movingly articulated in 1985 the relationship between Gethsemane and Calvary: "The cross was raised that all might see and gape and curse and deride. . . . There was a mighty storm, as though the very God of Nature was in agony. And truly he was, for *while he was hanging on the cross for another three hours, from noon to 3:00 P.M., all the infinite agonies and merciless pains of Gethsemane recurred*."[18]

Ezra Taft Benson, president of the church from 1985 to 1994, lauded the redeeming love manifest in both sites: "In Gethsemane and on Calvary, He [Christ] worked out the infinite and eternal atonement. It was the greatest single act of love in recorded history."[19]

At the 1996 First Presidency Christmas Devotional, President Gordon B. Hinckley stated that "we honor His birth. But without His death that birth would have been but one more birth. It was the redemption which He worked out in the Garden of Gethsemane and upon the cross of Calvary which made His gift immortal, universal, and everlasting."[20]

The above statements evidence that Latter-day Saints from the time of Joseph Smith have taught that Christ's suffering in the Garden of Gethsemane and his suffering and death on the cross of Calvary were both necessary in accomplishing his overarching mission—to make a substitutionary offering in behalf of all those who would accept him and his gospel.

The Grace of God. Most observers would agree that the Latter-day Saints seem to be focusing more and more as a church upon those scriptural passages that highlight the reality of man's weakness and mortal limitations, while at the same time attending to God's infinite and ever-available power to lift, to liberate, to lighten our burdens, and to change our nature. As church leader Bruce C. Hafen pointed out, "In recent years, we Latter-day Saints have been teaching, singing, and testifying much more about the Savior Jesus Christ. I rejoice that we are rejoicing more. As we 'talk [more] of Christ' (2 Nephi 25:26), the gospel's doctrinal fullness will come out of obscurity."[21]

Although we are "rejoicing more," in a strict sense nothing in the Latter-day Saint doctrine of Christ has changed in the last 175 years. The following are examples of words that came through or from Joseph Smith:

The Spirit is the same, yesterday, today, and forever. And the way is prepared from the fall of man, and salvation is free. (2 Nephi 2:4)

Wherefore, how great the importance to make these things known unto the inhabitants of the earth, that they may know that there is no flesh that can dwell in the presence of God, save it be through the merits, and mercy, and grace of the Holy Messiah. (2 Nephi 2:8)

Wherefore, my beloved brethren, reconcile yourselves to the will of God, and not to the will of the devil and the flesh; and remember, after ye are reconciled unto God, that it is only in and through the grace of God that ye are saved. (2 Nephi 10:24)

And now, my beloved brethren, after ye have gotten into this strait and narrow path, I would ask if all is done? Behold, I say unto you, Nay; for ye have not come thus far save it were by the word of Christ with unshaken faith in him, relying wholly upon the merits of him who is mighty to save. (2 Nephi 31:19; see also Alma 24:10, Helaman 14:13, Moroni 6:4, and Doctrine and Covenants 3:20)

And, if you keep my commandments and endure to the end you shall have eternal life, which gift is the greatest of all the gifts of God. (Doctrine and Covenants 14:7; see also Doctrine and Covenants 6:13).

The fundamental principles of our religion are the testimony of the Apostles and Prophets, concerning Jesus Christ, that He died, was buried, and rose again the third day, and ascended into heaven; and all other things which pertain to our religion are only appendages to it.[22]

One hundred and thirty-nine years after Joseph Smith elaborated on the centrality of Jesus Christ, one of his apostolic successors, Boyd K. Packer, put it this way: "Through Him [Christ] mercy can be fully extended to each of us without offending the eternal law of justice. This truth," Packer continued, "is the very root of Christian doctrine. You may know much about the gospel as it branches out from there, but if you only know the branches and those branches do not touch that root, if they have been cut free from that truth, there will be no life nor substance nor redemption in them."[23]

In addition, notice the following representative statements by other church leaders through the years on the vital matter of the grace of God.[24]

Joseph Smith's successor, Brigham Young, declared in typical forceful fashion:

> It requires all the atonement of Christ, the mercy of the Father, the pity of angels and the grace of the Lord Jesus Christ to be with us always, and then to do the very best we possibly can, to get rid of this sin within us, so that we may escape from this world into the celestial kingdom.[25]

> There are no persons without evil passions to embitter their lives. Mankind are revengeful, passionate, hateful, and devilish in their dispositions. This we inherit through the fall, and the grace of God is designed to enable us to overcome it.[26]

> In and of ourselves we have no power to control our own minds and passions; but the grace of God is sufficient to give us perfect victory.[27]

> All will have to come to the Lord and be sanctified through the grace of Christ by faith in his name; without this, I am happy to say, that none can be purified, sanctified and prepared to inherit eternal glory.[28]

President Joseph F. Smith discoursed on the relationship between grace and revelation: "Notwithstanding our many weaknesses, imperfections and follies the Lord still continues His mercy, manifests His grace and imparts unto us His Holy Spirit, that our minds may be illuminated by the light of revelation."[29]

Wishing all to partake of the grace of God, Heber J. Grant, president of the church from 1918 to 1945, entreated, "We call upon all men to come unto him [Christ], that through his grace they may attain to eternal life and an inheritance with him in the kingdom of his Father."[30]

"I am not unmindful," acknowledged David O. McKay, president of the church from 1951 to 1970, "of the scripture that declares, 'For by grace are ye saved through faith; and that not of yourselves: it is the gift of God.' (Ephesians 2:8.) That is absolutely true, for man in his taking upon himself mortality was impotent to save himself."[31]

Joseph Fielding Smith, among others, noted the differences between mortal beings and Jesus Christ that require us to rely upon grace. He gave this explanation while an apostle:

There is a difference between the Lord Jesus Christ and the rest of mankind. We have no life in ourselves, for no power has been given unto us, to lay down our lives and take them again. That is beyond our power, and so, being subject to death, and being sinners—for we are all transgressors of the law to some extent, no matter how good we have tried to be—we are therefore unable in and of ourselves to receive redemption from our sins by any act of our own.

This is the grace that Paul was teaching. Therefore, it is by the grace of Jesus Christ that we are saved. And had he not come into the world, and laid down his life that he might take it again, or as he said in another place, to give us life that we may have it more abundantly—we would still be subject to death and be in our sins. . . . So we are saved by grace and that not of ourselves. It is the gift of God.[32]

Then in contemporary times, Dallin H. Oaks, a current apostle of the church, remarked on the insufficiency of works to save even the best of us:

Men and women unquestionably have impressive powers and can bring to pass great things. But after all our obedience and good works, we cannot be saved from death or the effects of our individual sins without the grace extended by the atonement of Jesus Christ. . . . In other words, salvation does not come simply by keeping the commandments. . . . Even those who try to obey and serve God with all their heart, might, mind, and strength are unprofitable servants (Mosiah 2:21). Man cannot earn his own salvation.[33]

It is so easy to allow the theological pendulum to swing from one end to the other, to swing from religious legalism on the one hand to profligate libertarianism on the other. In the Book of Mormon and Doctrine and Covenants is found a more balanced approach to grace and works. The gospel of Jesus Christ is in fact a gospel covenant, a two-way agreement between God and man. On his part, God agrees to do for us what we could never do for ourselves—forgive our sins, cleanse our nature, purify our hearts, raise us from the dead, and glorify us hereafter. We agree, on the other hand, to do that which we can do, namely, to exercise faith in Jesus Christ—to have total trust, complete confidence, and a ready reliance upon him. Further, true faith always results in faithfulness, in obedience, in good works. It may be true that we are saved by grace alone, but grace is never alone.

Reasons for the Increased Emphasis

What has happened? What changes or developments have taken place that would lead the Latter-day Saints to see things with new eyes and appreciate some sacred matters that the general membership hardly noticed fifty years ago?

Greater Scriptural Literacy. In the 1970s the church began what has come to be known as a correlated scripture study program. In their Sunday School classes, all members of the church became involved in a sequential scripture study of one of the books within the Latter-day Saint canon: the Old Testament, the New Testament, the Book of Mormon, and the Doctrine and Covenants (including the History of the Church[34]). Whereas before this time much of the emphasis was upon the study of lesson manuals, now the text of study became the scriptures themselves. This has added immeasurably to the scriptural literacy of the Latter-day Saints. The doctrinal depth, familiarity, and personal application of scriptural truths is greater now among the Latter-day Saint people than at any time in the history of the church.[35]

When Ezra Taft Benson became the thirteenth president of the church in 1985, he placed a strong emphasis upon the use of the Book of Mormon, stressing that the doctrines and teachings of the Book of Mormon should be studied and discussed and applied more regularly by the Latter-day Saints. Whether one accepts the divine origin of the Book of Mormon or not, it does not take long in reading or perusing the text to discover that the Book of Mormon is grounded in redemptive theology. The church leaders have stressed its teachings for over twenty years now, inevitably resulting in a more Christ-centered emphasis in the whole church. For example, studies show that references to the Book of Mormon from 1942 to 1970 constituted about 12 percent of the total scriptures cited and then "jumped to 40 percent" after President Benson challenged the church to become more involved in the study of the Book of Mormon.[36]

Refinement. Further, as I have suggested elsewhere,[37] Mormons have changed in another way: there has been an important refinement over the years in regard to what they believe and teach. Few Latter-day Saints who are seeking to stay in the mainstream of the church and to remain orthodox in their teaching would feel free to just "grab anything by the tail" that was taught in our past and put it forward as the doctrine of the church today. Just because something was once said or written, even by someone in authority, does not make it fair game to teach as doctrine. Certain parameters allow us to discern what is deserving of our attention and our study: (1) Is it taught in the standard works? (2) Is it found in official proclamations or declarations? (3) Is it discussed in general conference today by apostles and prophets? and (4) Is it found in the church's general handbooks or the approved curriculum? Through adherence to these parameters, the Latter-day Saints' understanding of and emphasis on Christian doctrine has been shaped.

Desire to Be Understood. In one sense, Latter-day Saints have been the target of anti-Mormon propaganda since 1830. This is nothing new. But in the last few decades, the amount of polemical material has increased dramatically, some of it not only uncomplimentary but even blatantly false. The Church of Jesus Christ of Latter-day Saints has begun to emphasize its heartfelt acceptance of Jesus as the Christ so that people in society may not misunderstand its fundamental and core beliefs. Mormons believe what is in the New Testament and believe what God has revealed in the latter days concerning Christ. As indicated earlier, such teachings did not spring into existence within the last few years; they have been in the Book of Mormon, Doctrine and Covenants, Pearl of Great Price, and teachings of Joseph Smith and other church leaders from the beginning.

Specific Areas of Misunderstanding. The question that persons raise repeatedly is, Do the Latter-day Saints worship a "different Jesus"? Latter-day Saints accept and endorse the testimony of the New Testament writers and have done so since the days of Joseph Smith. His sermons were filled with biblical quotations and paraphrases. In short, the Latter-day Saints believe in the Jesus of history. They believe that the Jesus of history is indeed the Christ of faith.

From Joseph Smith's time on, Latter-day Saints claim to possess the glorious glad tidings of the Bible and also valuable insight into the work and wisdom of the Master through modern revelation and additional scripture. To put this into perspective, consider the following question: Did early Christians who accepted the Gospel of John "worship a different Jesus" than those who had for decades relied exclusively upon, say, the Gospel of Mark? The fourth Gospel certainly offered more and deeper insight into the power, premortality, and divinity of Jesus, but is the Savior John writes about a different Savior than Mark's? Supplementation is hardly the same as contradiction.

"As a Church we have critics, many of them," President Gordon B. Hinckley has stated.

> They say we do not believe in the traditional Christ of Christianity. There is some substance to what they say. Our faith, our knowledge is not based on ancient tradition, the [post–New Testament] creeds which came of a finite understanding and out of the almost infinite discussions of men trying to arrive at a definition of the risen Christ. Our faith, our knowledge comes of the witness of a prophet in this dispensation who saw before him the great God of the universe and His Beloved Son, the resurrected Lord Jesus Christ. . . . It is out of that knowledge, rooted deep in the soil of modern revelation, that we, in the words of [a Book of Mormon prophet named] Nephi, "talk of Christ, we rejoice in Christ, we preach of Christ, we prophesy of Christ, and we write according to our prophecies, that [we and] our children may know to what source [we] may look for a remission of our sins" (2 Nephi 25:26).[38]

The founder of the faith, Joseph Smith, said it this way: "Did I build on any other man's foundation? I have got all the truth which the Christian world possessed, and an independent revelation in the bargain, and God will bear me off triumphant."[39]

Another time, Joseph said, "One of the grand fundamental principles of 'Mormonism' is to receive truth, let it come from whence it may."[40] Along these lines, Rowan Williams, the Archbishop of Canturbury, has written the following touching and appropriate prayer about gaining "something fresh" of Jesus Christ:

Jesus,

help us not to hide in our churchy words;

when we worship, let us know and feel that there is always something new,

something fresh to see of you.

Do not let us forget that you will always have more to give us,

more than we could ever guess.

Amen.[41]

Then there is the matter of those who claim Mormons are not Christians. "Are we Christians?" President Hinckley asked on another occasion. "Of course we are Christians. We believe in Christ. We worship Christ. We take upon ourselves in solemn covenant His holy name. The Church to which we belong carries His name. He is our Lord, our Savior, our Redeemer through whom came the great Atonement with salvation and eternal life."[42] Latter-day Saints simply do not want to be misunderstood or misrepresented.

The Amsterdam Declaration (2000) includes an explanation that could resolve the debate:

A Christian is a believer in God who is enabled by the Holy Spirit to submit to Jesus Christ as Lord and Savior in a personal relationship of disciple to master and to live the life of God's kingdom. The word Christian should not be equated with any particular cultural, ethnic, political, or ideological tradition or group. Those who know and love Jesus are also called Christ-followers, believers and disciples.[43]

By that definition, I believe that Joseph Smith and most Latter-day Saints would consider themselves to be Christian, and their friends of other faiths would agree.

Less than a year before his death, Joseph Smith shared his perception of the differences between Mormons and other Christians: "The inquiry is frequently made of me, 'Wherein do you differ from others in your religious views?' In reality and essence we do not differ so far in our religious views, but that we could all drink into one principle of love."[44]

Conclusion

Frankly, to be baptized into The Church of Jesus Christ of Latter-day Saints is to enter a religious society that is anything but static; it is not, as Neal A. Maxwell, an apostle of the church, has observed, a "fossilized faith" but instead a "kinetic kingdom."[45]

So while Latter-day Saints hold tenaciously to the foundational doctrines and principles of revealed religion laid down by Joseph Smith, on the one hand, it will appear to many, on the other hand, that the Latter-day Saints are changing as they enter into and contribute to the religious discussions in the world. In fact, they just may be coming of age, taking their rightful place at the table, offering distinctive Christological insights to a world that may in time come to appreciate them. "Those who observe us say that we are moving into the mainstream of religion," President Gordon B. Hinckley observed. Then he declared:

> We are not changing. The world's perception of us is changing. We teach the same doctrine. We have the same organization. We labor to perform the same good works. But the old hatred is disappearing, the old persecution is dying. People are better informed. They are coming to realize what we stand for and what we do.[46]

Almost twenty years ago, O. Kendall White published a book entitled *Mormon Neo-Orthodoxy: A Crisis Theology*.[47] White drew a comparison between Protestant Neo-Orthodoxy—the effort during the twentieth century to return to the fundamentals of the faith stressed so solidly by the leaders of the Reformation—and a like effort by some Latter-day Saint writers who seemed to be leaning more and more heavily upon the Book of Mormon and such doctrines as the nature of fallen man, the need for spiritual rebirth, and salvation by grace. In my review essay of this work, I concluded with the following:

> Kendall White is correct in detecting a movement afloat in Mormonism in the latter part of the twentieth century. It is a movement toward a more thoroughly redemptive base to our theology, but a movement that is in harmony with the teachings of the Book of Mormon and one that may be long overdue. These

recent developments may represent more of a retrenchment and a refinement than a reversion. I believe that [quoting White] "few things portend a more ominous future" for us than to fail to take seriously the Book of Mormon and the redemptive theology set forth therein; the only real "crisis" to fear would be attempts to build Mormonism upon any other foundation.[48]

Fortunately, after two hundred years, Joseph Smith's Christology, is, if anything, apprehended more clearly than ever by the Latter-day Saints and expounded upon in public statements more frequently by their leaders. In other words, the doctrine of Christ has become, as Joseph Smith said it should be, the fundamental principle of our religion.[49]

Notes

1. "The Origin of Man," in *Messages of the First Presidency,* comp. James R. Clark, 6 vols. (Salt Lake City: Bookcraft, 1965), 4:203.

2. "The Father and Son: A Doctrinal Exposition by the First Presidency and Quorum of the Twelve," in Clark, *Messages of the First Presidency,* 5:34.

3. "Statement of the First Presidency on God's Love for All Mankind in 1978," February 15, 1978, in Church Archives, The Church of Jesus Christ of Latter-day Saints, Salt Lake City, reprinted in "I Have a Question," *Ensign* 18 (January 1988): 48.

4. "The Living Christ: The Testimony of the Apostles of The Church of Jesus Christ of Latter-day Saints," *Ensign* 30, no. 4 (April 2000): 2–3.

5. Dean C. Jessee, ed. and comp., *Personal Writings of Joseph Smith* (1984; repr., Salt Lake City: Deseret Book; Provo, Utah: Brigham Young University Press, 2002), 264–65, punctuation corrected.

6. See, for example, Joseph Fielding Smith, comp., *Teachings of the Prophet Joseph Smith* (Salt Lake City: Deseret Book, 1972), 119, 160, 269, 300, 312, 315.

7. See, for example, Gordon B. Hinckley, "The Work Moves Forward," in *Official Report of the 169th Annual Conference of The Church of Jesus Christ of Latter-day Saints* (Salt Lake City: The Church of Jesus Christ of Latter-day Saints, 1999).

8. This doctrine was taught from the very beginning. Some three millennia before the coming of Jesus to earth, Enoch saw in vision "the day of the coming of the Son of Man, even in the flesh; and his soul rejoiced, saying: The Righteous is lifted up, and the Lamb is slain from the foundation of the world." Enoch looked "and beheld the Son of Man lifted up on the cross, after the manner of men" (Moses 7:47, 55).

9. G. Homer Durham, comp., *The Gospel Kingdom: Selections from the Writings and Discourses of John Taylor* (Salt Lake City: Bookcraft, 1964), 114.

10. Wilford Woodruff, Joseph F. Smith, and Moses Thatcher, "Epistle of the General Superintendency," *The Contributor* 9, no. 8 (June 1888): 302–5; emphasis added.

11. Jerreld L. Newquist, ed., *Gospel Truth: Discourses and Writings of President George Q. Cannon, First Counselor to Presidents John Taylor, Wilford Woodruff, and Lorenzo Snow* (Salt Lake City: Deseret Book, 1987), 397.

12. Joseph F. Smith, *Gospel Doctrine*, 2 vols. (Salt Lake City: The Church of Jesus Christ of Latter-day Saints, 1971), 2:91, emphasis added.

13. George F. Richards, in *84th Semi-Annual Conference of The Church of Jesus Christ of Latter-day Saints* (Salt Lake City: The Church of Jesus Christ of Latter-day Saints, 1914).

14. Rudger Clawson, in *92nd Semi-Annual Conference of The Church of Jesus Christ of Latter-day Saints* (Salt Lake City: The Church of Jesus Christ of Latter-day Saints, 1921).

15. See Clark, *Messages of the First Presidency*, 5:208.

16. B. H. Roberts, *Seventy's Course in Theology, Fourth Year: The Atonement* (Salt Lake City: Deseret News, 1911), 126.

17. Joseph L. Wirthlin, in *123rd Semi-Annual Conference of The Church of Jesus Christ of Latter-day Saints* (Salt Lake City: The Church of Jesus Christ of Latter-day Saints, 1952).

18. Bruce R. McConkie, "The Purifying Power of Gethsemane," in *Official Report of the 155th Annual Conference of The Church of Jesus Christ of Latter-day Saints* (Salt Lake City: The Church of Jesus Christ of Latter-day Saints, 1985), emphasis added; compare *The Mortal Messiah*, 4 vols. (Salt Lake City: Deseret Book, 1979–81), 4:230; Bruce R. McConkie, *A New Witness for the Articles of Faith* (Salt Lake City: Deseret Book, 1985), 620; see also James E. Talmage, *Jesus the Christ* (Salt Lake City: Deseret Book, 1972), 613, 660–61.

19. Ezra Taft Benson, *The Teachings of Ezra Taft Benson* (Salt Lake City: Bookcraft, 1988), 14.

20. Gordon B. Hinckley, Christmas devotional, December 8, 1996; cited in Sarah Weaver, "President Hinckley: Jesus' Death Gave His Birth Meaning," *Church News*, December 14, 1996, 3–4; see also President Hinckley's remarks at a missionary devotional, December 15, 2002, in "Divine Mission of Jesus," *Church News*, September 3, 2005, 2. More recently, President Hinckley observed that the way we live our lives—patterned after the only sinless being to walk the earth—is the great symbol of our Christianity. He went on to add that "no member of this Church must ever forget the terrible price paid by our Redeemer, who gave His life that all men might live—the agony of Gethsemane, the bitter mockery of His trial, the vicious crown of thorns tearing at His flesh, the blood

cry of the mob before Pilate, the lonely burden of His heavy walk along the way to Calvary, the terrifying pain as great nails pierced his hands and feet. . . . We cannot forget that. We must never forget it, for here our Savior, our Redeemer, the Son of God, gave Himself, a vicarious sacrifice for each of us." Gordon B. Hinckley, "The Symbol of our Faith," *Ensign* 35, no. 4 (April 2005): 4.

21. Bruce C. Hafen, "The Atonement: All for All," *Ensign* 34, no. 5 (May 2004): 97.

22. Smith, *Teachings of the Prophet Joseph Smith*, 121.

23. Boyd K. Packer, "The Mediator," *Ensign* 7, no. 5 (May 1977): 56.

24. Some of the leaders who made definitive statements are Orson Pratt, B. H. Roberts, and Bruce R. McConkie. See Orson Pratt, "The True Faith," in *A Series of Pamphlets* (Liverpool: Franklin D. Richards, 1852), 6, 9; *Orson Pratt's Works* (Orem, Utah: Grandin Book, 1990); B. H. Roberts, *The Gospel: An Exposition of Its First Priniciples and Man's Relationship to Deity* (Salt Lake City: Deseret Book, 1966), 179–80; Bruce R. McConkie, *The Promised Messiah: The First Coming of Christ* (Salt Lake City: Deseret Book, 1978), 346; and Bruce R. McConkie, "What Think Ye of Salvation By Grace?" *Brigham Young University 1983–84 Fireside and Devotional Speeches* (Provo, Utah: Brigham Young University Publications, 1984), 48.

25. Brigham Young, in *Journal of Discourses*, 26 vols. (Liverpool: F. D. Richards, 1855–86), 11:301, February 3, 1867.

26. Brigham Young, in *Journal of Discourses*, 8:160, September 2, 1860.

27. Brigham Young, in *Journal of Discourses*, 8:226, October 21, 1860.

28. Brigham Young, in *Journal of Discourses*, 14:150, June 25, 1871.

29. Joseph F. Smith, in *Journal of Discourses*, 12:347, January 10, 1869.

30. "A Centennial Message," in *Messages of the First Presidency*, 5:286 (April 6, 1930).

31. *Gospel Ideals: Selections from the Discourses of David O. McKay* (Salt Lake City: Improvement Era, 1958), 10–11.

32. Bruce R. McConkie, comp., *Doctrines of Salvation: Sermons and Writings of Joseph Fielding Smith*, 3 vols. (Salt Lake City: Bookcraft, 1954–56), 2:309–10.

33. Dallin H. Oaks, *With Full Purpose of Heart* (Salt Lake City: Deseret Book, 2002), 75.

34. Joseph Smith Jr., *The History of the Church of Jesus Christ of Latter-day Saints*, ed. B. H. Roberts, 2d ed. rev., 7 vols. (Salt Lake City: Deseret Book, 1971).

35. The scriptures are impacting the youth, and the youth are maturing spiritually. Recent studies carried out at the University of North Carolina at Chapel Hill, for example, indicate that Latter-day Saint young people "know more about their faith, are more committed to it, and abide more closely by its teachings concerning social behavior than do their peers." Gordon B. Hinckley,

"Gambling," *Ensign* 35, no. 5 (May 2005): 61, referencing Christian Smith and Melinda Lundquist Denton, *Soul Searching: The Religious and Spiritual Lives of American Teenagers* (New York: Oxford University Press, 2005); reported in *Deseret Morning News*, March 15, 2005, A1, A3.

36. As cited in Bruce C. Hafen, *A Disciple's Life: The Biography of Neal A. Maxwell* (Salt Lake City: Deseret Book, 2002), 502.

37. Robert L. Millet, "What Is Our Doctrine?" *The Religious Educator: Perspectives on the Restored Gospel* 4, no. 3 (2003): 15–33; also in Robert L. Millet, *Getting at the Truth: Responding to Difficult Questions about LDS Beliefs* (Salt Lake City: Deseret Book, 2004), 43–69.

38. Gordon B. Hinckley, "We Look to Christ," *Ensign* 32, no. 5 (May 2002): 90–91.

39. Smith, *Teachings of the Prophet Joseph Smith*, 376.

40. Smith, *Teachings of the Prophet Joseph Smith*, 313.

41. Rowan Williams, *Christ on Trial: How the Gospel Unsettles Our Judgment* (Grand Rapids, Mich.: Eerdmans, 2000), 47.

42. Gordon B. Hinckley, "What Are People Asking about Us?" *Ensign* 28, no. 11 (November 1998): 71.

43. Cited in J. I. Packer and Thomas C. Oden, *One Faith: The Evangelical Consensus* (Downers Grove, Ill.: InterVarsity, 2004), 121–22.

44. Smith, *Teachings of the Prophet Joseph Smith*, 313.

45. Neal A. Maxwell, *Things As They Really Are* (Salt Lake City: Deseret Book, 1978), 46.

46. Gordon B. Hinckley, "Living in the Fulness of Times," *Ensign* 31, no. 11 (November 2001): 5.

47. O. Kendall White, *Mormon Neo-Orthodoxy: A Crisis Theology* (Salt Lake City: Signature Books, 1987).

48. Robert L. Millet, "Joseph Smith and Modern Mormonism: Orthodoxy, Neoorthodoxy, Tension, and Tradition," *BYU Studies* 29, no. 3 (1989): 66.

49. Smith, *Teachings of the Prophet Joseph Smith*, 121.

Part 5

Joseph Smith and the Making of a Global Religion

Spawned in the Burned-over District of upstate New York and classified by historians for decades as a western American church, The Church of Jesus Christ of Latter-day Saints now faces the challenge of broadening its scope and its reach into many countries of the world. In this context, scholars have examined some of the more poignant challenges that Latter-day Saints face in making the transition from being a regional sect to becoming a global religion in terms of teachings, practices, language, and cultural differences. What does it take, beyond a burgeoning membership, to become a bona fide world religion? To a certain extent, this globalization is attributable to Joseph Smith. He spoke in global terms of the work he set in motion, and he anticipated in many ways its international appeal and challenges. What, now, are its worldwide dreams and realities?

World Religion: Dynamics and Constraints

Douglas J. Davies

Mormonism as a world religion and Joseph Smith as its originating prophet furnish the subject of this paper. A brief theoretical reflection on approaching The Church of Jesus Christ of Latter-day Saints provides both an opening context for the quantitatively focused debate on Mormonism's potential for growth into world religion status and an introduction for a more extensive consideration of several factors of a more qualitative kind that may foster or inhibit that development. The paper then ponders the issue of identity in relation to Joseph Smith.

Approaching Mormon Religion

In his essay "The Concept of Scientific History," Sir Isaiah Berlin distinguished between "thin" and "thick" forms of information within different disciplines. "Thin" material, often single stranded, is relatively open to sociological, psychological, economic, or even medical research. "Thick" materials, by contrast, present the scholar, most especially the historian, with a "texture constituted by the interwoven strands." How to approach such "thick" material was, for him, a fundamental means of distinguishing between the natural and the human sciences.[1] In particular, history demands an active participation in the past lives of people with the common sense knowledge of our own life, age, and culture playing its part in our approach to the past. That very sense of "knowing oneself" provides the basis for knowing one another and constitutes Berlin's version of "nothing human being alien to me." This frames his appreciation of Max Weber's sociological theme of "understanding," or *Verstehen,* in approaching social life.[2] One intriguing mid-twentieth-century debate in British social anthropology reflected these issues when Evans-Pritchard, Berlin's Oxford contemporary, just a year after Berlin's essay linked history and anthropology as modes of engagement with humanity.[3] I invoke these intellectual visions both to curb oversimplification of Mormonism's numerical future and world-religion status and to prompt openness in pondering aspects of the life of its founder, Joseph Smith.

Another matter dealing with any approach to the subject lies in the vested interest of many Mormon commentators. It is important to appreciate and evaluate our bias: indeed, this is part of the calling of the scholar who sees study as part of the pursuit of the way things are—a phrase that, for me, represents "the truth" within one's intellectual endeavors. Church leaders see themselves charged with the preservation and expansion of the church and of dealing with those who would attack or undermine it. Apologists of other religious traditions often wish to devalue their attackers in order to assert their own confession of faith. Indeed, both protagonists and antagonists tend to create, emphasize, or ignore historical, organizational, and ideological-theological ideas each in their own distinctive fashion. This treatment is understandable but is also at times sad because of the conflict-grounded issues of identity, fear, and love that are involved. I acknowledge that perhaps my own vested interest as a scholar of Mormonism tends to stress positive aspects of its genius, life, and growth. I turn first to its growth.

Numbers

For some twenty years or so, Rodney Stark's statistical prediction of Mormonism's growth into a new world religion has prompted discussion.[4] His low and high profile predictions suggest that, for example, by 2020 the low membership would be thirteen million and the high, twenty-three million. By 2050 the low membership would be twenty-nine million and the high seventy-nine million. Further extrapolation, on the basis of growth from 1930 to 1980, led him to a figure of approximately 265 million by 2080.[5]

As I have argued elsewhere, and bearing the strong anachronism in mind, this would, in today's terms, make Mormonism nearly 75 percent the size of Buddhism and constitute some 13 percent of the total Christian world.[6] But those statistics do not consider the growth of mainstream Christianity and other religions by 2080, itself no small factor, even when compared to Mormonism's recent growth, especially in South America. Mormonism's growth parallels an explosive growth of numerous Protestant, Evangelical, and charismatic groups that are related to the offer of a faith that frames a purposeful and stable individual and family life, alongside a work ethic conducive to economic success.[7]

Be that as it may, the main point is that some church leaders have taken up Stark's projections as points of encouragement.[8] I have my doubts about his "thin" interpretation because of some of the "thick" factors of religious and cultural life. My interest today lies with some of the dynamics of this growth and the potential constraints inherent in its future.

A separate issue of a more technical kind in the history of religions concerns the meaning of a "world religion." I have discussed this elsewhere and argued, for example, that Buddhism, Christianity, and Islam constitute world religions while Sikhism and Judaism do not, with Hinduism being largely in the latter group.[9] This appraisal is based on a definition of world religion as involving a distinctive process of the conquest of death, a conquest rooted in ritual practice, explanatory doctrine, and an ethical pattern of life involving the generation of merit for soteriological ends. Crucially, it is also required that the movement develop from its original cultural source by engaging creatively with the cultures into which it expands and, in the process, generate diversifying textual, symbolic, and historic traditions.

Dynamics of Growth

Numerous scholars of Mormonism and commentators on American cultural life have, of course, seen in Mormonism a distinctive religious movement, even a distinctive American religion, and I do not wish to rehearse those well-known ideas here. Rather, I now turn to consider germane dynamics of and constraints upon growth in the Latter-day Saint world, factors that belong to the thickly complex nature of religion.

Death Conquest. From my perspective, a major feature in Mormonism's success to date lies in its extensive process of death conquest.[10] Its ritual provision, from genealogy to the temple and to eternity, furnishes a more extensive eternal soteriology than most religions, with the possible exception of medieval Catholicism. This is likely to be a major advantage for converts from contemporary cultural Catholicism or some traditional societies, such as New Zealand Maoris,[11] but a major disadvantage in Western Europe and other contexts where life after death is decreasingly a majority concern. An interesting paradox in secular Europe is that many are interested in genealogy for genealogy's sake but not for reasons of religious salvation—for the past and present and not for the future.

Migrant Commitment. For nineteenth-century European converts, however, death conquest was an attraction, especially in its early form of millenarianism. The inward and onward migration of converts during the first fifty or so years of the church's life, in particular the commitment expressed by many thousands of European Saints who abandoned their homeland, which they had come to define as "evil Babylon," for the New Jerusalem across the Atlantic, contributed a fundamental form of spiritual capital to the new development.[12]

Never had the classification of the "Old World and the New World" carried such a theological significance. Theologically speaking, the faith dynamic pervading their migration lay in eschatological hope. They were crossing the sea and, subsequently, would cross half of North America to prepare a place for the coming of Jesus Christ. They would be party to and celebrate in his joyous advent. Not that Christ had not already made his presence felt in North America. And here I do not refer to the well-rehearsed spiritual presence of Christ in and through waves of Protestant revivalism, but to the double belief that one of Christ's post-resurrection appearances had been in the New World (3 Nephi 11–27) and that he, along with his heavenly Father, had appeared to the boy Joseph Smith in the process of divine restoration of religious truth and authority. Indeed, in 1830, a book—the Book of Mormon—and a church had appeared as official expressions of these beliefs. Here, then, we see a variety of factors that express the overall Christological dynamic of earliest Mormonism.

Joseph Smith's Death. The murder of Joseph Smith in 1844, with all its potential for theological, social, and political interpretations as sacrificial martyrdom, lynch-mob rabble rousing, or Masonic vengeance, precipitated a critical reappraisal of leadership and divine intention. It marks a crucial dynamic in Mormonism's survival. The value of the spiritual capital brought by migrant converts was now tested, and while not all of it remained creditable, sufficient did for firm continued investment in the church's westward future under Brigham Young. The critical separations that occurred firmed those who remained, and it was with a quite different dynamic already reorienting itself upon the death of Joseph that devotees migrated further to a destination that would, under Brigham Young, become their proper place, for a century at least. Recognizing the mainstream of followers who went west, I do not wish to overlook the contributions made by other Mormon groups, for example, the Reorganized Church of Jesus Christ of Latter Day Saints—the Community of Christ—as it came to call itself in 2001, which was led initially by the martyred prophet's son, Joseph Smith III.

In mentioning spiritual capital, one is almost tempted into a further serious theoretical aside concerning rational-choice theory, favored by some sociologists of religion—that "religion supplies compensators for rewards that are scarce or unavailable" and that people make religious choices by "weighing the anticipated costs and benefits of actions and then seeking to act so as to maximize net benefits"[13]—and accordingly to explore the options available to those European migrants who were now without their "prophet dear." I resist that temptation, but only after highlighting the problem of rationality over faith, for while I am slightly unsure how to change the coinage of eschatological hope into that of rational choice, I am very unclear indeed how pragmatic rationality relates to the sense of truth and wonder inherent in some early Mormon spirituality. I fear that someone may lose out in the exchange. Indeed, this doubt is of some significance in relation to the death of Joseph Smith because it raises the issue of "understanding," of that *Verstehen* to which I alluded more theoretically in my introduction. If I may say so, the temptation of rational choice theory is to engage in too simplistic an appraisal of cost and value, and this will not do, I think, when one seeks to grasp something of the "thick" materials, of the complex yearnings of faith.

One element of Joseph Smith's dynamic contribution to Mormonism—his martyrdom—may be usefully isolated through the Catholic theologian Karl Rahner's interesting account of Christian martyrdom in general. In a direct and obvious way Rahner describes martyrdom as the uniting of "testimony" and "death" in the faithful decease of the believer. That would easily echo within Mormonism, given the primacy of place it affords to testimony as such, but Rahner also addresses the more nuanced way in which believers come to understand and grasp the inner dynamism of their faith.[14] Speaking specifically of Catholic spirituality with its stress both on Christ as the prime "faithful witness" and on the believer called to "follow in the bloody footsteps of his master and share the fate of the Word Incarnate unto death" and also on the "Spirit from above, the Holy Spirit of grace and strength," he adds that "anyone who really understands what is meant by these traditional expressions, has probably understood everything, for then his faith, his love, his fidelity comprehend more than words actually explicitly express."[15]

Moving from Catholicism to Mormon life, that kind of "understanding" (the epic *Verstehen* of the devotee) is also what binds believer to believer and, in all probability, bound many 1844 Saints to Joseph and to the ongoing mission assumed by Brigham Young. Of course not all were so bound, as the formation of other restoration groups attested, yet this martyr complex embracing testimony and death was of positive import in earliest Mormonism because of the death-conquest rites into which the prophet had already initiated some core-leadership families.

Vicarious Rites and Personal Endeavor. This brings me to the positive dynamic associated with vicarious ritual and personal endeavor in relation to death conquest, in particular the rites of baptism for the dead and of endowments that would become the charter forces of temple building and temple work. Theology and ritual combined in the church's desire that individuals should so enact their agency that, obediently, they might fulfill their covenants and obligations to the church and to God and attain their justly rewarded degree of celestial glory in the worlds to come.[16] In nineteenth-century Mormon life, with its strenuous endeavor to survive and to make the desert blossom as the rose, Latter-day Saints worked hard. And, developing this Mormon version of the Protestant ethic, there was also a parallel exertion in terms of eternal survival and flourishing. Doctrinally speaking, divine grace, focused on the atonement of Jesus Christ, would guarantee that every human being would attain resurrection. What followed the resurrection, however, would depend upon the life lived on earth. And since the degree of glory, the precise level of attainment achieved in the heavenly realms, was the crucially significant factor, it is perfectly understandable that Mormons should become an achievement-focused people.

Here was a powerful motivational dynamic fostering the very notion of "activity," with a desire to have as many as possible "active" in church and temple life.[17] This encouraged and motivated missionary work as it did leadership activity in a developing and expanding institution. Celestial glory and eternal progression were close partners of earthly activity and church expansion, not least in the second half of the twentieth century. In this sense a deeper insight lies in describing Mormonism as an exaltation religion rather than simply as a salvation religion, itself a term too often synonymous with "world religion."

Church and Sect. I take this Latter-day Saint theological distinction between exaltation and salvation and relate it to the organizational complement between temple and chapel as a further feature of dynamics and growth.[18] This distinction is helpful for the growth of the church in two ways. First, the ward, mission, and stake form of organization serves the missionary life of the church. In this form, missionaries and church members contact millions of people and can introduce them to a local form of congregational and community life. If successfully accomplished, the mission task results in the personal baptism of a new believer, repentance of sin, and the promise of divine grace to ensure a resurrection after death. But church membership does not end in and with local congregational life. Ideally, increasing involvement should lead to a reorganization of family life and, critically, to ritual action at the temple. So to practice the faith is to set upon the path of ultimate exaltation in the realms above, moving beyond the point of resurrection, provided by grace, into the domains of exaltation achieved by personal endeavor. One positive effect of the chapel-temple divide is to ensure a kind of church within a church or, in older sociological terms, a kind of sect within a church, fostering the intense levels of involvement required for an essentially voluntary organization.

Constraints

As is often the case, many a positive dynamic entails a negative constraint. Here I will consider three areas of such constraint.

Sensing Failure. The first constraint concerns Mormonism as an "exaltation religion" with its particular emphasis on grace, a feature noticeably addressed in recent decades within some Mormon circles.[19] This, it would appear, is the outcome as much of pastoral care as of any apologetics with Evangelical or Catholic Christianities over doctrine. Though I cannot explore the point here, "grace" is difficult to translate between traditions because of the difference in ethos of appropriation. I have described something of a similar problem of mutual comprehension elsewhere over the idea of the cross within theology and spirituality. Mormonism presents an interesting paradox when its ethic of achievement motivation encounters a desire to speak the language of grace.[20] This encounter can be perceived as a contradiction. How can one create a sense of the radical divine resource of love, forgiveness, and encouragement for energetic individuals, raised on an ethic of achievement, who have exhausted their personal resource in seeking to honor covenants and fulfill all family and church duties? It is not a new problem, of course. One manifestation of it lay in the debate between Augustine and Pelagius in the fourth and fifth centuries and, indeed, in later centuries, not least at the time of the Reformation.[21] This issue ever concerns the nature and degree of human and/or divine input into the living of a religious life. History suggests that the greater the hierarchical and ritual basis of a tradition, the greater the stress on human effort. Moreover, the larger the church grows, the more likely it is that an increase in central control will be necessary to maintain its doctrinal and organizational integrity as its particular type of restoration movement. This would imply that the greater the numerical success of the church and the greater the need for organizational control, the greater will be the incidence of this ethical-burnout experience. By contrast, moments of protest against hierarchy and ritualized access to divinity stress the freedom of believers in the reception of a divine outflow of salvation.

In terms of massive church growth, an obvious hypothesis would be that obedience to authority and to prescribed rites would take precedence over the idea of grace, especially when and if that idea is associated, in the minds of church leaders at least, with an individualized freedom easily open to a laissez-faire spirituality. An important issue here is one I outlined in my *Introduction to Mormonism* when comparing Evangelical, Protestant, and Mormon ideas of Jesus and describing how they differ according to the way each group views their church.[22] For many Evangelicals, Christ, and especially Christ in the heart, is more important than the actual denominational organization to which they belong. This is probably not the case for most Latter-day Saints, for whom Jesus is conceived of, and perhaps related to, as the one who frames, inspires, and ultimately leads this particular church rather than as an invited guest of the private heart.

Still it remains that some are exploring these issues and are developing what might be described as a reflexive insight on grace.[23] This reflexivity involves a transformation. It begins in the strenuous effort of obedience, discipline, and much activity—in family life, in mission, in church and temple work, as well as in career and community activity, and in added family responsibilities for the women. The faithful Saint works himself out and wonders whether he will ever attain an appropriate celestial degree of glory. Into such lives, the idea of divine love and acceptance may come as a force of considerable strength. This could be a breakthrough experience, easily describable as a new birth. It may involve a deeply personal sense of Christ or the Holy Spirit. Might this become a relatively new style of "Mormon conversion"? An intrachurch conversion? If so it might come to serve as a new resource of spiritual capital within the organization itself.

Inner Diversity: Sustaining and Opposing. Another element of constraint to which I wish to draw attention concerns the threefold relation between growth in numbers, the increase of inner diversity of the church, and the nature of centralized control. These I approach through the Mormon practice of the membership "sustaining" their leadership as God's called and appointed ones.[24] This process may be interpreted in terms of what we might call positive and negative forms of testimony. To sustain leaders is to engage in a type of positive, practical testimony. Saints raise the hand just as in the testimony meeting they vocally affirm that this is the true church and its leaders the chosen of God. A literary form of these manual and verbal types of assent appears at the front of the Book of Mormon in "The Testimony of Three Witnesses," "The Testimony of Eight Witnesses," and "Testimony of the Prophet Joseph Smith," himself. But there is another aspect of such testimony, for deep within the theological, historical, and psychological culture of Mormonism lies the phenomenon of negative testimony—of apostasy—which involves both the broad scheme of historical falling away from divine truth, corrected in the Restoration through Joseph Smith, and the more specific cases of individual apostasy.

One factor that might militate against Mormonism being identified as a world religion as defined above lies in the way that a hierarchical and centralized leadership could wish to control any diversity that might be viewed as dissent. Here one crucial issue concerns the way in which dissent is conceived, whether as faithful creativity or as apostasy. It may be that the pool of potential orientations inherited by the Utah church in relation to groups such as the Community of Christ or some groups self-defining as Latter-day Saint, but often designated as fundamentalist Mormon groups, will incline leaders more in one way than the other.

American Essence. In connection with this, the early Utah period of church life witnessed, quite naturally, a strong bonding between a distinctive type of American ethos and the message itself. This American-Mormon bond raises another vital factor that may constrain the world-religion status of Mormonism in the future, namely, the question of enculturation—itself one of the most powerful notions of Christian religious developments in recent decades.[25] Major world religions, as I define them, have largely broken their bond of origin and become encultured in many differing societies. This is, inevitably, a crucial question for the theme of Mormonism as a world religion. It was with that in mind that I preferred to speak of future Mormonism elsewhere as an "expansion as a denominational sub-culture but not as a world religion."[26] What might contradict that view, however, is the possibility that after its extensive expansion it will experience dissent, rupture, and extensive localization. Varieties of African, Indian, Japanese, Brazilian, or other forms of Mormon life would emerge, and the world religion idea would become a more realistic option.

Here I stress, with some personal fondness and intellectual respect, John Sorenson's interesting anthropological discussions of these significant issues, not least his 1973 essay "Mormon World-view and American Culture." As he put it then: "Broadly speaking, Mormons in the United States consider culture as something that foreigners have, while what they have here in 'Zion' are simply gospel truths."[27] Doubtless much has changed since then, but a genuine world-religion future would involve a great deal more. But to ponder that future is also to ponder the future of the United States of America. Many see the United States as a distinctive form of empire embracing globalizing economics and linguistic factors alongside a strong film and musical culture, not to mention the military engagements that some would view as invasion. Perhaps many within the United States also see it as a chosen country with a world mission. The twentieth century, especially its second half, was the era of the rise of the United States. Indeed, the early twenty-first century presents a complex picture of strongly mixed opinions of the United States and things American. Speaking as a Briton and Anglican who, even in a relatively short time, has lived through the fragmentation of the British Empire—itself in the nineteenth and early twentieth century one of the greatest empires the world has ever seen—I appreciate that the current status of the United States may not last. Certainly, one lesson of history is that kingdoms and empires rise and fall, and the religions they take with them also benefit and lose from those changing dynamics. One theological response to that is reflected in the final line of the hymn; "The Day Thou Gavest Lord Is Ended," which is much beloved by the Church of England:

> So be it Lord Thy Throne shall never,
> As earth's proud empires, pass away.
> Thy Kingdom stands and grows forever,
> Till all Thy creatures, own Thy sway.[28]

By 2080, for example, the United States might be like the United Kingdom of today: certainly Brazil, India, and China will experience great change by then. It is precisely such a view of the world that any scholar of religious futures needs to ponder, as indeed this view is pondered within contemporary politics and commerce and by the military. Statistical progression—itself a relatively thin form of analysis—may well falter as the cultural carriers of a message change. For all, but especially for religious leaders, such issues themselves demand some form of courage. And to this essentially thick complexity of human life and to the past, I now turn and return, in and through the life of Joseph Smith.

Courage, Identity, and Joseph Smith

Courage, as a theme worthy of religious studies, is of prime importance in the birth and growth of the church: here I raise it speculatively and provisionally because our subject concerns an individual man, a person whose life was, it seems to me, as mysterious to himself as sometimes our lives are to us. Precisely because church leaders can, perhaps, see Joseph too easily as part of the plan of salvation and church opponents decry him too readily as a misled and misleading individual, it is worth considering him as a man like the rest of us, albeit one who achieved something that the vast majority have not achieved, namely, founding a movement actively followed by millions as a means of living their life and approaching their death.

To focus on courage may seem odd, and the way I do so more curious still—odd, for example, given Fawn Brodie's trenchant assertion of Joseph's lack of courage in some events near the close of his life.[29] And perhaps curious because I am led to the theme of courage, prompted by the theological writing of Paul Tillich (1886–1965), the late-nineteenth- and mid-twentieth-century theologian, German by birth and American by adoption and cultural grace, who died just forty years ago and whose work I wish to note as worthy of solid reconsideration.

My wish to ponder courage is prompted by the opacity of many a great life to its acts and outcomes, and by the sympathy I consider a humane evaluation of each other to demand when seeking to understand others. One of the profounder aspects of Tillich's thought, emerging from his existential yet Protestantly rooted theological concerns, is what he calls the "courage of confidence." This confidence is "rooted in the personal, total, and immediate certainty of divine forgiveness." Tillich presses the point further, under the influence of Lutheranism, to describe the courage of confidence as "accepting acceptance through being unacceptable."[30] In taking this theme from Tillich, I am not simply trying to describe the Protestant form of the doctrine of justification by faith in different terms, nor am I introducing an idea that I think is directly intelligible to Mormonism. Rather, I am highlighting one dramatically important feature of human life: that of a transformation of self-identity in relation to belief in divine activity operative in and through the self. Tillich is very careful to argue that this courage is not simply a kind of psychological self-acceptance. "It is," he says, "not the Existentialist courage to be as oneself." Far from it, "it is the paradoxical act in which one is accepted by that which infinitely transcends one's individual self."[31]

And Tillich emphasizes the personal, and the person-to-person, nature of this relationship.

For the Reformation such a person was the "unacceptable sinner" being accepted into the "judging and transforming communion with God."[32] What was it for the Restoration? What was "the courage of confidence" of Joseph Smith? To answer this is too great a task for this paper, but the question is a worthy one. Part of the answer lies in Joseph's visions. These give a clear sense of an experience understood as a personal encounter within which he felt acceptance by the deity despite personal ideas of unworthiness. We should not simply read these motifs as some obvious framing of some inevitable form of religious experience in the Protestant Burned-over District of the 1820s. That kind of historical-psychological shorthand takes the color from the picture, the inspiration from the heart. It will not do when studying a prophet.

Unfortunately, I can spend no time developing this theme here. I simply enunciate it, for I must pass on to the courage of confidence as important in church growth, an issue that brings life to the missionary situation as to any level of the church as an organization. It may also be the basis of life in the missionary too, for such courage is likely to emerge only from crisis and hardship—it is seldom the product of homegrown simplicity. The mission field is as likely to be creative for the missionary as was the Palmyra grove for Joseph Smith. But there can be no formula for producing such courage. The lack of a formula or structure is, I think, a real problem for the church as an expanding organization, especially one in which central leaders are ever more distant, in personal terms, from the ordinary member. As the church becomes ever larger it increasingly depends upon formal organizational systems for its operation. Any growing church or society experiences this kind of developmental situation.

How do some church members perceive this expansion? For the majority, I suspect, this is deemed a great and good thing, a sign that the plan of salvation embraces the very organization of the church on earth. Attitudes of respect and a commitment to duty become prime, not least as the church is seen to grow in numbers and, as it were, to demonstrate its veracity through its very growth. For a few— perhaps especially for those who were young when the church was much smaller than it is today—this growth of a managed church can lead to a sense that formulae and a distanced authoritative hierarchy replace personal encounter. Authority, power, and control overwhelm the commitment, thought, and distinctive testimony of specific individuals.

At this point in the argument, I might be expected to express certain negative sentiments over this potential depersonalization of a community or even over the problematic nature of some forms of intellectualism or even dissidence within the church: indeed these are important arguments, but, by contrast, I intend to indicate quite another issue, one reflecting what might be viewed as a grand irony, namely, that such a sense of disquiet towards church leadership may become the arena out of which another kind of "courage of confidence" may, itself, be born. Joseph Smith's own spirituality seemed to have been fostered by his sense of dismay at the churches of his day, a dismay furnishing the seedbed of acceptance of revelation. By a strange analogy this might mean that some of the church's apparently disobedient sons and daughters are the best examples of the spirit of Joseph Smith. How can the church, as it grows, appreciate the resource of faith present in those few, especially when, quite understandably, the leadership is concerned about the lives of millions? That is a challenge for the church leadership bearing responsibility and desirous of directing a world religion. No easy answer can be summoned, certainly not here.

But the question is related to that characteristic of world religions involving the division into schools of interpretation and practice. Many and various are the reasons for that. One reason lies in the need of some individuals to gain power and influence and to carve a sector within the new world of truth; another lies in a real sense of possessing a more apt grasp of truth than the general truths obtained by all. Division is, historically speaking, not strange to the Restoration movement of the latter days. Its very presence is, however, a potential example of negative possibilities. This, it seems to me, is the profound problem of world-religion status. It could be that, with the centuries, Mormonism may become a deeply encultured faith with regional identity and organization separate from Salt Lake City, or relatively so. That would contradict my own sense of what is likely, but one cannot predict. It is wise to recall that after two thousand years most Christian traditions still utilize, dwell upon, and interpret not only the Mediterranean culture of the New Testament but also the previous millennium or so of Jewish antecedents. Alongside the challenge inherent in cultural diversity of change into, for example, an African Mormonism, Japanese, Korean, and Brazilian Mormonism, stands the potential for distinctive schools of thought.

But would these factors be totally negative? Not necessarily so. For what of a "courage of confidence" for the prophet, apostles, and key leadership? Such courage must not be ignored or hidden by talking only of hierarchy and formulaic organization. One form of courage of confidence would be to free the child from the parent so that its own form of restoration would be worked out. These great problems are, themselves, forces that prompt reconsideration, self-analysis, and the desire for divine direction. Human life is such that both dissident and apostle have to accept circumstance and in so doing find themselves accepted.

I leave that statement intentionally paradoxical as I come to my final point. It is one that has long intrigued me and lies in those words of Joseph Smith—"no man knows my history"—framed in the death-conquesting King Follett discourse. There are very few religious founders of whom we actually know more than we do of Joseph Smith. His history is exceptionally well known even if, as Brodie sixty years ago emphasized, it "is the antithesis of a confession."[33] But, for the scholar of religion, especially one both anthropologically and phenomenologically inclined, for whom the "thick material" of life with its interwoven strands are of the essence, that utterance is a proclamation of the mystery of self, of one aware of all that has befallen him in a world of extraordinary events. Those who are philosophically, psychologically, and theologically aware can, each in their own way, grasp the sense of the fact that no one knows his or her own personal history—despite extensive knowledge of one's biography. It seems to me that part of Joseph Smith's life lies in courage that is the equivalent of, and a frame for, not knowing "my history."

In concluding, then, it is precisely that courage of mysterious identity that I have wished to link with the status of an expanding movement within a complex world. The kind of organization that

Mormonism now is inevitably breeds a desire to control its growth. Yet it is precisely that desire that sits uneasily alongside the insight of unknowing. If Joseph could proclaim that no man knew his history when looking back over a much-examined life, it is not difficult to feel the hand of caution when pondering the future status of a church and its birthright culture. This contemplation has compelled me to set well-known statistics of group development alongside themes of human self-awareness and courage, and to be cautious of a world of changing empires.[34]

Notes

1. Isaiah Berlin, "The Concept of History," in *Isaiah Berlin, The Proper Study of Mankind* (London: Chatto and Windus, 1997), 17–58. First published as "History and Theory: The Concept of Scientific History," *History and Theory* 1, no. 1 (1960): 23.

2. Dirk Käsler, *Max Weber: An Introduction to His Life and Work* (Oxford: Polity Press, 1988), 175–79.

3. E. E. Evans-Pritchard, "Anthropology and History," in *Essays in Social Anthropology* (London: Faber and Faber, 1962), 46–65.

4. See the discussion by Jan Shipps and Gerald McDermott in this volume.

5. Rodney Stark, "The Rise of a New World Faith," *Review of Religious Research* 26, no. 1 (1984): 23; Stark, "The Basis of Mormon Success: A Theoretical Application," in *Latter-day Saint Social Life,* ed. James T. Duke (Salt Lake City: Bookcraft, 1998), 66.

6. Douglas J. Davies, *The Mormon Culture of Salvation* (Aldershot, UK: Ashgate, 2000), 243.

7. David Martin, *Tongues of Fire: The Explosion of Protestantism in Latin America* (Oxford: Blackwell, 1990); Henri Gooren, *Rich among the Poor: Church, Firm, and Household among Small-scale Entrepreneurs in Guatemala City* (Utrecht: Thela Latin America Series, 1998).

8. *Church Almanac 2001–2002* (Salt Lake City: Deseret News, 2000), 148–52.

9. Davies, *Mormon Culture of Salvation,* 214.

10. Davies, *Mormon Culture of Salvation,* 85–86.

11. Cf. Mette Ramstad, *Conversion in the Pacific: Eastern Polynesian Latter-day Saints' Conversion Accounts and Their Development of a LDS Identity* (Kristiansand, Norway: Norwegian Academic, 2003).

12. Douglas J. Davies, *Introduction to Mormonism* (Cambridge: Cambridge University Press, 2003), 28–31; Douglas J. Davies, "Aspect of Latter-day Saint

Eschatology," in *Sociological Yearbook of Religion in Britain*, no. 6, ed. Michael Hill (London: SCM Press, 1973); Douglas J. Davies, *Mormon Spirituality in Wales and Zion* (Nottingham: Nottingham Series in Theology, 1987), 1–20.

13. Rodney Stark and W. S. Bainbridge, *A Theory of Religion* (New Brunswick: Rutgers University Press, 1987); Stark, *The Rise of Christianity* (San Francisco: HarperCollins, 1997), 167, 169.

14. Davies, *Mormon Culture of Salvation*, 20, 128–30, 228–30.

15. Karl Rahner, *On the Theology of Death* (New York: Herder and Herder, 1972), 83.

16. Davies, *Mormon Culture of Salvation*, 70–72.

17. Davies, *Introduction to Mormonism*, 181.

18. Davies, *Mormon Culture of Salvation*, 152.

19. See Robert L. Millet, *Grace Works* (Salt Lake City: Deseret Book, 2003).

20. Davies, *Mormon Culture of Salvation*, 54–60.

21. Peter Brown, *Augustine of Hippo: A Biography*, rev. ed. (Berkeley: University of California, 2000), 497; John Hick, *Evil and the God of Love* (London: Macmillan, 1985); Robert F. Evans, *Pelagius: Inquiries and Reappraisals* (London: A. & C. Black, 1968).

22. See Davies, *Introduction to Mormonism*, 242.

23. Davies, *Mormon Culture of Salvation*, 56–57.

24. Davies, *Mormon Culture of Salvation*, 130–31.

25. Davies, *Introduction to Mormonism*, 252. See, for example, Phillip Tovey, *Inculturation of Christian Worship* (Burlington, Vt.: Ashgate, 2004).

26. Davies, *Mormon Culture of Salvation*, 241.

27. John L. Sorenson, *Mormon Culture: Four Decades of Essays on Mormon Society and Personality* (Salt Lake City: New Sage Books, 1997), 93.

28. Words by John Ellerton, 1870.

29. Fawn Brodie, *No Man Knows My History: The Life of Joseph Smith, the Mormon Prophet* (New York: Knopf, 1945; repr., New York: Vintage Books, 1995), 377.

30. Paul Tillich, *The Courage to Be* (1952; repr., London: Collins, 1962), 164.

31. Tillich, *The Courage to Be*, 165.

32. Tillich, *The Courage to Be*, 165.

33. Brodie, *No Man Knows My History*, vii.

34. Two further sources referenced but not directly cited are: Hans J. Mol, *Identity and the Sacred: A Sketch for a New Social-Scientific Theory of Religion* (Oxford: Blackwell, 1976); Max Weber, *The Theory of Social and Economic Organization* (New York: Free Press, 1947).

Testing Stark's Thesis:
Is Mormonism the First
New World Religion since Islam?

Gerald R. McDermott

In 1984, Rodney Stark startled the academic world with a claim that has kept sociologists and religion-watchers scratching their heads ever since. "The Church of Jesus Christ of Latter-day Saints, the Mormons," he predicted, "will soon achieve a worldwide following comparable to that of Islam, Buddhism, Christianity, Hinduism, and the other dominant world faiths."[1] Stark claimed that Mormonism has grown faster than any other new religion in American history.[2] Between 1840 and 1980, it had averaged a growth rate of 44 percent per decade; in the four decades 1940 through 1980, growth zoomed to an astonishing 53 percent. If it maintained a 30 percent growth rate, Mormons would exceed 60 million by the year 2080; if 50 percent, then 265 million by 2080.[3] "Today," he declared, "they stand on the threshold of becoming the first major faith to appear on earth since the Prophet Mohammed rode out of the desert."[4]

In 1996, twelve years later, Stark reported that his high estimate of projected growth was too low: by 1995 there were one million more Mormons than even a growth rate of 50 percent had predicted. Therefore he was still holding to his earlier projection of 265 million by 2080.[5] In 2001 he was saying the same: "By late in the twenty-first century the Church of Jesus Christ of Latter-day Saints will be a major world religion."[6]

In this paper we will test these claims by asking the following questions: Is Mormonism truly a new religion? Is it a world religion? Is it the first since Islam? What are its prospects for continued growth? I should add that when I discuss "Mormonism," I refer to the largest movement emerging from the life and teachings of Joseph Smith. There are many other smaller groups, such as the Community of Christ (formerly the Reorganized Church of Jesus Christ of Latter Day Saints), whose dynamics are different from the movement I am analyzing here.

Is Mormonism New?

In 1984, Stark insisted that, while Mormons "have retained cultural continuities with Christianity (just as Christianity retained continuities with Judaism and classical paganism), . . . the Mormons are a *new* religion."[7]

There is some disagreement here. Some Mormon scholars object that most Mormon distinctions can be found in earlier Christian thinkers and practices; some Mormon *believers* believe that the notion of Mormonism as new only feeds old and often-virulent prejudices that Mormonism is essentially unchristian and in fact a cult.

But there is an emerging consensus among both Mormon and non-Mormon scholars, that while Mormonism retains significant and central features of mainstream Christian thought and practice, it nevertheless diverges in ways sufficient to merit its characterization as a "new religious tradition."[8] Jan Shipps, who "has come to know the Saints better than any previous outside observer,"[9] has famously argued that Mormonism is a departure from the existing Christian tradition as much as early Christianity was a departure from Judaism. It abandoned both Roman Catholic and Protestant beliefs about the finality of the New Testament and particularly the Protestant principle of *sola scriptura*.[10]

Philip Barlow's recent study of Latter-day Saint use of the Bible reinforces Shipps's contention. Like Shipps, he believes Mormonism departs from *sola scriptura*: the new tradition puts limits on biblical authority and rejects the Bible as a sufficient religious guide.[11]

Since the time of Joseph Smith, the Mormon use of scripture has combined a traditional faith in the Bible with more "conservative" elements (like a more than occasional extra dose of literalism), some liberal components (such as Joseph Smith's Bushnell-like insistence on the limitations of human language), and, at least in an American context, some radical ingredients (an open canon, an oral scripture, the subjugation of biblical assertions to experimental truth or the pronouncements of living authorities).[12]

According to Barlow, Mormon apostle Bruce R. McConkie taught that while the Bible was originally inspired by God, it has since been corrupted and so now contains "only a shadow of the clearer, unmarred revelations Joseph Smith wrote and spoke." Elder McConkie said, "[Our present Bible] contains a bucket, a small pail, a few draughts, no more than a small stream at most, out of the great ocean of revealed truth that has come to men in *ages more spiritually enlightened* than ours."[13] McConkie felt the most enlightened age was that of Joseph Smith, who, as Grant Underwood notes, has been given by Mormons the same canonical status as the apostle Paul.[14] Barlow also points out that McConkie's views often dismayed some Mormon leaders, but over time were thought to be generally orthodox.[15]

There are other significant departures from mainstream Christian thought, such as "the possibility of people evolving into gods,"[16] the bodily nature of God, and "Latter-day Saints' erasure of unassailable walls of separation between matter and spirit and humans and gods."[17] For Eric Eliason, these doctrinal differences are possibly "serious enough to make Mormonism ultimately irreconcilable with traditional Christianity."[18]

Two scholars beg to differ. Terryl Givens, citing Stephen Robinson, uses Stark's outline of seven marks of orthodox Christian belief and finds that "in all seven cases, Mormon belief is in unambiguous accord with these core beliefs." Even the Mormon idea of deification is not new, he argues; it is no different from what can be found in Clement of Alexandria, Irenaeus, Justin Martyr, Athanasius, and Augustine. Givens cites Truman Madsen's assertion (but without accompanying argument) that Mormon beliefs anticipate thinking held by Bonhoeffer, Hartshorne, and (Avery) Dulles.[19]

Yet at the same time, Givens suggests that Mormonism rejects what Kierkegaard called the "infinite qualitative difference" between the human and the divine: "The [Mormon sense of the] divine, in other words, was not characterized by the radical otherness that [mainstream Christian] religious tradition equated with the sacred. For this reason, [Smith's] religious innovation was more the naturalizing of the supernatural than the other way around."[20] For Givens, then, the Mormon sacred is not, after all, the traditional understanding of *mysterium tremendum et fascinosum*. Religion is not mystery; God in a sense has been reduced (at least in difference from humanity) and humanity exalted. As Milton Backman puts it, Mormons teach an "anthropomorphic God and theomorphic man."[21] On the ontological nature of humanity and deity, then, even Givens suggests significant departure.

Christie Davies is another scholar who says Mormonism is not a new religion. Instead, he argues, it "is best regarded . . . as merely a forward position on a Protestant line of advance away from Roman Catholicism and back towards the traditions of the Old Testament."[22] But Davies adds that if Mormonism maintains an ultra-Protestant concern for abstention from mild drugs of sociability (alcohol for fundamentalist Protestants, caffeine for Mormons), it nevertheless guards a Jewish, "and very non-Christian, mode of defining its boundaries and identity through dietary taboos and an obsession with genealogy and descent."[23]

If Givens claims too much for the Mormon doctrine of deification (the Greek Fathers never broke down the wall of ontological separation between creature and Creator[24]), he is nonetheless right to emphasize continuities between Mormonism and traditional Christianity.[25] After all, these have often been obscured by religious polemics. Evangelicals in particular need to hear that Mormons teach basically the same moral theology which John Paul II called the "gospel of life"; that they believe in the (original) Bible as the Word of God, Jesus as God the Son and not just the Son of God, Jesus as the only means of salvation, and the substitutionary atonement. They also need to know that Mormon scriptures assert that salvation is not earned by human effort but that Christ took our sins, we take his righteousness, and we are saved by grace through faith.[26]

At the same time, however, the newness of this religious tradition cannot be denied. There is, in Barlow's phrase, an "enduring difference."[27] Mormons enlarge the biblical canon, accept new revelation, claim that God the Father had his own father, hold that eternal law is independent of and coeternal with God, deny ontological difference between creature and Creator, and reject *creatio ex nihilo*. In addition, Mormons and traditional Christians differ on whether creatures can share God's "incommunicable" attributes, whether there are nonmaterial beings, and whether there were preexistent spirits coequal with the Father of Jesus Christ.

Is Mormonism a World Religion?

Before investigating whether Mormonism is the newest world religion, one needs to acknowledge that the term *world religion* is anything but clear. Scholars have been debating its meaning for some decades now. The trouble is that they cannot agree on what it means.

The biggest problem is the word *religion* itself. Many in the West have defined it in terms of belief, especially belief in a supernatural deity. But many in other parts of the world challenge that assumption. Scholars of south Asian religion often observe that Hindus do not agree on any single belief, including belief in a personal god.[28] It is well known that philosophical Hindus reject belief in any personal deity, preferring impersonal nondualism. Theravada Buddhists, probably closest in belief to Gautama Buddha himself, are functional atheists as well. Yet surely we cannot say that these folks are not religious.

Some Western thinkers have defined religion in other ways. Schleiermacher and Tillich, for example, have focused on experience—either the feeling of absolute dependence or the attitude of ultimate concern.[29] Others find the essence of religion in its function. Freud, for example, said religion is based on repression of childhood sexuality and projection of these feelings on a god figure.[30] Durkeim proposed that religion is the way society seeks cohesion.[31]

Even the use of the singular *religion* is problematic, for it assumes an essence that is found in all the religions or even in the different versions of a single "religion," just as basic toothpaste is found in all the brands thereof. But what is the essence of Hinduism when there is no one thing on which all Hindus agree? Is there a common essence that unites Nigerian Anglicans and the American Episcopalians who consecrated an actively gay bishop? The Nigerians emphatically deny it. They also deny that they share anything religiously essential with their fellow Nigerian Muslims. Nigerian Muslims say the same about Nigerian Christians.

These definitional problems are what have led comparative religionist John Hinnells to say that religion is simply what people do who call themselves religious.[32] If *religion* is slippery, *world religion* is no easier to grasp. Most nontraditional groups prefer the term because its reputation is obviously superior to *sect* or *cult* and suggests broad appeal. Yet it, too, is hard to pin down, and scholars have been unable to reach consensus.

Does *world religion* mean that there are devotees scattered across the world? This alone cannot count, for there are hundreds of religious groups with insignificant numbers that no one would call world religions. Yet some religions that have significant numbers located in many countries are still inaccessible to most. Judaism, Zoroastrianism, Sikhism, and Hinduism, for example, are mostly ethnic and endogamous. This is why Douglas Davies, among others, says they are great religions of the world but not world religions.[33]

What then do we mean by *world religion*? A religious group in a variety of countries, accessible to newcomers, and of significant numbers? Even this last feature, which seems the most obvious, is suspect, for many religions cannot be counted easily. In East Asia, for example, millions would call themselves Buddhists. But most of these same people would also call themselves Confucianists and many, especially in China, also Taoists. Most estimates of religious demographics assume religious exclusivism for their surveys of world religions, but these Asian millions are clearly not exclusive in their religious attachments.[34]

These are some of the reasons Hinnells concludes that no label, neither *religion* nor *world religion*, is clear or transparent or perhaps even coherent.[35] Hence more work needs to be done defining what is meant by the terms before we say with any certainty if Mormonism qualifies. If the number of adherents can be misleading, it is nevertheless the easiest way to measure the size of a religious group. And if it is not the only measure of a world religion—whatever that may be—it is nevertheless an important and useful one. Since membership is the leading criterion Stark uses, we will use it to help us answer the next question.

Is Mormonism the First New Religion since Islam?

If we use the number of adherents as our primary measure of what we agree to call a world religion, it is impossible to say that The Church of Jesus Christ of Latter-day Saints is the first new world faith since Islam. Since the seventh century, a number of other new faiths have arisen of comparable or larger size. Each was sufficiently different from its parent religion to merit its moniker as a new tradition.

For example, True Pure Land Buddhism arose in the thirteenth century, inspired by Shinran's Protestant-like theological innovations. In the 2001 edition of David Barrett's *World Christian Encyclopedia*, which is one of the most reliable sources of comparative religious demographics, Mormons number 11 million while True Pure Land Buddhists total 14 million.[36] The twentieth-century new Japanese religion, Soka Gakkai, already outstrips the Mormon Church, 18 million to 11 million. Baha'is, who originated in the nineteenth century, numbered 7.1 million in 2000, while Sufism, which dates its origins to some time between the eighth and tenth centuries, claims a whopping 237 million.[37]

Shipps seems to agree with Stark's claim, but she limits her comparison to new American religious traditions. She proposes that every other new American religion was sectarian, which means that they did not change the mainstream Christian story in fundamental ways. Since Mormonism changed the story fundamentally by opening the canon with a new prophet and new revelation (and recapitulating key events in both Hebrew and early Christian histories in such singular ways that its history itself became a new text), it is a new religious *tradition*.[38]

But what about Jehovah's Witnesses? Did they not change the dominant religious story in fundamental ways? Mormons added new incarnations to the story, but Jehovah's Witnesses denied the concept of incarnation entirely. Mormons rejected traditional understandings of the origin of God the Son, but the Witnesses denied the *existence* of God the Son. Mormons disavow the Trinity but retain three "personages" of Father, Son, and Holy Spirit, each fully divine. Witnesses, on the other hand, do not even come close: Jesus is ontologically inferior to the Father, and the Spirit is an impersonal force.[39]

If Mormons qualify as a new tradition because of their changes to the dominant religious story, Jehovah's Witnesses also deserve the label. In terms of numbers, Jehovah's Witnesses are doing even better. Despite starting later (1872 vs. 1830), they have more adherents and are in more countries. Barrett reports that in 2000 there were 11 million Mormons in 116 countries, compared with 13 million Jehovah's Witnesses in 219 countries.[40]

Stark suggests that only Mormons have what it takes to become the next major world faith, listing ten marks of such a community. Careful consideration, however, reveals that the Jehovah's Witnesses also fare well when judged by these same criteria.

1. "Cultural continuity with the conventional faith(s) of the societies in which they seek converts."[41] Stark himself says that Jehovah's Witnesses will have an advantage over the Latter-day Saints in Christian societies because of novelties in Latter-day Saint theology: an infinite number of universes, multiple gods and their wives, and the potential of today's humans to become gods.[42] But the advantage may not be significant, given the Jehovah's Witnesses' discontinuity with modern culture on other scores: their pacifism, discouragement of higher education, and refusal to participate in civic groups or politics.

2. "Nonempirical" doctrines.[43] Here Jehovah's Witnesses are at a disadvantage because of their long history of failed attempts to predict the end of the world.[44] Mormons fare better on this score.

3. A modicum of tension with the surrounding environment: "strict but not too strict."[45] Mormons and Jehovah's Witnesses are probably comparable here: Jehovah's Witnesses do not celebrate birthdays or holidays, but they can drink alcohol. Mormons drink

neither coffee nor beer, but they are viewed by "Gentile" Americans as responsible citizens.

4. "Legitimate leaders with adequate authority to be effective."[46] This also means opportunity for members to assume authority. Both churches use self-taught laity, not seminary-trained clergy, to lead. Hence every member, at least among males, has the chance to take a leadership position.

5. Volunteer labor, who also evangelize. Both churches are remarkable on this score, with Jehovah's Witnesses having a slight edge, since they enlist all ages to go door to door, not just the young for two years.

6. High fertility rates. Both churches emphasize the importance of large families, and fertility rates are higher than average in each.[47]

7. Weak competition in a political context of religious freedom. For both Jehovah's Witnesses and Mormons, there is greater growth in regions where there are higher numbers of the unchurched. Stark has shown that where there is a healthy percentage of those who list their religious affiliation as "none," new Latter-day Saint membership is higher.[48] The same can be said for Jehovah's Witnesses in Europe, which has been secularized by the Enlightenment and communism.

8. "Strong internal attachments, while . . . able to maintain and form ties to outsiders."[49] Both groups seem adept at networking friends on the inside. But Mormons are better at forming ties to outsiders. Jehovah's Witnesses are less connected to the outside world because they reject a larger number of cultural institutions—not only politics, just war, and higher education, but also blood transfusions and blood products, religious holidays, extracurricular school activities, saluting the flag, and working in hospitals.

9. They "remain sufficiently strict."[50] Although Jehovah's Witnesses are more rigorous in terms of lifestyle, both churches maintain more than minimal tension with their surrounding cultures—especially in nations outside the United States where the Latter-day Saint church is perceived as an American religion.

10. Religious education that persuades the young not to defect or seek to eliminate the tension with their culture. Stark points out that since Latter-day Saints are well connected to outsiders and

mainstream American society, "the message to ambitious young Latter-day Saints [is that] successful people are religious people."[51] Hence they are not unduly tempted to think they need defect in order to find worldly success. This will be more problematic for Jehovah's Witnesses, who discourage higher education.

All in all, the differences between these two churches on these criteria are not great. The two churches are fairly even for six of the criteria, while Latter-day Saints have the advantage in three and Witnesses in one. This rough parity is evidenced by worldwide growth: the two churches are remarkably close in numbers of adherents, with Witnesses having a slight edge. Because the Witnesses have planted communities in 88 percent more countries and are not as associated theologically with America in this increasingly anti-American world, their prospects for further growth might be a little better.

Taking stock of the argument so far, Mormonism is indeed a new religious tradition, but it cannot be said to be the first new tradition since Islam. Other religious traditions with broad appeal have arisen since the seventh century, not only among non-Christian religious families but even within the American Christian congeries of traditions. The term *world religion* is problematic; there is no scholarly consensus on its meaning. But if we stipulate that it refers to a religious movement of significant numbers and is accessible to a broad number of peoples, then Mormonism takes its place not among the great world religions (all of which dwarf it in size[52]) but among a fair number that may someday reach that status.

Is Mormonism "Translatable"?

The question is, then, will Mormonism grow as Stark suggests? Perhaps we can learn from its parent, apostolic Christianity. According to Lamin Sanneh and Andrew Walls, the two most notable thinkers in the study of what has come to be called "world Christianity," the key to Christianity's growth has been its ability to transcend its Jewish-Palestinian culture and use the language and even concepts of new and different cultures.[53] In a word, the key lay in Christianity's "translatability."

Sanneh and Walls have argued that when Christian faith takes the word of Christ into a new culture—which more often than not is animated by a religious vision—it uses the language and almost invariably the concepts of the new culture. In the process, the faith is reshaped and sometimes even expanded by "translating" its message into the vocabulary and concepts of the new culture.

Scholars have noted that this process took place even during biblical periods. In the Old Testament, for example, God used previously existing Mesopotamian religious rituals (sacred torches and censers in initiation and purification rites, and circumcision) to teach new religious concepts to Abraham and his progeny.[54] God also seems to have used Persian religious traditions to teach his people in Babylonian exile new understandings of cosmic warfare and life after death.

In the New Testament, we can see the influence of Hellenistic religion: the Hellenistic *theos* was often understood to be a single godhead behind many names and mythologies or an impersonal One behind all that is. New Testament authors used the word, already invested with the suggestion of the ground and force behind everything that exists, and added a new layer of meaning denoting the epitome and source of personhood. Such "translation" is always risky: while something may be gained, something may also be lost by importing foreign connotations that corrupt the original meaning. The use of the new term "Lord" for Messiah (Christ) in Antioch (Acts 11:20), by unnamed believers from Cyprus and Cyrene speaking to Greeks, ran the risk of reducing Jesus to one more cult divinity alongside Lord Serapis or Lord Osiris. But because the new community was saturated in the Hebrew scriptures, the Greco-Roman *kyrios* was reshaped into a new kind of *kyrios*, recognizably Jewish.[55]

Sanneh has argued recently that translatability was therefore written into the fabric of the apostolic faith. It was not an accident that Christianity was the only world religion transmitted without the language or culture of its founder.[56] Jesus's followers believed the gospel ought to be translated into other languages and cultures. "There was nothing God wanted to say that could not be said in simple everyday language," and therefore be translated into other languages and cultures. All cultures were created equal; no language or culture had privileged access to the divine.[57]

The question then becomes whether, or to what degree, Mormonism is translatable. There are some positive indications that it has several comparative advantages in its translatability. First, as Douglas Davies has contended repeatedly, Mormonism promises the transcendence of death.[58] Indeed, Mormonism's transcendence comes "value-added." It goes beyond mainstream Christianity by not only offering some sort of salvation to nearly everyone—even non-Mormons—but also providing detailed descriptions of the afterlife. There are a variety of heavens available and the assurance of being reunited with family and other loved ones. On top of all that, it promises godhood to faithful Mormons. This is attractive to people in some cultures, particularly those in religions such as Theravada or Zen Buddhism that have little or no hope of conscious life after death.

Also, Latter-day Saints are able to tell residents of Latin America and the South Pacific that God did not neglect them. Recent interpretations of the Book of Mormon assert that Jesus's "other sheep" (John 10:16) were people in "ancient America," which is now said to include Central and South America and perhaps Pacific islands.[59] Stark has shown that many Latin American Saints believe they are direct descendants of Abraham through Lehi and that the Book of Mormon is "the authentic history of pre-Columbian times."[60] Hence Christie Davies confidently predicts, "Mormonism is set to become a new world religion because it reaches parts other religions cannot reach."[61]

Moreover, as Armand Mauss has pointed out, Mormonism has an enormous capacity for change. When the Latter-day Saints received poor reception in various times and climes, it changed its doctrine about blacks, Jews, and the identity of the Lamanites. In the process, "a provincial—even tribal—movement was gradually transformed into a universal religion in which lineage of all kinds became essentially irrelevant."[62] As Mormons adopted a greater Christocentric focus in the twentieth century and emphasized the apostle Paul's universalism, they dropped their nineteenth-century belief that Anglo-Saxon and German Mormons had an "inborn propensity, in their very blood, to recognize the teachings of Christ as delivered by Latter-day Saint missionaries."[63] This change bore "some apparent relationship to the results of church programs for proselyting and retention in various parts of the world."[64]

Similar pressures preceded the elimination of the ban on the priesthood for blacks. When the Nigerian government in the early 1960s refused Mormon missionaries because of the church's ban on black priests, and growth in the Brazilian church necessitated a new temple (which would have been closed to black converts), "President [Spencer W.] Kimball, in an inspiring combination of spiritual and political astuteness, brought his colleagues in the leadership to an acceptance of his own understanding of God's will in the matter."[65] The result was the 1978 elimination of the ban on blacks in the priesthood.

Emphasis on Jewish conversion has diminished as Jews have shown themselves "impervious" to the same, and the identity of Lamanites gradually shifted from North to South America "as church growth has bogged down among the Indians of North America and (by contrast) mushroomed in Latin America."[66]

Since Mormon theology is still in process (Lawrence Young laments "its limited formal theology"[67]), one wonders what would happen if it would continue some recent trends toward mainstream Christian theology.[68] There is some precedent here. In 1997, the Worldwide Church of God dropped both its objections to the doctrine of the Trinity and certain Pelagian tendencies and was accepted as a member of the National Association of Evangelicals.[69] Now, Mormon-Evangelical differences are greater than WCOG-Evangelical differences. Nevertheless, one guesses that if Mormonism were to affirm the incommensurability of the human and divine natures,[70] and the eternal deity of the godhead, Mormonism would be more translatable in regions (such as Africa and China) where there is increasing familiarity with historic Christian thought.

Despite these positive possibilities, Mormonism faces a number of obstacles as it seeks to become a world religion. Perhaps the most formidable is its close association with American history and culture. Mormons believe that God's new prophet was from New York and that the Millennium will begin in Missouri. When America had a better public image internationally, this may have been a drawing card for Mormon missionaries working abroad. But in recent years, it has become a liability. Growing anti-Americanism will hinder the promotion of a religion that is American not only culturally but theologically. Therefore the question is whether, as Douglas Davies poses it, Mormonism will be able to transcend indigenous culture or remain essentially North American.[71]

As we have already discussed, new understandings of Lamanites have helped Mormon missions in Latin America. But even here, resentment toward the northern superpower may hamper missionary efforts. In Asia and Africa, it will be more difficult. Lamin Sanneh has argued that mainstream Christian translatability has enabled African Christians to feel more African.[72] Will Mormon theology enable them to do the same, when they learn that Christ came to North and South America but not Africa?

This theological and cultural connection to America may help explain the second obstacle, which is what seems to be a low retention rate outside of the United States. In 1994, Lawrence Young observed that outside of the South Pacific, Mormonism was numerically marginal. In all countries except Chile (2.5 percent of the population), the Mormon population was usually significantly under 1 percent. Weekly attendance rates in Latin America and Asia were half of the rates in the United States. Young predicted that most new members outside the States would not be integrated successfully and that Mormonism would remain marginal in those societies.[73] Mauss was similarly pessimistic, noting in 1991 that retention rates for the second generation outside North America ranged "from modest to abysmal."[74] It is not clear that these problems have been resolved.[75]

Ironically, one of Mormonism's strengths is now a weakness: its lack of a formal theology.[76] Without a clearly identified set of core beliefs, it is harder for Mormonism to compete in areas with religions that have clear doctrine—mainstream Christianity and Islam, for example. In other words, if Mormonism's doctrinal fluidity were to work itself out of a job by clarifying its theological core, and particularly in the direction of mainstream Christian theology, it would become more competitive. But without those sorts of changes, it may be difficult to overcome its cultural embeddedness.

Conclusion

In summary, Mormonism is indeed a new religious tradition, with significant differences from mainstream Christianity. But it is not the first major faith to have arisen since Islam,[77] and it has not grown faster than any other new American religion. True Pure Land Buddhism, Sokka Gakkai, Baha'i, and Sufism are all religious movements that are of comparable or greater size and have also arisen since the seventh century. Each is an important departure from its religious parent. The Jehovah's Witness tradition, another new American religion, has grown even faster than Mormonism and boasts larger worldwide membership in many more countries. The Church of Jesus Christ of Latter-day Saints and Jehovah's Witnesses are comparable in their fulfillment of ten criteria that Stark proposes are necessary for religious growth.

Hence Mormonism is not among the great world religions (of course, Stark only claimed it is on its way), but it is one of a number of religious communities that are growing. Its potential to rank among the five or six largest religions depends on its translatability, that is, its ability to transcend its American provenance and theological character. It has the advantages of (1) teaching a near-universal salvation with an attractively detailed afterlife, (2) a proven capacity for adaptation, and (3) theological appeal to those who live in the Americas.

But precisely because of this American history and theological structure, its recent growth may start to level off, as its poor retention rates outside the United States suggest is possible. This trend may continue in parts of the world where anti-Americanism is growing and global Christianity's increasing prominence in the Third World is heightening sensitivity to differences with historic Christian beliefs. Unless it can transcend these cultural barriers, and reduce theological dissonance between its doctrines and mainstream Christian understandings of creation and ontology, it may prove difficult to sustain its growth outside the Americas.[78]

Notes

1. Rodney Stark, "The Rise of a New World Faith," *Review of Religious Research* 26, no. 1 (September 1984): 18.

2. Stark, "New World Faith," 19.

3. Stark, "New World Faith," Table 2, 22.

4. Stark, "New World Faith," 19.

5. Rodney Stark, "So Far, So Good: A Brief Assessment of Mormon Membership Projections," *Review of Religious Research* 38, no. 2 (December 1996): 178.

6. Rodney Stark, "The Basis of Mormon Success: A Theoretical Application," in *Mormons and Mormonism: An Introduction to an American World Religion,* ed. Eric A. Eliason (Urbana: University of Illinois Press, 2001), 239.

7. Stark, "The Rise of a New World Faith," 23. The emphasis is Stark's.

8. Jan Shipps, *Mormonism: The Story of a New Religious Tradition* (Urbana: University of Illinois Press, 1985), 149.

9. Philip Barlow, "Jan Shipps and the Mainstreaming of Mormon Studies," *Church History* 73, no. 2 (June 2004): 412.

10. Jan Shipps, *Sojourner in the Promised Land: Forty Years among the Mormons* (Urbana: University of Illinois Press, 2000), 331; Shipps, "Is Mormonism Christian? Reflections on a Complicated Question," in *Mormons and Mormonism*, 83; reprinted from *BYU Studies* 33, no. 3 (1993): 439–65.

11. Philip L. Barlow, *Mormons and the Bible: The Place of the Latter-day Saints in American Religion* (New York: Oxford University Press, 1991), 220.

12. Barlow, *Mormons and the Bible*, 227–28.

13. McConkie, cited in Barlow, *Mormons and the Bible*, 193, emphasis added.

14. Grant Underwood, "Mormons and the Millennial World-View," in *Mormon Identities in Transition,* ed. Douglas J. Davies (New York: Cassell, 1996), 141.

15. Barlow, *Mormons and the Bible,* 190.

16. Colleen McDannell and Bernhard Lang, "Modern Heaven . . . and a Theology," in *Mormons and Mormonism*, 145.

17. Eliason, "Introduction," in *Mormons and Mormonism*, 10.

18. Eliason, "Introduction," 10.

19. Terryl L. Givens, "'This Great Modern Abomination': Orthodoxy and Heresy in American Religion," in *Mormons and Mormonism*, 101–2. The seven points (the first four of which are regarded as essential) are "existence of a personal God, the divinity of Jesus Christ, the authenticity of biblical miracles . . . the existence of the Devil, . . . life beyond death, the virgin birth, and Christ's walking on water."

20. Givens, "'This Great Modern Abomination,'" 116.

21. Milton V. Backman, cited by Terryl Givens, "The Book of Mormon and Religious Epistemology," *Dialogue: A Journal of Mormon Thought* 34, no. 3 and 4 (Fall–Winter 2001): 53–65.

22. Christie Davies, "Coffee, Tea and the Ultra Protestant and Jewish Nature of the Boundaries of Mormonism," in *Mormon Identities*, 43.

23. Davies, "Coffee, Tea," 44.

24. Norman Russell's new authoritative study of deification among the Greek Fathers shows that deification language was used "in one of three ways, nominally, analogically, or metaphorically." The first used the word "gods" for human beings simply as a term of honor. The second stretched the nominal by saying that humans can become "sons or gods 'by grace' in relation to Christ who is Son and God 'by nature.'" The metaphorical use takes two approaches, the ethical and realistic. In the ethical, humans attempt "likeness" to God by moral imitation. In the realistic, humans participate in God's being. But the relationship even here is "asymmetrical," bringing together beings of "diverse ontological type"—the opposite of Mormon claims that God and humanity share the same ontology. Norman Russell, *The Doctrine of Deification in the Greek Patristic Tradition* (Oxford: Oxford University Press, 2004), 1–2.

Justin Martyr used Psalms 82:6 ("You are gods, and all of you sons of the Most High") to argue that "all human beings are deemed worthy of becoming gods and of having power to become sons of the Most High" (*Dialogue with Trypho* 124). But he relates deification only to John's statement that "to all who received [Christ], who believed in his name, he gave power to become children of God" (John 1:12). He never developed this statement into a doctrine resembling Mormon deification (Russell, *Doctrine of Deification*, 96–101).

Irenaeus linked Psalms 82:6 not to Johannine "children of God" but to Pauline adoption. His doctrine of deification ("Because of his infinite love he became what we are in order to make us what he is in himself" [*Against Heresies* 5. Preface]) therefore "involves an exchange of properties, not the establishment of an identity of essence. He who was Son of God by nature became a man in order to make us sons by adoption (*Against Heresies* 3.19.1)" (Russell, *Doctrine of Deification*, 106, 108).

Clement's deification is similar. It is "not ontological—human nature per se is not transformed by the Logos—but exemplary. . . . Christians who have attained perfection will be enthroned in glory with the highest grade of the saved, but still on a lower level than Christ. As Butterworth points out, this shows 'how careful Clement is to distinguish between the most exalted men or angels and Christ (1916:161). *The divinity of the perfect is a divinity by title or analogy*" (Russell, *Doctrine of Deification*, 137, 133–34; emphasis added).

Even Origen, who is widely considered to have been more deeply influenced by Hellenistic notions of divinization, maintains this ontological distinction. According to Origen, a "fundamental distinction should be made between that which is immortal, rational, good, etc. of itself and that which merely participates in these attributes, although the term 'god' may be predicated equally of both. . . . Although like the Logos they are recipients of divinity, [those made in the image of God] are much further removed from God. The Logos alone abides intimately with God in ceaseless contemplation of the Fatherly depths. . . . Origin maintains that men are virtuous in a contingent sense by participation in a goodness which is self-subsistent" (Russell, *Doctrine of Deification*, 145, 147).

Athanasius, whose exchange formula is most often quoted ("He became human that we might become divine" [*On the Incarnation* 54]), shows most emphatically that Mormon deification is qualitatively different from patristic deification. Athanasius argued that "recipients of adoption and deification have simply received the name of sons and gods; Christ, however, is Son and God 'by nature and according to essence.'" Athanasius insisted on a "radical division" between the "agenetic" Godhead and the "genetic" created order, the ἀγένητος and the γενητά. "If to be deified by participation must be contrasted with true divinity, then the Logos is certainly not deified." The Christ is the Father's "only own and true Son deriving from his essential being." Hence the participant is essentially different from the participated. In Athanasius's determination to defeat Arianism, he denied any similarity at all between Christ and those who are participate in Him. In those discussions, he "played down the designation of men as gods." Hence for Athanasius there was no question of humans ever becoming the same as God. "They are sons and gods only in name" (Russell, *Doctrine of Deification*, 171, 170, 182, 181, 185, 186).

Augustine is little different. In the *City of God* he writes, "It is one thing to be God, another thing to be a partaker of God" (22:30). In *On Nature and Grace* we find the following: "The creature will never become equal with God even if perfect holiness were to be achieved in us. Some think that in the next life we shall be changed into what he is; I am not convinced" (33:37) (Russell, *Doctrine of Deification*, 332). Of course, the fact that Augustine needed to make this clarification suggests that the ontological line between humanity and deity was not clear for some in the church of his day.

25. See Terryl L. Givens, "Joseph Smith: Prophecy, Process, and Plenitude," in this volume, 63–64.

26. For Mormon understandings of grace, see 2 Nephi 2:3, 5–8; 33:6; Doctrine and Covenants 20:30–31. These understandings nevertheless differ from what one finds in most Protestant circles. For example, most Mormons seem to interpret 2 Nephi 25:23 ("It is by grace that we are saved, after all we

can do") in semi-Pelagian manner, consistent with the Mormon Third Article of Faith: "We believe that through the Atonement of Christ, all mankind may be saved, by obedience to the laws and ordinances of the Gospel." More charitably, this could be viewed as an Arminian position. For further discussion of evangelical and Latter-day Saint differences on salvation, see Craig L. Blomberg and Stephen E. Robinson, *How Wide the Divide? A Mormon and an Evangelical in Conversation* (Downers Grove, Ill.: InterVarsity Press, 1997), 143–88.

Latter-day Saint scholars at Brigham Young University have sought to minimize the disparity between Mormon and mainstream Christian soteriologies. Robert L. Millet, for example, has argued that the intent of the 2 Nephi 25 passage is that "above and beyond all we can do, it is by the grace of Christ that we are saved"; see Robert L. Millet, *Grace Works* (Salt Lake City: Deseret Book, 2003), 131; Robert L. Millet, *The Mormon Faith: A New Look at Christianity* (Salt Lake City: Shadow Mountain, 1998), 69–79, 168–69; Robert L. Millet, *By Grace Are We Saved* (Salt Lake City: Bookcraft, 1989); see also Stephen E. Robinson, *Are Mormons Christians?* (Salt Lake City: Bookcraft, 1991), 104–8; and Robinson in Robinson and Blomberg, *How Wide the Divide?* esp. 143–66.

27. Barlow, *Mormons and the Bible,* 228.

28. See, for example, Vasudha Narayanan, "The Hindu Tradition," in *World Religions: Eastern Traditions,* ed. Willard G. Oxtoby (New York: Oxford University Press, 2002), 16.

29. Friedrich Schleiermacher, *The Christian Faith* (Edinburgh: T. and T. Clark, 1928); Paul Tillich, *Systematic Theology,* vol. 1 (Chicago: University of Chicago Press, 1951).

30. Sigmund Freud, *Totem and Taboo* (1913–14; repr., New York: W. W. Norton, 1962).

31. Emile Durkheim, *The Elementary Forms of the Religious Life* (1912; repr., New York: Free Press, 1995).

32. John Hinnells, "What Is a World Religion?" unpublished paper author shared with me.

33. Douglas J. Davies, *The Mormon Culture of Salvation* (Aldershot, England: Ashgate, 2000), 259; see also Douglas J. Davies, "World Religion: Dynamics and Constraints," in this volume, 255.

34. See, for example, Julia Ching, "East Asian Religions," in *World Religions,* 348–49.

35. Hinnells, "What Is a World Religion?" 259.

36. David B. Barrett, George T. Kurian, and Todd M. Johnson, eds., *World Christian Encyclopedia,* 2d ed., 2 vols. (New York: Oxford University Press, 2001), 2:5, 7. According to the Latter-day Saint church almanac, total membership in 2004 was 12,207,000; *Deseret Morning News Church Almanac* (Salt Lake City: Deseret News, 2004), 6.

37. Barrett, *World Christian Encyclopedia*, 2:5, 7. Each of these religious movements represented significant departures from previous traditions. Shinran's rejection of all "ways of effort" (*jiriki*) was a radical divergence from the Gotama's endorsement of self-effort: "Be ye lamps unto yourselves" (Farewell Address, in Mahaparinibbana Suttanta). Soka Gakkai followed Nichiren in regarding other religions as false and other Buddhist sects as heretical. The Baha'is believe other divine messengers have come since Muhammad and will come in the future, implicitly rejecting traditional Islam's insistence that Muhammad was the "seal" (last) of the prophets. For this and other reasons Islamic authorities have persecuted Baha'is. Although Sufis have comprised large percentages of Muslims, they have often been condemned by "mainstream" Islamic groups for practices such as praying to Muhammad and the saints, and since the eighteenth century have been denounced by the Wahhabiya—now one of the most potent Islamic movements—as foreign to "true" Islam.

38. Shipps, *Mormonism*, 49.

39. For Jehovah's Witnesses beliefs about the Trinity, Jesus and the Spirit, see "Should You Believe in the Trinity?" (Brooklyn: Watchtower Bible and Tract Society, 1989).

40. Barrett, *World Christian Encyclopedia*, 2:664.

41. Stark, "The Basis of Mormon Success: A Theoretical Application," in *Mormons and Mormonism*, 216.

42. Stark, "The Basis of Mormon Success," 225–26.

43. Stark, "The Basis of Mormon Success," 221.

44. Joseph F. Zygmunt, "Prophetic Failure and Chiliastic Identity: The Case of Jehovah's Witnesses," *American Journal of Sociology* 75, no. 6 (May 1970): 926–48; M. James Penton, *Apocalypse Delayed: The Story of Jehovah's Witnesses* (Toronto: University of Toronto Press, 1985).

45. Stark, "The Basis of Mormon Success," 222.

46. Stark, "The Basis of Mormon Success," 226.

47. Stark, "The Basis of Mormon Success," 234. According to Stark, it has been "carefully documented many times" that Latter-day Saints have larger families.

48. Stark, "The Basis of Mormon Success," 234–35. This may not be true in Europe, however, where the Latter-day Saint church has not prospered and is dominated by expatriates.

49. Stark, "The Basis of Mormon Success," 236.

50. Stark, "The Basis of Mormon Success," 237.

51. Stark, "The Basis of Mormon Success," 239.

52. Barrett and Johnson, in *World Christian Encyclopedia*, 3, Table 7–1, report Christianity (2 billion), Islam (1.2 billion), Hinduism (811 million), and Buddhism (360 million) as the great world religions, with the Sikhs (23 million) and Jews (14 million) as two notable but ethnic religions.

53. Andrew F. Walls, *The Missionary Movement in Christian History: Studies in the Transition of Faith* (Maryknoll, N.Y.: Orbis, 1996); Lamin O. Sanneh, *Translating the Message: The Missionary Impact on Culture* (Maryknoll, N.Y.: Orbis Books, 1989); and Sanneh, "Gospel and Culture: Ramifying Effects of Scriptural Translation," in *Bible Translation and the Spread of the Church: The Last 200 Years*, ed. Philip C. Stine (Leiden, Netherlands: Brill, 1990), 1–23.

54. McDermott, *Can Evangelicals Learn from the World Religions? Jesus, Revelation and Religious Traditions* (Downers Grove, Ill.: InterVarsity Press, 2000), 80–82.

55. Walls, *Missionary Movement*, 34–35.

56. Lamin Sanneh, *Whose Religion Is Christianity? The Gospel beyond the West* (Grand Rapids, Michigan: Eerdmans, 2003), 97–98, 120. One might ask how Islam grew so quickly while insisting the Qur'an cannot be translated. Sanneh contends that Islam spread so quickly in its first century because, unlike Christianity in its first three centuries, it was able to harness the powers of the sword and the state.

57. Sanneh, *Whose Religion Is Christianity?* 98.

58. See, for example, Davies, *The Mormon Culture of Salvation*, 264; see also Davies, "World Religion: Dynamics and Constraints," 256.

59. "The Living Christ: The Testimony of the Apostles," *Church Almanac*, 20. Many Saints now believe that the central characters in the Book of Mormon lived in Central America; John L. Sorenson, *An Ancient American Setting for the Book of Mormon* (Salt Lake City: Deseret Book, 1985).

60. Stark, "The Basis of Mormon Success," 218–19.

61. Christie Davies, "Place, Time, and Family in Mormonism," *Dialogue* 34, no. 3 and 4 (Fall–Winter 2001): 18.

62. Armand L. Mauss, "Mormonism's Worldwide Aspirations and Its Changing Conceptions of Race and Lineage," *Dialogue* 34, no. 3–4 (Fall–Winter 2001): 103.

63. Mauss, "Mormonism's Worldwide Aspirations," 109.

64. Mauss, "Mormonism's Worldwide Aspirations," 105.

65. Mauss, "Mormonism's Worldwide Aspirations," 123–24.

66. Mauss, "Mormonism's Worldwide Aspirations," 125.

67. Lawrence A. Young, "Confronting Turbulent Environments: Issues in the Organizational Growth and Globalization of Mormonism," in *Contemporary Mormonism: Social Science Perspectives,* ed. Marie Cornwall, Tim B. Heaton, and Lawrence A. Young (Urbana: University of Illinois Press, 1994), 61. In 1996 Mauss noted that core Mormon doctrines had not been identified. See Armand L. Mauss, "Identity and Boundary Maintenance: International Prospects for Mormonism at the Dawn of the Twenty-First Century," in *Mormon Identities,* 13.

68. For example, theologian Robert L. Millet's efforts to reorient Mormon soteriology toward grace and away from Pelagian conceptions. See note 26.

69. Mark A. Kellner, "Worldwide Church of God Joins NAE," in *Christianity Today* 41, no. 7 (June 16, 1997): 66.

70. This need not conflict with Mormon deification, if the latter were to be redefined in accord with historic Christian understandings. See my discussion of this earlier in note 24 above.

71. Davies, *Mormon Culture of Salvation*, 238; see Davies, "World Religion: Dynamics and Constraints," 11–12.

72. Sanneh, *Whose Religion Is Christianity?* 43.

73. Young, *Contemporary Mormonism,* 56–60.

74. Mauss, "Identity and Boundary Maintenance," in *Mormon Identities*, 13.

75. Professor Tim Heaton, a leading scholar of Mormon demographics at Brigham Young University, told me he does not know of any study since that time (mid-1990s) that documents retention rates outside the United States. Phone conversation, April 21, 2005.

76. Nor has there been delineation of "core Mormon doctrines." Mauss, "Identity and Boundary Maintenance," 13.

77. Stark's comparison of Mormonism to Islam suggests more similarity than actually exists. The apparent analogies at first appear remarkable—both traditions suggest the best evidence for their faith is their book of revelation; both claim the Christian scriptures have been corrupted; both founders were prophet-statesmen who set up a religio-political order; both tout their theologies' simplicity as evidence of their superiority to the arcane complexities of traditional Christian theology; and both founders taught and practiced polygamy. But the differences are more significant: Mormons proclaim Jesus as God in the flesh, the Savior of the human race, who was crucified and raised from the dead. Muslims deny each of these propositions.

78. This is particularly true as Christianity has become centered in the southern hemisphere. See Sanneh, *Whose Religion Is Christianity?* and Philip Jenkins, *The Next Christendom: The Coming of Global Christianity* (New York: Oxford University Press, 2002).

Joseph Smith and
the Making of a Global Religion

Jan Shipps

In regard to the other "worlds" of the first Mormon prophet, Joseph Smith was certainly "in that world *and* of it." He was clearly in attendance "in his own time;" he attempted to recover past worlds; he was and is present in his own and in the personal worlds of others; and he challenged the theological world of his day.

In the sense that his gospel vision was expansive enough to impel his sending members of the Quorum of the Twelve as missionaries to England and continental Europe—and even sending Orson Hyde to Jerusalem—Joseph Smith put down the foundations for reaching out to the entire world.[1] Yet when he was murdered in 1844, Mormonism essentially remained an indigenous North American faith.[2] Joseph the prophet was not present when Mormonism became what some now describe as a "global religion."

Smith's initial prophetic vision had been that the gathering of the Saints would make possible the building of the "New Jerusalem" in Jackson County, Missouri, a place that would have a temple at its center (Doctrine and Covenants 57). After the construction of a temple surrounded by a Mormon kingdom became impossible there, the Saints built a kingdom on the Mississippi and constructed their second temple, this one in the city they called Nauvoo. But events transpired such that this place of habitation, too, had to be abandoned.

Following the splintering of the Mormon movement, which occurred after Smith's death, the largest body of the Saints followed Brigham Young and most of the members of the Quorum of the Twelve to the Intermountain West.[3]

Once settled in the Great Salt Lake Valley, they again became very serious about spreading the gospel to foreign parts. Missionaries were again sent to the British Isles, all through northern Europe, and even to the South Seas. But as Mormonism was still in its gathering phase—living in the "winding-up scene"—the church's missionaries encouraged all those who accepted the gospel message to join the body of the Saints in the Great Basin. Establishing the Perpetual Emigrating Fund and assisting in many other ways, the church helped converts come to the valley in the tops of the mountains. Rather than spreading across the globe, the form of Mormonism whose institutional manifestation is The Church of Jesus Christ of Latter-day Saints centered itself in the Intermountain West, where it became a provincial faith.

Leonard Arrington and many other scholars who have paid close attention to the life of Brigham Young have argued convincingly that as the "Lion of the Lord" presided over the Saints in the intermountain region, he turned his beloved Joseph's prophetic vision into reality.[4] In doing so, he created a kingdom that turned on its head the persecution the Saints had faced as long as they were in the United States. Before they departed the settled United States, they had lived in a land that, despite the separation of church and state, was virtually a Protestant establishment. In the West, The Church of Jesus Christ of Latter-day Saints became the established church. Other religious bodies were "tolerated" in territorial Utah in about the same way that sects were tolerated in the British Empire with its established church at that time. Consequently, for at least a decade, the kingdom was truly a Mormon theocratic state, and, to some of the Saints, the Millennium seemed to be over the next horizon.

When the United States government sent the army to intervene in the kingdom-building process in 1856–1857, Brigham Young directed the church's foreign missionaries to return to their home-base in the Intermountain West. This, however, was only a brief temporary remission of the missionary effort. Rather than giving up on gathering the Saints, the Saints never lost sight of the injunction found both in the New Testament and in revelations given through Joseph Smith instructing them to "go ye into all the world." In "whatsoever place ye cannot go ye shall send [missionaries], [so] that the testimony may go from you into all the world unto every creature" (Mark 16:15; Doctrine and Covenants 84:62).

Those who heard the message and responded by converting to the new faith were not only asked to accept a new understanding of what it meant to be Christian, but also to prepare to gather with the Saints in the intermountain region of the United States. The Great Basin became a new place of gathering both for the Saints who had become part of the movement during the lifetime of Joseph Smith and those who responded to the gospel message after his death.

Salt Lake City became the new center of God's earthly kingdom, and within what subsequently became mountain Mormonism, the geographical trajectory from periphery to center was maintained until the early decades of the twentieth century. Many vibrant Latter-day Saint congregations were established outside the Intermountain West.[5] But until long after the end of World War II, the Mormon world was divided into the "kingdom" in the Intermountain West and Mormonism elsewhere, which was popularly known as "the mission field."

This faith community's construction of itself as a truly significant player on the global religious scene really began during the presidency of David O. McKay (1951–1970). His attention to the church's restructured missionary program; development of an extraordinary building agenda; creation of a correlation program that, in time, would function to ensure that Mormonism would be the same no matter where it materialized, with enough strength and vitality to be organized into wards and stakes; and his circumnavigation of the globe were all essential elements in beginning the transformation of Mormonism from provincial tradition to global religious force.[6] A signal alteration that carried this transformation forward came during the presidency of Spencer W. Kimball when in 1978 a new revelation made priesthood ordination available to all "worthy" males, thereby universalizing the Mormon message (Doctrine and Covenants Official Declaration 2). And practically the entire ecclesiastical administration of Gordon B. Hinckley (including his many years of service as proto-president) has been devoted to completing the "conversion" that would make the church and its gospel message universal enough to make itself at home in myriad places and many different cultures.

When and in What Sense "Global"?

The complete history of twentieth-century Mormonism has yet to be written. But armchair observers seem to agree that the growth and geographical expansion of Mormonism is primarily due to the program initiatives and policies of Presidents McKay, Kimball, and Hinckley. If these presidents are responsible for the growth, then why have a session on Joseph Smith and the making of a global religion in this Library of Congress conference on "The Worlds of Joseph Smith?" It is true that the first Mormon prophet said he wanted to take the gospel to the entire world. But other than organizing the "traveling high council" and sending out missionaries to accomplish the gathering of potential Saints scattered throughout the nations, just how much did Joseph Smith do to begin the process of turning Mormonism into a global religion?

If this question is considered in practical and strategic terms, the answer is "not much." But in getting beyond such a superficial response that treats the query as if it were posed in ordinary common sense terms, Douglas Davies's paper is of considerable benefit to students of Mormonism. It is helpful first of all because he draws a valuable distinction between *global* religions (understood primarily with regard to the geographical dispersion of various faith communities all across the world) and *world* religions (understood not only in terms of geographical dispersion, but with how fully faith communities are assimilated into the cultures where they are located). In Davies's typological scheme, Buddhism, Christianity, and Islam are clearly world religions while Judaism, Sikhism, and perhaps Hinduism—all great religions of the world—probably do not merit classification in the world religion category.[7]

In addition to making distinctions based on geographical dispersion and levels of assimilation, Davies defines a true world religion as one that is ultimately concerned with the conquest of death. But as his discussion of the dynamics of world religions makes clear, he is aware that elements other than theology and ritual help to determine whether a religion is or is not a world religion. Both Davies and Gerald McDermott say that religions that are true world religions do not remain embedded in their own particular geographic places and idiosyncratic cultures. Instead, they become encultured, making themselves genuinely at home in myriad places and many different cultures. On the other hand, those religions that do not fit into the world religion class may also be widely dispersed geographically. But they never become fixed more or less firmly as an integral part of the surrounding host cultures where they are located.[8]

Away from their home cultures, religions in this second category preserve enough of their home cultures to make them always seem somewhat foreign to whatever host culture they encounter. This is what seems to have happened to Mormonism. While it has gone global in the past half-century, it continues to struggle with its Americanness. As one German Saint said in a recent email message to me, "[probably because of correlation, Mormonism's] message, metaphors, and images are retained without adaptation." Texts are translated, of course, but this particular "un-gathered" Saint believes that the persistent uniformity of Mormon programs and materials across cultures makes it difficult to use culturally appropriate images in other countries. Perhaps time will remedy this, but until it is remedied, Mormonism is likely to retain a status similar to Judaism— a great religion of the world—but not a religion that belongs in Davies's world religion category.

For all that, the reference to Mormonism as a global religion compelled Davies to grapple with Rodney Stark's prediction that Mormonism will be the next great world religion and with his argument that rational choice is the best way to account for the almost exponential growth and geographical expansion of Mormonism that took place between 1930 and the end of the twentieth century.[9] In referring to the work of this sociologist, whose published work has had such a high profile among Mormon ecclesiastics, bureaucrats in the church's Public Affairs division, and the Latter-day Saint intellectual community, Davies points out that Stark's analysis primarily rests on church growth as measured in membership numbers. But he does not—as many of his sociologist colleagues are now doing—make reference to the way that the rate of Mormonism's growth has slowed in recent years or to his failure to take membership retention into account.[10]

Instead Davies uses Sir Isaiah Berlin's distinction between "thin" and "thick" forms of information within different disciplines to point to how much Stark's argument rests on single-stranded material (membership statistics) and how even his application of rational choice theory to the Mormon case does not measure up to the creation of a texture constituted of many interwoven strands. Challenging Stark effectively, but less directly than does Gerald McDermott, Davies offers his own understanding of what a world religion is, reiterating his firm distinction between a world religion and a global religion before turning to the question: What is the relationship between Joseph Smith and the making of a global religion?

Because his observations on the latter matter are brought together around the concept of *courage,* Davis rapidly moves into the experiential arena. He credits Joseph Smith with the courage to accept his prophetic call, which Davies connects with the First Vision. He refers as well to how, despite considerable taunting and the cruel behavior directed toward him, Smith was willing to function as a seer and translator, as well as prophet. Throughout this section of his paper, Davies echoes Richard Bushman's argument, describing a prophet who moved forward without fully understanding what was happening to him.[11]

As significant as were the prophet's profound encounters with deity, there is another way to address the matter of the connection between Joseph Smith and the Mormonism of today, a different way of asking what the first Mormon prophet did to prepare the way for this faith community to be what it is two hundred years after his birth.

Before I turn to this method of connecting Joseph Smith to modern Mormonism, I must add to the discussion of typology by pointing to yet another way of thinking about religious movements. We need to add and define a different term: *religious tradition*. The most expeditious way to capture the meaning of this term is to think chronologically.

New religious movements come into existence when followers coalesce around a charismatic leader. But unless the charisma at their centers is somehow preserved through a process that the eminent theoretical sociologist Max Weber described as the "routinization of charisma," such movements—sociologists call them cults—do not survive the death or disappearance of their leaders.[12] If the charisma is somehow preserved, religious movements take on the shape of sects, denominations, churches, or much more rarely, religious traditions. While preserving much of existing traditions, new traditions differ from them in fundamental ways. Before they can move on to become either global or world religions, however, they must be firmly grounded in the real world. Only after they are fully realized as new traditions does the question of whether they can or cannot modify and adapt to host cultures come into play.

In What Sense "Religion"?

A little historical aside is probably in order here. Much was changing in Mormonism around the time of its sesquicentennial in 1980. An almost unaccustomed spirit of optimism was infecting Latter-day Saint communities throughout the nation and across the world. What appeared to be an infinite number of missionaries were converting what appeared to be an infinite number of persons to the Mormon faith. Such a rapid rate of church growth suggested to some observers that this faith community had entered what the economic historian W. W. Rostow called the "take-off" stage, after which truly extraordinary membership growth would be a normal condition.[13]

Although church growth and geographical expansion were causing headaches for general authorities and church bureaucrats alike— what a fascinating story all of this is—the future for Mormonism looked brighter than it had for many generations. It was at this point that Rodney Stark, a University of Washington sociologist, began to pay attention to Mormonism. At the same time, the Mormon intellectual community was experiencing what Davis Bitton has denominated Camelot, a glorious time when the sources of the church's history were open to scholarly appraisal and new communities of inquiry (the Mormon History Association, *Dialogue, Sunstone*) were coming into existence, bringing all sorts of Saints, inactive as well as active, mountain Saints and prairie Saints, plus a few interested non-Mormon scholars together to seek answers not only to questions about what happened in the formative years of Mormonism and in the pioneer period, but also questions about Mormonism as religious phenomenon.

One large part of the scholarly community had a ready answer to the question of what Mormonism was/is: it was/is the true Church of Jesus Christ. Another equally significant part of the body of scholars who were studying American religion was not so sure. Was it a sectarian movement—a sect to end all sects as the distinguished scholar of Protestantism, William Clebsch, asked in one of the very first issues of *Dialogue*?[14] Was it "a sect, a mystery cult, a new religion, a church, a people, a nation, or an American subculture" or all of the above, asked "Mr. American Religious History," the eminent Yale professor Sidney Ahlstrom.[15] Or, as Mario DePillis, another well-known non-Mormon scholar, proposed, along with Will Herberg, was Mormonism simply one more way to be American?[16] Although Stark may not have been as aware of this heated debate as were historians and scholars of religion, in 1984 he weighed in with the news that Mormonism would be the next great world religion.

The very next year, in my first book I argued that Mormonism was a new religious tradition, one that stood apart from Christianity in its Protestant, Catholic, and Orthodox forms and was more connected to Christianity's Hebraic roots than existing Christian traditions.[17] Because Stark's proposal was put into print less than six months before my argument appeared in book form, it is not surprising that my argument about what Mormonism is and Stark's prediction about what it might become in the future became confused. Many folks apparently thought that the arguments were one and the same.

For years I have been trying to say that this is not correct and to clarify the difference. Happily, the distinction that Davies makes between how some arguments are made on "thick" and others on "thin" materials spells out the difference in my argument and that of Stark's much more clearly. Stark's conclusion that Mormonism will be the next world religion was based on "thin" material, on statistics describing the church's membership growth and geographical expansion. My argument that Mormonism is a new religious tradition was based on a much "thicker" examination of Mormon materials.

Drawing on the theoretical (not theological) analyses of the eminent religious studies scholar Ninian Smart and the history of religions specialist Mircea Eliade, I set about examining Mormonism in order to determine whether in it I could identify the six dimensions of religion that are found in such existing religious traditions as Christianity and Judaism, as well as religions that—having passed from the scene—are now artifactual religious traditions.[18] These dimensions are the mythological, doctrinal, ritual, social/institutional, ethical, and experiential. Once this agenda was set, the data I had gathered in the previous twenty years of research convinced me that in Mormonism not only do all six dimensions of religion exist; they are also distinctive.

Added to the biblical story, the Book of Mormon enriches the mythological dimension of Mormonism, a dimension that is also augmented by the life stories of those who first believed. Mormon doctrine is distinctive both in its character and in the way it was settled—not through councilor deliberations but by way of revelation. The building of a temple rather than a church in Kirtland and the Prophet's translation of the Bible and other texts generated the development of a unique configuration of ritual practice as well as a particularly distinctive theology. Mormon social patterns were profoundly affected by the introduction of plural marriage, and although Mormonism's ecclesiastical manifestations resembled Catholicism and certain forms of Christian primitivism, its priesthood structure and lay clergy made the social/institutional dimension of the Mormon religion exceptional as well. Except for the Word of Wisdom, the ethical dimension of Mormonism is not as atypical as are all the other dimensions of this religion. (But this is a huge exemption because one of the functions of the Word of Wisdom has always been that it signifies Sainthood.[19]) The gathering and the subsequent creation of a Mormon village lifestyle even in the urban areas of the great intermountain Mormon corridor made the everyday experience of the Saints unique. Finally, that part of the experiential dimension of religion that forged connections between the divine and human realms was so often characterized by the sorts of revelation that Dallin H. Oaks describes in his contribution to this volume, plus the oft-described revelatory response to Moroni 10:4, that the experiential dimension of religion in Mormonism is likewise exceptional. It is both comparable to and different from the experiential dimensions of other religious faiths.

Separating these six dimensions in this manner is artificial. But the way they work together to create a peculiar people with a shared language and symbol system is an indication that Mormonism is more than a cult, sect, denomination, or church. It is a religious tradition, one that was new when it came into being in nineteenth-century America. And here is where one answer to what Joseph Smith had to do with the making of a global religion comes in.

Both Charismatic and Practical

The Mormon prophet was absolutely central to the creation of virtually all of the dimensions of Mormonism, both doctrinal and practical. Whether its source was golden plates or some inspired production process, the Book of Mormon came forth through the agency of Joseph Smith. He was a seer and translator as well as prophet and leader. As one who spoke for God, Smith was likewise the agent through which the revelations that established the church's theology and organization were introduced. The fundamental ritual patterns were also established through prophetic action.

Although the architectural plans of the social and institutional and even the ethical structures that the Saints turned into reality came through prophecy, Joseph Smith was, one might say, the general contractor. His leadership was practical and farsighted as well as prophetic. Without him, Mormonism—had it lasted—would be something else entirely. While he did not do what he did single-handedly, he was the originator, designer, and engineer responsible for the creation of this new religious tradition.

Even though fairly firmly established, many new religious movements never get beyond the stage of being led by a charismatic leader. The leader's death spells the eventual demise of the movement. That this did not happen in the wake of Joseph Smith's death may well be his greatest contribution to the making of modern Mormonism. Early on, his role as prophet was conflated with his role as ordained priest and as prophet-priest he was likewise the president of the church as well as the president of the high priesthood.[20] This meant that, unlike many other religious systems brought into being by charismatic leaders, Mormonism had three quite separate streams of authority already in place when Smith was murdered.

The organization of the church was complete enough that the mantle of the prophet did not have to fall on a new charismatic leader in order for the movement to survive. Of equal significance, because of this conflation of the roles of prophet and priest, Mormonism was not constrained by the need to wait until some extended "routinization of charisma" was completed for the tradition to get on with the business of carrying the gospel message to the world.

In the end, however, it is critical not to overlook the reality that Joseph Smith was a charismatic figure and that it was through his agency that the heavens were opened and the divine once again spoke in a language that humans could understand. Without the reopening of that conversation, Mormonism would likely be just one more restoration movement that started out, as did the Disciples of Christ, claiming to be the only true Church of Jesus Christ, but all too quickly took its place on the religious landscape as an idiosyncratic Protestant denomination.

Although something of that nature might well be happening in the Community of Christ, there seems little danger that this could happen to the Mormonism of the mountain Saints.[21] But it is too soon to know what is likely to happen to The Church of Jesus Christ of Latter-day Saints (and Joseph Smith) headquartered in Salt

Lake City. What appears to this "Mormon watcher" at present is that its categorical home is something between a global religion and a great world religion. Somewhat like Judaism, it is fully realized as a religious tradition, but it is one not able to be fully encultured in some parts of the world. Whether it is a proto-world religion, one that will yet lengthen its stride enough to attain world religion status, remains to be seen.

Notes

1. Grant Underwood, *The Millenarian World of Early Mormonism* (Urbana: University of Illinois Press, 1993), 26.

2. Canada was almost as much a part of the Mormonism of Joseph Smith's day as was the United States.

3. A surprising proportion of Smith's followers remained in the Midwest and elsewhere east of the Mississippi River. In addition to the Saints who "reorganized" the church in 1860 under the leadership of Joseph Smith III, Mormon organizations came into existence under the leadership of Sidney Rigdon, James J. Strang, Charles B. Thompson, Alpheus Cutler, and others. In addition, a substantial group of Saints followed Lyman Wight to Texas. See Steven L. Shields, *Divergent Paths of the Restoration: A History of the Latter-day Saint Movement*, 3rd ed. (Bountiful, Utah: Restoration Research, 1982) and Michael Scott Van Wagenen, *The Texas Republic and the Mormon Kingdom of God* (College Station: Texas A&M University Press, 2002).

4. Leonard Arrington, *Brigham Young: American Moses* (New York: Knopf, 1985); see also Ronald K. Esplin, "The Emergence of Brigham Young and the Twelve to Mormon Leadership, 1830–1841" (PhD diss., Brigham Young University, 1981).

5. Except stakes (dioceses) organized in Canada and Mexico in 1895, most of the stakes outside the United States were organized after 1960.

6. Gregory A. Prince and William Robert Wright, *David O. McKay and the Rise of Modern Mormonism* (Salt Lake City: University of Utah Press, 2005).

7. Douglas Davies, "World Religion: Dynamics and Constraints," in this volume, 255.

8. Davies, "World Religion," 263.

9. Davies, "World Religion," 254–55, 257; Rodney Stark, "The Rise of a New World Faith," *Review of Religious Research* 26, no. 1 (September 1984): 18–27.

10. Ryan Cragun, "A Re-examination of Stark's LDS Church Growth Projections by Individual Countries;" Rick Phillips, "Rethinking the International

Expansion of Mormonism;" Henri Gooren and Erik Sengers, "Assessing Secularization and Religious Market Approaches to Religion: The Case of Mormon Growth in Europe," papers presented at the Annual Meeting of the Social Scientific Study of Religion in Kansas City, October 22–24, 2004; David Clark Knowlton, "How Many Members Are There Really? Two Censuses and the Meaning of LDS Membership in Chile and Mexico," *Dialogue: A Journal of Mormon Thought* 38, no. 2 (Summer 2005): 53–78.

11. Richard Bushman, "Joseph Smith's Many Histories," in this volume, 12–15; Davies, "World Religion," 264–65.

12. Max Weber, *The Theory of Social and Economic Organization,* trans. A. M. Henderson and Talcott Parsons (New York: Oxford University Press, 1947), 363–86.

13. W. W. Rostow, *The Stages of Economic Growth: A Non-Communist Manifesto* (Cambridge, England: Cambridge University Press, 1960), 36–58.

14. William A. Clebsch, "Each Sect the Sect to End All Sects," *Dialogue: A Journal of Mormon Thought* 1, no. 2 (Summer 1966): 84–89.

15. Sydney E. Ahlstrom, *A Religious History of the American People* (New Haven: Yale University Press, 1972), 508.

16. Mario S. De Pillis, "Mormonism and the American Way: A Response [to William A. Clebsch]," *Dialogue: A Journal of Mormon Thought* 1, no. 2 (Summer 1966): 89–97; Will Herberg, *Protestant, Catholic, Jew: An Essay in American Religious Sociology* (Garden City, N.Y.: Doubleday, 1955).

17. Jan Shipps, *Mormonism: The Story of a New Religious Tradition* (Urbana: University of Illinois Press, 1985). See especially chapter 3, "History as Text."

18. Ninian Smart, *Worldviews: Crosscultural Explorations of Human Beliefs* (New York: Scribner's, 1983); Mircea Eliade, *The Sacred and the Profane: The Nature of Religion,* trans. Williard R. Trask (New York: Harcourt Brace, 1959).

19. "The practice of abstaining from all forms of alcohol, tobacco, coffee, and tea, . . . may outwardly distinguish active Latter-day Saints more than any other practice." Joseph Lynn Lyon, "Word of Wisdom," in *Encyclopedia of Mormonism,* ed. Daniel H. Ludlow, 4 vols. (New York: Macmillan, 1992), 4:1584. This 1833 revelation was adapted to the "weakest of all Saints" (Doctrine and Covenants 89:3).

20. See Doctrine and Covenants 107:9, 65.

21. The Community of Christ is the new name of the Reorganized Church of Jesus Christ of Latter Day Saints, an ecclesiastical manifestation of Mormonism headquartered in Independence, Missouri.

Authority and Worldwide Growth

Roger R. Keller

Although Davies stands outside the Latter-day Saint tradition, he stands outside with respect. The tools he uses are those of the anthropologist, sociologist, and theologian. Being from outside the Latter-day Saint tradition gives him a perspective that those within the tradition find hard to replicate, and that is precisely Davies's strength. He sees things "Mormon" in a slightly different way than those within the tradition and raises interesting questions that should be answered.

On the other hand, this strength is also a weakness. I know the limitations of his approach, having tried to be fair to the Mormon tradition when I stood outside of it myself at one point in my life. No matter how hard I tried then to be fair to Joseph Smith and Mormonism—or for that matter to Islam or Hinduism or Taoism today—as an outsider I can never articulate another's tradition quite the way that a practitioner of that particular faith could or would. I might come close, but there will always be something I overlook or do not completely comprehend. Similarly, Davies has served all readers well in his thoughtful paper, but a few things he has said bear reevaluatation from the standpoint of a practicing Latter-day Saint.[1]

A Personal View of Priesthood Authority

When my wife, Flo Beth, and I were considering becoming members of The Church of Jesus Christ of Latter-day Saints, Flo Beth had the opportunity to meet with one of the members of the Quorum of Twelve Apostles. In that meeting, he told her that we could join the church because we enjoyed the fellowship and the spiritual support. However, until we understood the concept of authority, we should not join. After that meeting, Flo Beth was puzzled, for she was confident that I already had authority as a minister in the Presbyterian Church.

And in one sense I did have authority. It stands to reason that God does not call persons to do something on his behalf without giving them the authority to do what he has called them to do. He had called me to the Presbyterian ministry; I know that as surely today as I knew it thirty-five years ago. Thus, I had the authority to bring people to Christ through the spoken word and the sacraments of the Presbyterian Church. That was the limit of my authority, however. When I saw that I did not have the authority to administer the saving ordinances of the gospel of Jesus Christ through the priesthood of God restored by Joseph Smith, that made all the difference for us, and we became Latter-day Saints.

In a similar vein, Latter-day Saints have often said to me, "We are so glad that you found the gospel." My response has always been, "I knew the gospel long before I was a Latter-day Saint. What I have found is the fullness of the gospel." The essence of that fullness is that the authority of the priesthood is found only within The Church of Jesus Christ of Latter-day Saints. It is this authority that gives power to the taking of the sacrament on Sunday and to every ordinance within the temple.[2] As Joseph Smith stated: "All the ordinances, systems, and administrations on the earth are of no use to the children of men, unless they are ordained and authorized of God; for nothing will save a man but a legal administrator; for none others will be acknowledged either by God or angels."[3]

This understanding of authority is absent from Davies's paper, and this absence colors what he has said about the dynamics and constraints of Latter-day Saint church growth. The return of the authority to administer the saving ordinances of the gospel is the heart of the Restoration. Likewise, the loss of that authority, with the loss of the original Quorum of the Twelve Apostles, is the heart of the Apostasy or "falling away" (2 Thessalonians 2:3) that made a restoration necessary. This concept of authority affects the way Latter-day Saints understand the first principles of the gospel, the organization of the church, and what it will mean for Mormonism to be a world religion. My comments will focus on these three headings.

First Principles of the Gospel

Davies has suggested that Mormonism is an achievement-based religion, and that is true to a certain degree.[4] But that is the "thin" understanding of the Latter-day Saint religion. The first principles and ordinances of the gospel are a better measure of Mormon theology than any superficial "achievement"-based identity.

The first principle of the gospel according to Joseph Smith is "faith in the Lord Jesus Christ" (Article of Faith 4). In Joseph Smith's words:

> The fundamental principles of our religion are the testimony of the Apostles and Prophets, concerning Jesus Christ, that He died, was buried, and rose again the third day, and ascended into heaven; and all other things which pertain to our religion are only appendages to it.[5]

In other words, everything about Mormonism is Christological to the core. The focal point is faith in the Lord Jesus Christ because Christ worked the atonement.[6] We are saved only by the atonement of Jesus Christ (Article of Faith 2)—not by faith, repentance, baptism, the gift of the Holy Ghost, or the temple. Each of these is a channel of grace provided by the Lord so that one may tap ever more deeply into the Savior's atoning sacrifice. Each channel that people refuse creates a diminution in their ability to fully appropriate the atonement into their lives. Thus, having met Jesus Christ, believers see the need to repent and reorder their lives. With that realization, they comprehend the need for the essential saving ordinance of baptism by immersion, which can be administered only under the hands of one holding the authoritative priesthood of God (Articles of Faith 4 and 5). Baptism then leads to the ordinance of confirmation, by the laying on of hands by one holding the authority of the Melchizedek Priesthood, with the command to receive the Holy Ghost.[7] These public ordinances are then followed by the private ordinances of the temple, which deepen one's relation with and knowledge of the Savior and his Father, ordinances again administered by persons holding the priesthood of God. None of these ordinances or rites, as Davies calls them,[8] would have any eternal effect, divine validity, or salvific power if they were not administered by priesthood authority to act in the name of God.

This sequence of ordinances shows how Mormon theology is a priestly and sacramental theology. In this way, Latter-day Saints are very much like the Catholics or the Anglicans, who observe sacraments or ordinances as special points in their lives, through which divine grace may be encountered and appropriated. Grace may be seen and appropriated in other ways, but Joseph Smith held out the prospect that only in and through the ordinances administered by priesthood power can people know that they will meet Christ and "obtain celestial thrones."[9]

Where then does the concept of achievement enter of which Davies spoke? It lies in a life of Christian discipleship. I do not know any thinking Christians who do not realize that their lives have to change if they are going to follow the Savior. Unfortunately, too many Christians today try to live with one foot in the church and the other in the worldly arena. The word of God found in the scriptures has, for many, become relative. Modern principles of tolerance for almost anything take the place of scriptural principles.[10] The sense that there is a divinely revealed truth and lifestyle is becoming lost, and sadly that is true even among some Latter-day Saints. But the gospel, revealed in and through Jesus Christ and subsequently through his prophets, demands certain standards of behavior and works. People must respond to God's grace with discipleship, or to put it another way, grace without works is dead.

There is a synergy or cooperation between the Christian and God, which concept many Evangelicals may find offensive, but both the Old and New Testaments demand response and responsibility from people of faith.[11] Most of the Christian world understands this synergy, particularly those of the Roman Catholic and Eastern Orthodox traditions. Humans do participate in their own salvation through following the commandments of God and accepting the ordinances that he offers to all. However, some Latter-day Saints have lost the balance between grace and works. Some feel they must work out their own salvation. That is incorrect Latter-day Saint doctrine as both Stephen E. Robinson and Robert L. Millet have shown in their respective writings on the relationship between grace and works.[12] Discipleship is works. It is the outgrowth of our encounter with the Savior, and anyone who claims differently stands outside the biblical tradition. From a Latter-day Saint perspective, discipleship is the application of priesthood to daily life.

But can Latter-day Saints ever know how they stand with the Lord? Are they not always wondering if they are good enough, as Davies suggests?[13] Some do wonder, but that may be because they do not understand the atonement well enough. To a Latter-day Saint, the presence of the Holy Ghost in his or her life is God's personal witness and assurance that that individual is acceptable before the Father, because he or she has put on Christ. In God's eyes, he or she is perfected because of Christ.[14]

Having said this, however, the Holy Spirit will never permit people to stay where they are but will shove and push them to grow. That, too, is part of discipleship; there should always be some discomfort with where we are in our Christian lives. Out of discomfort comes growth, and the Spirit is good at creating that discomfort, a discomfort, however, which should never overshadow the basic assurance that is rooted in Christ and his atoning work. Are Latter-day Saints, therefore, an achievement-oriented people? Yes, but not in the way that Davies states it, but rather as a natural product of discipleship that has been a part of historic Christianity from its inception. For many people in the world, the opportunity to work authoritatively together with

God in bringing to pass the eternal lives of human souls is a strong dynamic of attraction and growth.

Church Structure

Davies seems to feel, however, that the hierarchical priesthood structure of the Latter-day Saint church may stand in the way of its becoming a world religion.[15] Again, this overlooks an essential aspect of authority as seen by those within the Latter-day Saint tradition. Authority must flow through channels. For Latter-day Saints, this flow begins with the living Prophet of God and proceeds through the First Presidency, the Quorum of the Twelve, the Quorums of the Seventy, Area Presidencies, stake presidents, bishops, and other priesthood and auxiliary leaders. Thus, the worldwide church lives on the same page. As Joseph Smith taught on April 6, 1836, priesthood orders and offices are necessary, just as in the human body "which has different members, which have different offices to perform; all are necessary in their place, and the body is not complete without all the members."[16]

Does that limit dissent? Yes, especially when church members believe that there is on the earth today a living prophet who is just like Abraham, Moses, Elijah, Isaiah, or Peter. Those who would challenge that basic, fundamental principle will find themselves marginalized by the church.

Ours is a revealed faith, not one derived from rational reflection. Ours is a theology not generated in the academy, but a theology given through and derived from revelation given to living prophets. The church structure is the vehicle of transmission, and that will not change. The church has what no other Christian tradition has except perhaps the Roman Catholic Church, that is, a clearly defined magisterium to which one can turn for answers to questions on faith and morals.

Given this hierarchical structure, will members feel divorced from the leadership as the church grows? No, and I am sure of that, having experienced the priesthood training sessions that have been conducted by the First Presidency and the Quorum of Twelve over the last three years. The entire Latter-day Saint church was connected together by the miracle of satellite. Each of us participated personally as President Hinckley spoke to us from Salt Lake City, Elder Dallin H. Oaks from the Philippines, and Elder Jeffrey R. Holland from Chile. Just as the world is shrinking, so is The Church of Jesus Christ of Latter-day Saints on a worldwide basis. Priesthood power can flow more easily through the church today than it could in the early years of the church as we take advantage of the miracles of modern-day transportation and communication.

Mormonism: A World Religion?

Davies's principal question is whether we can see The Church of Jesus Christ of Latter-day Saints as a worldwide church, either today or in the future. He uses an interesting definition for a world religion. He states:

> This appraisal is based on a definition of world religion as involving a distinctive process of the conquest of death, a conquest rooted in ritual practice, explanatory doctrine, and an ethical pattern of life involving the generation of merit for soteriological ends. Crucially, it is also required that the movement develop from its original cultural source by engaging creatively with the cultures into which it expands and, in the process, generate diversifying textual, symbolic, and historic traditions.[17]

It is clear from this statement that numbers alone do not define a world religion. Certainly, Mormonism has a clear answer ritually and doctrinally to the problem of death, as Davies notes. There is also a well-defined ethical pattern for life, which does have bearing on our ultimate destiny. The issue over which Davies wonders whether The Church of Jesus Christ of Latter-day Saints can ever be a world religion is its ability to engage with other cultures. Here, as with the other issues I have addressed, the unifying force will be authority.

From Davies's point of view, a world religion seems to be one in which there is not only cultural diversity but also diversity in doctrine, organization, and opinion. Protestantism certainly has that diversity; there is little unity to it. Roman Catholicism has a much stronger worldwide organization, but due to a long history when communication was limited, Catholicism has immense diversity. Buddhism is quite diverse with its three major schools of thought—which are also internally diverse. Islam is unified by the Five Pillars, but true Qur'anic principles have not always permeated cultures as the varied treatment of women or the various attitudes toward jihad would indicate.

What then of the possibility that Mormonism might be a burgeoning world religion? Can it adapt to new cultures? I know that this cultural question was of particular concern to Elder Neal A. Maxwell, who worked with others to determine what was essential to the gospel message and what was merely American culture that did not need to be exported. I think we are still working on that issue, and we will learn over time how to address it more adequately.

That which will never be changed, however, is the concept of central authority flowing down from the living prophet through the priesthood channels of the church. But those channels are becoming more and more composed of persons from the cultures into which the church has entered. The church has now established the Seventh and Eighth Quorums of the Seventy. The former is in Brazil, and the latter encompasses part of Asia and the Pacific Islands. In other words, a majority of the church's general officers now live among the people whom they serve. They do precisely so that practice and doctrine remain unified worldwide. The Restoration first and foremost means unity in doctrine, organization, and attitude—not diversity.

What areas of life can be open to diversity? Music would be one. Our western musical forms are not the only ones available with which to praise the Lord. Some of the traditional hymns of the Restoration will cover the globe, but I can see a day when a portion of the hymnbook in Thailand is different from that in India or Japan, not only in words but also in music. I believe we will also see variety in diet. Converts to the church in India or south Asia may choose to continue vegetarian diets, which are probably more in harmony with the Word of Wisdom and what will be eaten in the Millennium than are our traditional western diets of today. I am sure there are many areas of cultural accommodation that can be made. But that accommodation will not be at the expense of central authority.

Conclusion

Davies's paper seems to be a critique rooted in the failed, decentralized Protestantism of Western Europe. Davies disagrees, saying that his view of a world religion is rooted in a broad survey of those faiths that are recognized today as world religions, namely, Christianity, Islam, and Buddhism. Be that as it may, my critique still holds, for Davies's worldview is that of decentralized faith traditions. It appears that from his perspective, if Latter-day Saints wish to become a true world religion, they must become like his decentralized, diverse models. Obviously, that will never happen, because the heart of the Restoration—restored authority to administer the saving ordinances of the gospel through a divinely revealed structure—will not permit us to do so. We will maintain structure, order, and unity in doctrine and organization, while at the same time permitting regional and cultural diversity when that diversity does not violate the principles of the revealed order of things. In my view, The Church of Jesus Christ of Latter-day Saints will indeed become a world religion, but it will be like none before it, because it will have a central authority and cohesion unknown in the rest of the religious world. Those will be the parameters of this growing world religion, and in the end, I am happy to leave its expansion in the hands of God.

Notes

1. Davies recognizes that the issues he raises are not simple. To use his word, they are "thick," a fact too many commentators on the Mormon tradition do not recognize. Too often Latter-day Saint and non-Latter-day Saint scholars alike couch their comments in much too simplistic terms. If one of the aspects of being a world religion is "thickness," then we qualify along with several others. Douglas J. Davies, "World Religion: Dynamics and Constraints," in this volume, 253–54.

2. See Doctrine and Covenants 107:8, 20.

3. Joseph Fielding Smith, comp., *Teachings of the Prophet Joseph Smith* (Salt Lake City: Deseret Book, 1972), 274.

4. Davies, "World Religion, Dynamics and Constraints," 259, 260–61.

5. Joseph Smith Jr., *History of The Church of Jesus Christ of Latter-day Saints*, ed. B. H. Roberts, 2d ed., rev., 7 vols. (Salt Lake City: Deseret Book, 1971), 3:30.

6. See Douglas E. Brinley, "Faith in Jesus Christ," in *Encyclopedia of Mormonism*, ed. Daniel H. Ludlow, 4 vols. (New York: Macmillan, 1992), 2:483–85.

7. Joseph F. Smith, *Gospel Doctrine: Selections from the Sermons and Writings of Joseph F. Smith* (Salt Lake City: Deseret Book, 1939), 94–106.

8. Davies, "World Religion: Dynamics and Constraints," 259.

9. Smith, *Teachings of the Prophet Joseph Smith*, 362.

10. For example, Christian Smith, ed., *The Secular Revolution* (Berkeley: University of California Press, 2003); D. A. Carson, *The Gagging of God: Christianity Confronts Pluralism* (Grand Rapids, Mich.: Zondervan, 1996); and Philip Jenkins, *The Next Christendom: The Coming of Global Christianity* (New York: Oxford University Press, 2002).

11. See the story of David and Goliath in the Old Testament in 1 Samuel 17, or the instruction given by Jesus to the rich young ruler who sought eternal life in Matthew 19:16–26.

12. See Stephen E. Robinson, *Are Mormons Christians?* (Salt Lake City: Bookcraft, 1991); Robert L. Millet, *Grace Works* (Salt Lake City: Deseret Book, 2003); Robert L. Millet, *The Mormon Faith: A New Look at Christianity* (Salt Lake City: Shadow Mountain, 1998); Robert L. Millet, *By Grace Are We Saved* (Salt Lake City: Bookcraft, 1989).

13. Davies, "World Religion: Dynamics and Constraints," 262.

14. Bruce D. Porter, "Gift of the Holy Ghost," in *Encyclopedia of Mormonism*, 2:543–44.

15. Davies, "World Religion: Dynamics and Constraints," 262–63.

16. Smith, *Teachings of the Prophet Joseph Smith*, 112.

17. Davies, "World Religion: Dynamics and Constraints," 255.

Contributors

Randall Balmer *is the Ann Whitney Olin Professor of Religion at Barnard College, Columbia University, and the author of many best-selling books on the history of religion in America.*

Margaret Barker, *of Derbyshire, England, is a Methodist preacher and former president of the Society for Old Testament Study. She has delivered lectures and workshops at Brigham Young University and around the world.*

Richard L. Bushman *is the Gouverneur Morris Professor of History emeritus at Columbia University and author of three books and multiple articles on Joseph Smith.*

John E. Clark *is Professor of Anthropology at Brigham Young University, director of the New World Archaeological Foundation, and a specialist in Book of Mormon geography.*

Douglas J. Davies *is Professor in the Study of Religion at Durham University in England and the author of three books on Mormonism.*

Terryl L. Givens *is Professor of Literature and Religion and the James A. Bostwick Chair of English at the University of Richmond and the author of two books on Mormonism published by Oxford University Press.*

Richard T. Hughes *is Distinguished Professor of Religion and Director of the Center for Faith and Learning at Seaver College, Pepperdine University, and a specialist in restorationist movements.*

Roger R. Keller *is Professor of Church History and Doctrine at Brigham Young University, an expert on world religions, and a former Presbyterian minister.*

Gerald R. McDermott *is Professor of Religion at Roanoke College in Virginia and an expert on the writings and life of Jonathan Edwards.*

Robert L. Millet *is the Richard L. Evans Professor of Religious Understanding and former dean of the College of Religious Education at Brigham Young University.*

Richard J. Mouw *is President and Professor of Christian Philosophy at Fuller Theological Seminary in Pasadena, California, and has been engaged in an ongoing Evangelical–Latter-day Saint dialogue for the last five years.*

Dallin H. Oaks *is former president of Brigham Young University and professor at the University of Chicago Law School. He is a member of the Quorum of the Twelve Apostles of The Church of Jesus Christ of Latter-day Saints.*

David Paulsen *is Professor of Philosophy at Brigham Young University and specializes in the philosophy of religion. He has published several articles in the* Harvard Theological Review *on the corporeality of God.*

Robert V. Remini *is Emeritus Professor of History at the University of Illinois at Chicago, Distinguished Visiting Scholar of American History in the John W. Kluge Center at the Library of Congress, and an expert on the Jacksonian Era.*

Jan Shipps *is Professor Emerita of History and Religious Studies at Indiana University–Purdue University at Indianapolis and Senior Research Associate for the POLIS Center, former president of the Mormon History Association, and the author of numerous books and reviews on Mormonism.*

Grant Underwood *is Professor of History at Brigham Young University and the author of multiple books on Mormon history.*

John W. Welch *is the Robert K. Thomas Professor of Law at the J. Reuben Clark Law School, Brigham Young University, and the editor-in-chief of* BYU Studies.

Index

A

Abraham, Book of, 55, 65, 78, 107, 113, 114, 121, *139*

Adam and Eve, 65, 74

Adams, James, letter of, *123*

Agency of man, 193

American Religion: The Emergence of the Post-Christian Nation, The (Bloom), 9, 11, 20n22

Ancient scripture, revealed to Joseph Smith, 55, 64–66, 78, 107, 113–14, 131, *139. See also* Book of Mormon

Angel Moroni Delivers the Gold Plates to Joseph Smith on Hill Cumorah, by Lewis Ramsey, 129

Antebellum America. *See* Jacksonian era

Anthon, Charles, 15, 60

Anti-Americanism, affecting growth of Mormonism, 284, 285

Apocalypse of Weeks, 72–78

Apostasy, Christian, 63–64, 184, 262, 309

Apostles, and authority, 182–84

Articles of Faith, 145

Atonement of Jesus Christ
as foundational message of Mormonism, 232–38, 309, 311
as symbolized by the cross, 234–38

Augustine, 57, 64

Authority
in Christianity, 182–85, 206n30, 223–25
Joseph Smith's source of, 112–14, 183–84, 213–14
loss of apostolic, 176, 178, 184, 223–25, 309
in The Church of Jesus Christ of Latter-day Saints, 308–15
through Peter, 184, 224–25

B

Baha'is, compared to Mormonism, 277

Baptism for the dead, 119–201, 259

Beecher, Lyman, on America, 37

Berlin, Isaiah, 253–54